T0191424

FIRST CLASS

The

LEGACY *of* DUNBAR,
AMERICA'S FIRST
BLACK PUBLIC HIGH SCHOOL

ALISON STEWART

foreword by MELISSA HARRIS-PERRY

Lawrence Hill Books
Chicago

Copyright © 2013 by Alison Stewart
Foreword copyright © 2013 by Melissa Harris-Perry
All rights reserved
First edition
Published by Lawrence Hill Books
An imprint of Chicago Review Press Incorporated
814 North Franklin Street
Chicago, Illinois 60610

ISBN 978-1-61374-009-5

Interior design: PerfecType, Nashville, TN

Library of Congress Cataloging-in-Publication Data
Stewart, Alison, 1966-
    First class : the legacy of Dunbar, America's first Black public high school
      / Alison Stewart ; foreword by Melissa Harris-Perry.
      pages cm
    Summary: "An analysis of the first US high school for African Americans,
      the publication of which will coincide with the opening of the school's
      new facility"— Provided by publisher.
    ISBN 978-1-61374-009-5 (hardback)
    1. Dunbar High School (Washington, D.C.)—History. 2. High schools—
      Washington (D.C.) 3. African Americans—Education—Washington
      (D.C.) 4. African Americans—Education. I. Title.
    LD7501.W3S84 2013
    373.753—dc23
                                    2013008818

Printed in the United States of America
5 4 3

To my family

CONTENTS

FOREWORD

Melissa Harris-Perry

———————————— ⚬✦⚬ ————————————

IN 2007, CONTROVERSIAL EDUCATION reformer Michelle Rhee and Mayor Adrian Fenty embarked on an aggressive, and short-lived, era of education reform in Washington, DC. Within four years Rhee had resigned and Fenty was defeated in his bid for reelection in a campaign that centered on his school-reform efforts.

In subsequent years, multiple interpretations of their story have fueled an ongoing debate about what is broken in American education and what it will take to fix it. Driven by ideology rather than information, the reform debate tends to offer more heat than light. *First Class* enters into this moment in an entirely unique, wholly surprising, and especially illuminating way.

Alison Stewart is a journalist by training and craft. She has spent her career reporting on the cultural, social, and political life of contemporary America. As a journalist, she trades in the urgency of the relentless twenty-four-hour news cycle, reporting on breaking political events, interviewing key newsmakers, and offering insights on the issues of our moment.

Given this esteemed career, you might expect that her book about education in Washington, DC, would begin in 2006, when Adrian Fenty staked his nascent mayoral administration on reforming the city's schools. And you might expect to find, beneath of the covers of such a book, a series of interviews with the young reformers who have galvanized public attention in the past decade.

That might be a good book, but it would be a wholly ordinary one—one whose relevance would barely exceed the shelf life of a magazine. Alison Stewart did not write that book.

Instead, Stewart takes us back to the nineteenth century, when most blacks below the Mason-Dixon were still enslaved and when DC's Black Codes ensured that free coloreds in the city remained disenfranchised, impoverished, segregated, and most importantly, uneducated. She begins in that moment with one story, the story of a small group of education reformers who founded a small project that ultimately becomes Dunbar High School, the first public high school for blacks in America. And then she tells us what happens to Dunbar. It is one story that spans more than a century and illuminates everything we think we already know about education.

Through Stewart we learn that Washington, DC—capital of the nation, site of the preservation of the Union—is also the original laboratory for African American education. Stewart's long, historical sweep destroys any easy assumption that deeply politicized, ideological battles over education, race, and reform are new. Instead, as you read this tale, you will learn that teachers, principals, families, neighborhoods, students, and whole communities have long tied their identities and their dreams to their education. School is a place of making meaning, and in no place is this truer than in Dunbar High School.

In the beginning, educating "colored" children in DC was the private crusade of a handful of courageous white teachers. But with the founding of Dunbar High School at the turn of the twentieth century, educating black students was part of a national movement for justice and citizenship. Classically educated black pupils who knew Greek, physics, mathematics, and literature were incarnate examples of the inherent equality of the races. Their excellence proved that notions of essential racial inferiority were patently false. Dunbar High School committed itself fully to the radical mission of proving black worthiness by cultivating black academic excellence. Dunbar had stunning achievements and produced a startling share of black leaders.

But Dunbar's story is not wholly triumphant. When Stewart's book begins, the performance of Dunbar's marching band at the inauguration of President Obama evokes pity and shame rather than pride from DC's black middle class. The deteriorating physical plant of the school is a monument to decades of collective disinvestment in Dunbar's core mission. The proud Dunbar alumni do not exist, even as faded stories, for the current Dunbar students. The legacy of accomplishment has been supplanted by the realities of underachievement.

But even as it falters, Dunbar retains a spirit of struggle and an attachment to community that promises to see it through the latest epoch of reform. There is still a cadre of teachers, parents, students, and alumni who believe in pursuing the mission of exemplary public education for students who have been relegated to second-class status. There are just enough to write a new chapter in Dunbar's history and, therefore, in the history of American education.

There is no one better suited to tell this story than Alison Stewart. She is the child of Dunbar graduates, and introduces us to this school with the passion and love that can emerge only from an early childhood attachment to a story and to a place. To read *First Class* is to glimpse Stewart's love letter to a complicated and sometimes disappointing beloved. Her narrative situates Dunbar in the long history of American educational reform, the ongoing struggle for racial equality, and the deeply personal history of a family that has contributed so much to the tapestry of America.

INTRODUCTION

FIRST CLASS IS A collage of memories, news articles, ephemera, interviews, research, reporting, and observations about one of the most spectacular success stories in education. The genesis of this project was a conversation around the dinner table. My parents were reminiscing about what a good education meant to them as African Americans and how Dunbar High School had shaped their future.

One day in early 2003, I was in DC for work, and I decided to go take a look at the school I had heard so much about as a child, the segregated high school that became a mecca of African American education. Dunbar had produced doctors, legal scholars, educators, and civil rights leaders. Dunbar graduates had been honored with postage stamps bearing their portraits and had argued in front of the US Supreme Court, changing history. They were men and women who had refused to let the disgusting practice of segregation limit their ambitions. Dunbar was a defining institution for African Americans of a certain age. It was such a part of their lives that Dunbar is often listed in the obituaries of its older graduates. Dunbar meant something in DC. I *had* to see Dunbar. When I mentioned to a colleague where I was going, his response was, "Dunbar—hey, they have a great basketball team."

After visiting Dunbar, I understood his response. The Dunbar I visited that day, unannounced and unquestioned by staff as I walked the halls, was not like the place my parents described. The students weren't in class. Correct grammar was optional. Teachers were doing their best under adverse conditions. The only remnants of Dunbar's former academic glory could be seen in a dusty display case filled with faded pictures and tarnished trophies. What had happened to Dunbar? How had it managed to be successful when the laws and social mores of the nineteenth and early twentieth centuries worked against its students and their families? How had it managed to deteriorate in the twenty-first century?

And why didn't more people know about the school's reputation? Where were the graduates of Old Dunbar today? And what would happen to their stories if someone didn't write them down? Those who lived the Dunbar story were in their later years, and their numbers were diminishing. It was important that their history be remembered. In this age where we are all looking for education reform, there is a blueprint that could be followed: Dunbar's blueprint.

Please consider these three points as you read this book:

First, after consulting veteran African American journalists and college professors of African American studies, I chose to include the language of the eras about which I wrote. Sometimes it was hard to write the words and perhaps it will be hard to read them, but that is part of the story, the struggle for respect and recognition through education. In the nineteenth century the word "colored" was in standard use, as was the word "nigger." Sometimes a person might have the status of a "free black" or "free colored." In 1930 the *New York Times* and the *Atlantic Monthly* changed their stylebooks and began to use "Negro" in their articles. Following the black power movement of the 1960s, again the *New York Times* made a shift—this time to "black," as did the Associated Press. In the late 1980s, "African American" became more prevalent. You will see the language change throughout the book as the story progresses.

Second, the school went through several name changes over the years. From 1870 to 1892 it was called the Preparatory High School for Colored Youth. From 1892 it was known as the M Street High School, and in 1916 it took on the name Dunbar. Until the 1954 Supreme Court decision Dunbar was segregated and was the only purely academic public high school available to African American children in Washington, DC. The fact that Dunbar High School was a winner during a time of segregation does not in any way suggest that racial segregation in the United States was anything but a demeaning, cruel, and unconstitutional system. Dunbar made the best of the limiting practice of segregation—but this does not make segregation palatable or condonable in any way.

Finally, all quotes (unless otherwise noted) come from first-person interviews I conducted for this book. For this book I traveled from a rough neighborhood in Chicago to the historical home of a nineteenth-century poet in Dayton, Ohio, to the White House. I am enormously grateful to all of the Dunbar graduates and educators who welcomed me into their homes and offices. Not every story could be included in the book, but every interview, conversation, e-mail, and phone call informed the narrative. The number of graduates who accomplished extraordinary things is long and includes achievements in medicine, the arts, the military, education, politics, civil service, and the law. At the Charles Sumner School and archives, the official museum and archives of Washington, DC, public schools, there are folders several inches thick with biographies and obituaries that celebrate the life and accomplishments of M Street/Dunbar graduates.

The story of Dunbar shows what can happen in spite of huge legal, societal, and professional hurdles. It shows what is possible when a group of people focus and band together to make something better. Dunbar shows what happens when a stable middle class exists. And Dunbar shows us that politics pollutes education. And through all this, Dunbar helped create the greatest generations of African Americans.

Dunbar High School

Courtesy of Charles Sumner School Museum and Archives

PROLOGUE

IF YOU STAND ON the corner in front of Dunbar Senior High School and look down New Jersey Avenue, you can clearly see the front of the Capitol, where history was made on January 20, 2009. That day Joe and Carol Stewart watched on television with nearly 38 million other American viewers as Barack Obama was inaugurated. What made their experience distinct was that sixty-five years earlier, just ten blocks from where the first black president of the United States was being sworn in, they had attended a segregated high school—the first public high school for blacks in the United States.

In the 1940s, Joe and Carol were teenagers in the southern city of Washington, DC, at a time when they and their friends couldn't grab a hamburger in some restaurants or buy a pair of shoes from certain stores. Now, in their lifetime, a black man had been elected to the highest office in the land.

"What a magnificent display of what *Homo sapiens* is capable of in his most civilized state, you know?" marveled Carol, ever the biology teacher, as she settled in on the couch. "I enjoy the whole thing, the whole concept—the mass of humanity, without any fights or pushing or screaming, but with everybody smiling. Everybody just wants to be hopeful, and there's just so little to lift your spirits these days. So, if he can lift the spirits, God bless him. God bless him. God bless him. He's got a lot on his plate, you know."

Joe Stewart, who as a young black kid had almost slipped through the cracks, was visibly moved by President Obama's inaugural address. "It was the tenor of the speech—that for the first time since Ronald Reagan, it is 'We are together and we are going to get it done,' and that these divisions between us are nowhere near as important as the things we have in common. And I think that spirit has been missing for at least the last eight years—and time before that, from the time of Newt Gingrich and maybe back to Reagan. Because, while Reagan said it was 'morning in America,' he also in a sense said that we weren't responsible for one another. So, I'm glad to see a return to the idea that it's one country and the idea that diversity is a good thing. That's truly the idea, that diversity is a good thing instead of just lip service."

"Daddy, did you think you'd live to see the day that there would be a black president?" I asked Joe, my father.

"I don't know that I did. It is stunning, just stunning." But he did live to see the first black president; he lived to see it by seventy-one days.

Later that evening I called my mom to see if they had watched Dunbar High School marching band in the parade.

"I can't believe those girls were switchin' their behinds," my mom said in the curt way that high school teachers do. Oh, yes, she had seen it. "That was not what young ladies should do!"

1 | IT IS WHAT IT IS

ON SEVERAL COLD, DARK mornings, and a few weekends too, the Dunbar Senior High School marching band practiced, practiced, and practiced some more for the historic day. Within six weeks Dunbar's band, the Crimson Tide, would participate in the inaugural parade for the forty-fourth president of the United States.

A high-profile performance like this was something band director Rodney Chambers couldn't have pulled off four years earlier, when he arrived at Dunbar. "We had sixteen kids in the band. That was everybody."

In the summer of 2004, Chambers, a transplanted North Carolinian, was working in DC with a music-education nonprofit when he heard through the grapevine that Dunbar didn't have a band director. "This was like a week, two weeks before school started. I'm like 'What?' I said, 'Well, I'll see if I can find somebody.'"

Sporting a shaved head and a goatee, the forty-year-old Chambers has the manners of a southern gentleman and the physique of a former football player. "I talked to the principal and told her I would do it for a month or two. She said, 'There's no need to volunteer; you might as well get paid.' And I've been here four and a half years."

Chambers didn't realize what he had signed on to do. The principal who hired him left the school, as did her successor—and her successor's successor. The twenty-first-century Dunbar Senior High School had problems—academically, physically, and, it could be persuasively argued, spiritually. The almost forty-year-old facility, a hulking "greige"-colored building that had clearly been designed in the 1970s, was in bad shape all the way around. The alarms on the doors didn't work. The escalators between the cavernous floors rarely worked. Kids ran wild in the parts of the building that were no longer in use due to dwindling attendance. The library had encyclopedias from the 1990s and computers that could be museum pieces.

In the lobby, pictures of illustrious alumni hung in broken plastic picture frames. It was a hall of fame featuring strong African American leaders such as Senator Ed Brooke and Dr. Charles Drew, looking out at students who couldn't recognize them as role models because the kids didn't recognize them at all. The halls echoed with the sounds of "motherfucker" and mangled variations the verb "to be." Truthfully, the academic picture wasn't unique for an urban high school facing persistent economic and social challenges, but the sight was indeed shocking given Dunbar's rich history. Shocking and sad.

Once upon a time, not so long ago, Dunbar High School was a nationally known, academically elite public high school. Its graduates were among the most educated and most productive Americans of a generation. Flying in the face of racist stereotypes and restrictive segregation laws, Dunbar graduates broke through glass ceilings and shattered assumptions. The first black general in the US Army was a Dunbar graduate, as was the first black federal court judge and the first black presidential cabinet member. Once upon a time, not so long ago, expectations for Dunbar students were extremely high. By the early 2000s expectations were depressingly low.

"When I got here, it was, like, so much they needed," band director Chambers recalled. Things like instruments. When Mayor Adrian Fenty and Schools Chancellor Michelle Rhee took over the school system in 2007, Chambers was already a year into wading through streams of red tape, trying to redirect some funds his way. "They gave us $3.7 million, and we got uniforms and instruments for everybody. It took almost three years to get those things. It has been really tough." He had forty band members by the end of September 2004. He said he recruited forty-five students by the end of 2005. There were persistent rumors and whispers that Chambers used ringers—any kid who would show up, a warm body—to supplement the band, not that anyone would have noticed.

However he did it, Chambers grew the band to sixty-five students by the end of 2007. He wanted to convey the message that music can take you to places you've never been. "Kids want to travel, to go places. Sometimes the only way to get there is to be a part of a band or football or something because some of the kids have never even been to the south side of Washington. They don't cross the river."

By the fall of 2008, there were about eighty-five kids in the band. That's when Chambers put into action his plan to be a part of the inauguration. It would give the kids a goal. He worked on the band's résumé, listing the awards it had won for indoor dance and drum-line competitions, and made a DVD. "The DVD kind of told the story, not just the DVD of performance, but told the story of where we've come from and what we've done, and we had some really good recommendation letters," Chambers said.

Dunbar alumni, including then DC city council chairman Vincent Gray and Congresswoman Eleanor Holmes Norton, weighed in with their support. But Chambers knew the odds were long. There were 1,382 applications submitted for only a handful of slots. Chambers wanted to protect the kids and himself from disappointment. "We told everybody we weren't going to apply like the other high school bands. If we didn't get it, then we'd have egg on our face. So we were telling everybody, 'No we're not applying, we're not applying.' "

Chambers got the official invitation on December 9, 2008.

The media flocked to the story. It was an irresistible headline. MARCH-ING INTO HISTORY read the *Washington Times*. D.C.'s DUNBAR, THE FIRST BLACK HIGH SCHOOL IN THE U.S., PREPARES TO HONOR THE NATION'S FIRST BLACK PRESIDENT read the banner on one website. Barack Obama had been elected exactly 138 years to the day after the country's first black public high school opened its doors.

The inaugural eve concert would take place on Martin Luther King Jr. Day and would be dedicated to America's children. The story wrote itself. C-SPAN covered the band's preparation four days before the big event. Chambers instructed the kids to keep their lines straight and to keep their knees high. "It's going to be twenty degrees on Tuesday!" he yelled. One young student named Lynwood told the C-SPAN interviewer, "I'm honored to do it for Barack Obama. He's a black president and now that shows hope—that now black kids can now say I can grow up and be a black president because, you know, we never really had no black president before."

"We understand it is a privilege," a nervous but smiling Chambers told the C-SPAN interviewer.

On January 20, 2009, at 5:09 PM, the Dunbar Senior High School marching band made its way past the First Family on the reviewing stand. It was a feat, given what had happened that morning.

Earlier in the day, the band joined the other parade participants, lining up for the big event. It was a bitterly cold day with the wind chill in the teens. People were lining up along the parade route as early as 7:00 AM, even though the parade didn't begin until 2:30 PM. "We had to wait so long out there in the cold, and the kids, not all of them, behaved poorly," Chambers said. "They were tired and cold, and there's not a lot of parental support, so they think they are adults. And they were cussing and stuff like that."

Chambers recalled the story a week later, hunched over with his forearms on his knees, hands clasped and fingers laced as if praying, his shaved head hanging low. He almost hadn't shown up for the meeting. A week after the inauguration he had agreed to a post-parade interview but initially was nowhere to be found in the Dunbar school building. He wasn't in the band room or in the main office. Repeated calls and text messages to his cell phone went unanswered. He finally surfaced around noon and explained that he hadn't answered the messages because he had been in his car getting a few minutes of peace before heading back to the classroom. "I guess all the excitement is over now, so I guess I'm a little melancholy," he said with a shrug.

One would expect Rodney Chambers to be completing a victory lap after the big day, but he really didn't want to talk about what had happened. "It was bittersweet. We had a lot of problems that day with the kids."

The morning of the inauguration, while the band was getting into formation, Chambers realized that some band members were missing. They'd all arrived together, but now his head count was off. Some of his students had taken off into the crowd of a million and a half people. "And then they got lost. And then the military picks them up. We had to wait three hours after the parade, on our buses, for the military to deliver those kids." Chambers looked pained retelling the story. "It wasn't a good day."

Without its renegade members, the rest of the group, which had practiced so hard for this big day and wanted to do the best job possible, did what they went there to do. The Crimson Tide reached the viewing stand where the President, First Lady, and their then ten- and seven-year-old daughters watched the parade. Three pretty girls in red, shiny, formfitting track suits and white knit caps were energetically high-stepping as they held the gold and red D-U-N-B-A-R sign. Behind them came ten more girls, the Dunbar Dolls, clad in tight white spandex unitards, faux white fur vests, and white headbands. They looked simultaneously cute and a tad mature. The high energy drum majors were next, followed by musicians with a heavy horn and drum sound. The flag team brought up the rear.

As the Dunbar Dolls reached the stand, their drop-it-like-it's-hot moves reflected the times—and in a few instances might have impressed an exotic dancer. Two young men, the drum majors, couldn't be missed with their Trojan warrior helmets with foot-long white feather plumes. They looked more confident than the others and tried to keep the spirits high and the musicians on beat.

In two minutes, the big moment in front of the president was over. However, thanks to the Internet, moments like the Dunbar band's brush with the new First Family last forever. The video of the band's performance was uploaded to YouTube within a day, and the viewer's comments were blunt.

southeasttink wrote: "Dunbar was a disgrace"

delemadiance wrote: ". . . luckily there were other black schools to counteract the raunch and filth displayed."

bluephil82k wrote: "I disagree with most of you, its not about the way they danced in front of the President because that's what they normally do. Don't get upset with the band staff and parents now."

Ripshanky08 wrote: "All yall that is hatin on dunbar, fuck yall, yall just mad because yall cant wear something like dat . . . they was good so fuck all yall all that don' like them and how they performed."

CT4L wrote: "Poor kids. Blame the band director."

There's plenty of blame to go around for Dunbar's troubles. The band director blamed the students' difficulties on an inadequate school system and strained home environments. "The kids struggle. They have a lot to do. . . . They go home and take care of young brothers and sisters." As if having an epiphany, he added, "Out of the eighty-five kids I had, I could only think of one kid who has the mother and father at home. And her behavior is so much better than all the rest."

The poor behavior of the students was on display as he spoke. He repeatedly had to raise his considerable voice and request that a couple of unwelcome loungers leave the band room. The loiterers ran off, for the moment, and he continued his train of thought, speaking like a man who needed to get something off his sizeable chest.

"Some of these kids I've taught for four years—I've never met a parent. What is that about? I took the band to Florida for six days. We went to Ohio, and New York, North Carolina, and some of the parents I've never met. I wouldn't know who they were if they were to walk in the door now." He said he personally paid for kids' food on many of these trips. "I've never been in a place where parents don't seem to care. But the only time you see parents really here is when the kids get in a fight, and then their parents come to fight. The parents come to school to fight."

He went on, "When I grew up in North Carolina, if I got in a fight, my mother gave me a good whipping." Chambers expressed despair about what happened at the inauguration, what had been happening at the school, the loss of good teachers, and the school's changing principals. He was contemplating leaving, maybe before the end of the school year. "I'm not sure. I keep praying on it. I'm still taking some mental time to try to decide where I want to go from here."

As his next class began to trickle in, a huge commotion broke out in the hallway. The band room was on the first floor by one of the school's exits. Suddenly a man's voice came over the P.A. It was the principal.

"Pardon me for the interruption. At this time I need for all my security administration to make sure that they are walking the halls and [to] remind some of our students if there are any fights in my building today, I'm going to make you aware that I am putting you up for involuntary transfers, so today will be your last day at Dunbar Senior High School. I will be doing involuntary transfers. So, staff, please give me their names, I'll just pull them out of here."

At the time, according to Section 2501.1 of the disciplinary code for the District of Columbia Public Schools, educators have several choices for discipline:

> Disciplinary options for intervention, remediation, and rehabilitation shall include, but are not limited to, the following strategies: in order is as follows: (a) Reprimands; (b) Detention; (c) Additional work assignments; (d) Restitution; (e) Mediation; (f) In-school disciplinary centers; (g) Alternative educational programs and placements; (h) Rehabilitative programs; (i) Crime awareness/prevention programs; (j) Probation; (k) Exclusion from extracurricular activity; (l) Peer court; and (m) Transfer.

Dunbar's principal said that day he'd choose the last option, transferring out whoever had started that fight. That student would be someone else's problem tomorrow. According to Rodney Chambers, "A lot of people don't want to work in DC. It's rough. You hear all the things on the news and then once you get inside and experience it . . ." His voice trailed off.

An ambulance arrived shortly after the announcement. Chambers gave me a sidelong glance and said, "You say your mom went here?" Pause. "It's not the same Dunbar."

2 | TEACHING TO TEACH

APRIL 16 IS A legal holiday in Washington, DC: Emancipation Day. The only reason anyone outside the District might know this is that occasionally the District-wide day off pushes back the income tax deadline. On a spring day in 1862, President Abraham Lincoln signed the Compensated Emancipation Act, which ended slavery for the estimated thirty-one hundred slaves in Washington, DC—a small number compared to the four million in the country at the time. The move happened almost nine months before Lincoln's more well-known Emancipation Proclamation. The official language of the DC act read, "Be it enacted that all persons held to service or labor within the District of Columbia by reason of African descent are herby discharged and freed of and from all claims to such service or labor." The compensation part of the law referred to local slave owners who would be given $300 for the loss of their human property. Washington, DC, was now a city with a large population of free colored men, women, and children, which meant old systems would have to adjust. Just one month later, on May 21, 1862, Congress would pass a bill requiring public funding for schools for all free coloreds in the District.[1] It was what a small community in Washington and Georgetown had been wanting for for years.

While DC had a very healthy slave trade, it also had a good number of free blacks, as they were also called, living among whites and slaves, dating as far back as the early 1800s. Some had purchased their freedom; others had been freed by manumission. Still others were the free sons

9

or daughters of slaveholders or coloreds who perhaps had never been enslaved at all. By the time DC's Emancipation Act was passed there were about eleven thousand free colored people in the district, about 20 percent of the entire population.

While their status was "free," their lives were hardly characterized as ones enjoying liberty. A free colored person was not owned by anyone, but did not have the rights or protections of a white Washingtonian. They were subjected to degrading Black Codes, laws that restricted where they could live, what jobs they could hold, and even when they could walk down the street. All free blacks were required to register with the city and have whites bear witness to the registration on their behalf. For example, on September 11, 1840, this entry was made to the District of Columbia Free Negro Register under Certificate of Freedom.

> Hannah Cooke, a credible white person, swears that she has known Lucy Duckett, the wife of Augustus Duckett, for many years and she is free. Lucy's two children, Richard Edward, who is about twelve years old, and William Augustus, who is about eight, were born free.

On May 6, 1842, Henrietta Carroll registered for her free status when the lady of the house saw fit to let her go:

> Maria Ford frees her servant woman named Henrietta Carroll, who she has held as a slave for a term of years. Henrietta is a bright mulatto woman about thirty years old.

Nighttime curfews were established. A free black person could be arrested if he or she wasn't carrying the correct identification, and that could land a person a six-month jail term. And everyone knew you did not want to wind up in the infamous District Jail, a hideous institution regularly condemned by some northern senators as inhumane.[2] Sometimes a free black man or woman would have to pay an inexplicable fine just for existing, a fee called a peace bond to insure continued "good" behavior.[3]

The Black Codes were meant to deter runaway slaves from coming to Washington and to keep free blacks in their place. But, given the oppressive nature of the restrictive codes, there was a glaring omission: while there were no laws supporting the education of free blacks in the District, there were no laws *restricting* their education either, as there were in much of the South.

Imagine the sheer will of a free black carpenter, George Bell, and two other free men, Nicholas Franklin and Moses Liverpool, skilled caulkers—all illiterate but determined to build a schoolhouse for their children, decades before Emancipation Day. Bell's wife, Sophia, sold produce and meals at local markets and she made enough money to buy her husband's freedom for $400 when he was forty years old.[4] Six years later, in 1807, Bell, Franklin, and Liverpool partnered with a white abolitionist named Lowe who accepted the teaching position at the newly built Bell School. It is thought to be the first physical schoolhouse built for colored children in the District.[5]

Over time, more and more schools were formed in black churches and in private homes with progressive Northerners serving as teachers. Among them were Mrs. Mary Billings's School, St. Frances Academy for Colored Girls, the McCoy School, and the Ambush School, to name a few. This shadow education system was necessary because, very simply, the original law requiring public schools in the District of Columbia clearly stated that the funds would support public schools for whites only.

Two years after the District's government was established in 1804, the charter was amended to provide a permanent educational institution for white children ages six to seventeen, paid for by the government. The city elders believed there was "an inseparable connection between the education of youth and the prevalence of pure morals."[6] The money would come from taxes on "slaves and dogs and licenses for carriages and hacks, ordinaries retailing wines and spirituous liquors, billiard tables, theatrical hawkers and peddlers."[7] Tax the sins to pay for budding virtue.

President Thomas Jefferson, who was also president of the first DC School Board of Trustees, contributed $200 to start an endowment that would help defray the cost.[8] For some of the more class-conscious Washingtonians, the idea of public schools seemed on par with how some people feel about public toilets. Detractors of the government-sponsored education plan thought that the "public" academies were low class and conjured up a structure of "pauper and charity schools."[9] For several years, wealthy parents were told not to send their children to these schools so that there would be room for only the most destitute.

It wasn't until the 1860s that the idea of free education was presented in a way that made it palatable to most Washingtonians. The new movement—complete with a rebranding campaign, "Schools for all: Good enough for the richest, cheap enough for the poorest"[10]—pushed for the construction of substantial buildings for children who lived in the nation's capital, but still only for white children. As one former superintendent of schools acknowledged, "It may be stated at the outset that the colored children of the District of Columbia were not included among the beneficiaries of the public schools in any legislation by the Congress or the city council prior to the abolition of slavery in 1862."[11]

A small woman from the North disagreed with this position.

It was hard for Myrtilla Miner to work on her family's farm in Brookfield, New York. Compared to her twelve hale siblings, she was small, thin, and pale, and she suffered from a weak spine. However, she tried to work the fields, picking hops so that she could afford the luxury of occasionally buying a book. Most of the time she borrowed them from the library. She often joked that in her lifetime she had every book from the library in the family home at some point.

The Miners lived in poverty like most people in the Oneida region. Her father saw to it that his children had just enough education and learned to read, but the farm life came first. Myrtilla, or Myrtle as she was known to family and friends, was permitted to go to school for a brief time. It was a distance from her home on the hill, and getting there was a challenge, given her back problems. Still, as often as she could, she hiked down from her house and across a footbridge, crossing from the farmland into a small town where she could take a seat in an old red schoolhouse.

Given her active mind and frail body, Miner searched for a way to extend her education, at one point even writing to Governor Seward of New York to ask if there was some way a girl like her could acquire a liberal education. The outcome presented a good news/bad news scenario. The good news was that the governor actually wrote her back. The bad news was his message: such programs and endowments did not exist for women at that time.[12] Undaunted, she continued to self-educate as the years passed. She tried to teach some younger girls, but Miner became aware of her own academic limitations. She knew needed to go to school, serious school, so she resorted to begging.

The principal of Young Ladies' Domestic Seminary in Clinton, New York, found himself facing a delicate brunette woman with huge eyes and a sallow complexion, whom he later described as "pathetic," pleading with him to allow her to attend his school for free.[13] She hoped the principal would let her defer payment for a year until she could work it off. Something in him recognized her passion was real.

Once admitted under this arrangement, Miner would let nothing keep her from her classes or lessons, even as she underwent a procedure to have setons inserted near her spine.[14] She wrote to her brother Seth that sometimes she was so sore she could barely move. Although physically weak, she began to develop a strong voice, a feminist one, which in turn awakened an abolitionist leaning. At school she observed three classmates, free colored girls, who were treated the same as she was. The extent to which her feminism and abolitionism would fuse would not be fully clear until after she left school and, in 1847, accepted her third teaching position, at Newton Female Institute in Whitesville, Mississippi. She was thirty-two years old.

Miner was not prepared for the sound of the whip. Slaves were being herded, and in some cases beaten, not far from where she was teaching the charming daughters of the area's wealthy plantation owners. While the young ladies were learning ornamental knitting and ancient languages, young girls their age worked the fields. When she quietly approached the field master about more humane treatment for the slaves, he replied it was out of his power and that "they are but grown up children and must be whipped or they will not work and we cannot sustain them without."[15] The conditions horrified Miner; she could not eat or sleep. She also couldn't leave her lucrative job. She was very much in debt due to her schooling. To pay back her loan she would have to endure the experience—and it would change her life forever.

In the South the idea of teaching slaves or even free blacks to read was anarchic. As one former slave named Elijah Green remembered, "For God's sake, don't let a slave be catch with a pencil and paper. That was a major crime. You might as well had killed your marster or missus."[16] If a slave in the Deep South dared to learn to read, the harsh penalty could be a whipping, branding, or the painful removal of a finger. South

Carolina's slave code prohibited slaves from gathering without white supervision, learning to read and write, and growing their own food. Some whites feared slave uprisings if their property became educated.

After two years of watching the plight of young enslaved women, Miner thought she had uncovered a way to help. She approached the principal of the institute, Dr. D. L. Phares, to ask about teaching the young slave girls in her free time. Phares reminded Miss Miner that doing so was illegal in Mississippi under penalty of fine or imprisonment. Undaunted, she appealed to their shared strong religious convictions.

"I am convinced that they should be properly instructed or the belief in their immortality be relinquished be persons professing to be guided by Christian principles. . . . I beg leave to teach them."

"Have you ever taught colored people at home?" the principal asked.

"Not as a class but only as individuals in white schools."

Dr. Phares quietly responded, "I have often thought that northern philanthropists have a great field of labor among their own colored people and if they would convince us of their sincerity they should instruct and elevate them first." The truth in those words struck Miner, and later she recalled, "It was that hour I resolved to open a normal school for colored youth."[17]

Miner knew her best chance at success was elsewhere. She was aware that within the Washington, DC, city limits, it was illegal for "coloreds" to attend white schools but it was not illegal to teach them. But Myrtilla Miner's mission was bigger than simply teaching colored girls to read and write. She was looking for a long-term solution to both the horror she'd witnessed in Whitesville and the benign neglect of the North. She believed if a colored woman learned to teach, she could then teach her own people, especially in the South. It was Miner's take on the proverb "Give a man a fish, and you feed him for a day. Teach a man to fish, and you feed him for a lifetime." As she prepared to open a school in Washington, she wrote to a friend:

All who look upon with curiosity rather than earnest sympathy I distrust for it is evident they are attracted to me by my peculiar ties and not by the spirit within me. I am really going to Washington to secure a school for the colored missus there. . . . Our intention is to educate a class of teachers who shall be efficient and exert an influence that in ten years may be felt. We go forth anticipating vast obstacles and many trials but a friend in Washington writes, he thinks we can undisturbingly teach colored children there.

Some thought the idea preposterous, and it was clearly dangerous. When word from the tiny woman with the huge plan reached the famed abolitionist Frederick Douglass he told her the plan was "reckless, almost to the point of madness."[18]

On December 6, 1851, in a rented room owned by a free black and paid for by money from northern Quakers, Miner's school opened: the

Myrtilla Miner, founder of the Normal School
for Colored Girls.
Library of Congress, John Angel James Wilcox, engraver

Normal School for Colored Girls. Her first students, just six of them, were barely literate, and some left almost immediately. Within a month, however, there were fifteen pupils. And as colored families learned of the extraordinary news that there was a school where young girls could learn more than just rudimentary addition and reading, Miner was inundated with requests. She soon had forty pupils. Parents approached her, some desperate. One pleaded with Miner, "Will you educate my daughter? I have so many children I can hardly feed and clothe them, much less give them learning, but I want this one taught and if you educate her you may have her."[19]

As grateful as some were for her work, others were equally hateful. Her home was set on fire and bricks were thrown through her windows.[20] She was forced to move the school several times because of threats. One morning she arrived at school to find a note that read, "If you are not out of that house with your niggers by the tenth of April you and all your effects will be set in flames." It was signed "Citizens of the First Ward."[21]

Things came to a head four months after the school opened. A group of local white neighbors began to harass Miner's students as they left at the end of the day. The group gathered outside the school and verbally assaulted the young girls as they tried to walk home. The angry whites blocked the sidewalks and forced the girls to go around them. One lawyer spread his elbows out in an effort to knock the girls off the walkway. When his arm made contact with one of the young misses, he then cursed the girls, calling them "impertinent hussies." White Washingtonians were not as progressive as Miner had hoped. The words of Frederick Douglass were coming true. Her students worried. One of her students, a girl named Marietta, wrote to her teacher, "Sometimes a dark cloud seems to overshadow me. The cloud appears thicker and darker. I say will slavery forever exist? But a voice says, it shall cease. It shall and it must be abolished! I think blood will be shed before all and be fair. The question is are we willing to give up our lives for freedom?" [22]

On the morning of her thirty-seventh birthday, Myrtilla Miner dressed in her best clothes. She was not going to a party or to a show. She was going to confront the lawyer with the sharp elbows. He had threatened the school's landlord, an older colored woman who told Miner she feared for her property and for herself. He told the old woman that she might expect to see her house torn down over her head, and if she escaped she should think herself well off. The old woman had come to Miner distraught.

"The Lord save us! O the Lord have mercy! I can't endure this. I shan't have no home that ole masssa lef me during my lifetime. Then I'll be so desolate. What will I do ?" The old woman was wringing her hands.

"Why, what is the matter Aunty? I think the Lord will save and have mercy, too, if we trust Him," Miner tried in vain to console her.

"But they threaten to mob this house 'cause I let in the school and I can't afford to be mobbed and turned out in my old age."

"O, don't be so troubled. If they mob this down, the Lord will give you a better one. There are friend whose will not see you suffer to such a cause."

"But the thing'd be to get it. I'se 'fraid to trust." But the old woman did trust Miner, who regularly paid the rent of ten dollars a month. And in a moment of strength the older woman informed the man that as long as the teacher paid the rent, Miner had the right to stay and no one could turn her out. The attorney was an upper-crust sort who thought he knew how to intimidate the old colored landlady and the spinster teacher.

Myrtilla Miner recalled in a detailed letter to a friend that the lawyer received her politely on that day, her birthday, when she introduced herself. However, once she inquired about his contention that her pupils were disturbing the peace, their conversation became heated.

"Your pupils?" the lawyer responded.

"Yes, the colored girls."

"What, you keep that nigger school?"

"Yes and hold myself responsible for their deportment in the street."

"Well, I'll tell you we are not going to have this nigger school. Anyhow for they are saucy and impudent and shove white people off the walks! It is contrary to all rules to have them gathered in such companies and we shan't have it!"

"Did more than one answer you?"

"Yes they all answered as saucy as possible!"

"It tells too much," Miner countered. "For I have forbidden my pupils to even answer the insults of white men. What did you say to my scholars?"

"We are not going to have you Northern Abolitionists coming down here to teach our niggers. We know better what to do with them than you do."

"What do you propose to do with them?"

"Send them out of the country. We don't want them here."

"But you cannot do that in a day, and while you are prosecuting your plans, I shall prosecute mine."

"I have an idea that they have grown more impertinent since you came among."

"Very likely, for they have not had time to outgrow their ignorance and folly, but wait two years and see how they will appear."

"Who sent you here to teach niggers?"

"A higher power than man directed me and man shall not defeat me."

"But who pays you?"

"The scholars pay a regular tuition and I am infringing no law, so the mayor tells me."

"Well you will be mobbed; that will be the consequences."

"It seems to be a new version of Southern chivalry that you would mob a defenseless woman who violates no law of God or man, merely because she dare earn her living in a philanthropic way and insult her pupils because they wish to acquire knowledge to earn their livelihood and be independent of the aid of those who despise and degrade them."

The lawyer responded, "I shall not do it but you will be mobbed and that is certain."

"Who will mob me?"

"Why—the rowdies!"

"No, never! They do not care what or whom I teach and never take the responsibility of violating the laws except when instigated by such men as yourself! It would be well to remember that we are on national domain and the laws are for me as well as for you."

The man stamped his foot.

"No! This is every inch my own soil. Every inch mine we stand on."

"But you can make no law because they are made by legislation of the country for my protection and for my scholars as well as for you. Besides, these free colored people are not your niggers and you have no more right to say what I shall or shall not do with them than I have to say what you shall do. Inasmuch as I do not presume to dictate to you neither shall you interfere with my plans."

The lawyer tried a different tack.

"But what good will it do to teach them? They will never thank you. They are a most ungrateful set and will only turn and despise you for all you do."

"I should so suppose from the treatment they have received, but I am not seeking thanks, and these considerations are of little consequences compared with the law of right."

"Paying all deference, Madam, to your judgment which I undoubtedly hold in the highest respect, I must be allowed to differ and assure there is no right in the case and you will be disappointed in your expectations. Some morning it will come out in the 'Baltimore Sun' that the white abolitionist that came down here to teach a nigger school was mobbed. The house torn down and all the books and furniture burned."

"The next morning it will come out that the famous Mr. Lawyer instigated the mob and then we shall no longer remain in obscurity but stand side by side before the world for judgment and I shall be more willing to take my sentence than you."

"But I shall not mob you," he offered as a defense. Plausible deniability. He would get the poor whites to do his work. Still, Miner would not be distracted.

"Then it will not be done. For you are the first who threatened it and you will have the glory and if Washington can afford a mob because one lone woman wishes to teach a few of its neglected free colored people I can afford to meet the mob. You will be obliged to mob many times unless you mob my head off and as you are not prepared do that, it will be better to make no attempt."

"They will not hurt you, but they will tear down the house and I would not like to see you in it at the time."

"I hope I may be there. It must be sublime. Quite like an ocean story."[23]

The conflict lasted about an hour.

Miner stayed in the building only another month before leaving out of respect for the terrified landlord. By this time, Myrtilla Miner had learned how to use a pistol.

Funding was another issue. Because there were no public funds available for her school, Miner constantly needed to solicit donors to keep the school afloat. Another concern was the exclusiveness of her student body. She wanted her school to be a place where all could learn but, in her own words, "confessed" to a friend that she sought out more educated girls for her school and often sought out girls of mixed race. A fund-raising letter revealed why. Reverend William H. Beecher, one of her biggest supporters, trustee of the school, and brother to Harriet Beecher Stowe, was able to collect impressive sums for the school from northern abolitionists. He received $375 from the Plymouth Church in Brooklyn and $33 from the Congregational Church in Guilford, Connecticut, as well as many more donations. At one point he was able to collect $1,262 in just two months.[24] His fund-raising letters touted the virtue and the moral position of educating colored citizens. In one pitch he painted a dramatic scenario, describing that, in addition to the general population of the District, the school would

> hope to reach a class of girls of peculiar interest, often the most beautiful and intelligent and yet the most hopelessly wretched. Receiving from the mother beauty, grace, and gentleness and from the master-father the Saxon energy, intelligence, and fire, they are often object of strong paternal affection and gladly would he educate and save them. But no place of refuge is there on all the earth; domestic peace drives them from his hearth; he cannot emancipate them to be victims of violence or lust; he cannot send them to Northern schools. . . . We would open an asylum near them where they may be brought, educated in housewifery as well as science, and thus be prepared to be teachers among their own race and places of usefulness guaranteed to them.

That many of the girls had access to reading or basic education by virtue of their access to whites, perhaps through a white parent, apparently made for an effective—and perhaps latently racist—fund-raising pitch. As did the tragic mulatto theme.

The fund-raising over the years was successful. Miner was able to purchase three acres near N Street and New Hampshire Avenue NW for $4,300, a fourth of which came from Harriet Beecher Stowe—royalties from *Uncle Tom's Cabin*.

In March 1854 the school opened on its own property. That year more than a hundred people from around the country visited the school. They came from as far away as Kentucky, Massachusetts, New Hampshire, and even Canada to see the work for themselves.[25] It was a Miner miracle. Miner's standards were high. Her students learned geography, history, and languages. Each girl tended her own garden. Miner was fastidious about cleanliness and required her students to bathe daily. Her students thought of her as their guardian angel.[26] She too believed that she was protected by God, and she also believed herself to be clairvoyant, a fact that informs the substance of this letter to a friend:

> I love this school of mine profoundly, and have really no idea, when I am with them, that my students are not white, recognizing their spiritual more than their physical. Some, indeed, many spirits with whom I come in contact here seem far darker than they.[27]

Given her success against the odds, Miner was emboldened to pursue a secondary school, something akin to a high school, for colored children. She and a contingent of abolitionists sought to buy land to build a new facility that would accommodate 150 students. It would include a dormitory for teachers and students who wanted to come from neighboring states.

Miner's increased ambition touched a nerve. An all-girls school to engage the existing semiliterate colored population was barely tolerated. A magnet that would draw more coloreds from other parts of the country was something else entirely. In a letter to a local paper, one of the city's elders, former mayor Walter Lenox, clearly articulated what many white Washingtonians thought and said to each other about *their* city, free coloreds, and abolitionists. The mayor's 1,319-word piece was published in the *National Intelligencer* newspaper, appearing in the May 6, 1857, edition. On the subject of the proposed school's course of study, he wrote:

> The standard of education which is proposed is far beyond the primary branches, and will doubtless from time to time be advanced. Is it, then, just to ourselves or humane to the colored population for us to permit a degree of instruction so far beyond their political and social condition and which must continue to exist in this as in every other slaveholding community? With this superior education there will come no removal of the present disabilities, no new

sources of employment equal to mental culture; and hence there will be a restless population, less disposed than ever to fill that position in society which is allotted to them. In my judgment these two objections—the increase of our free and the indiscriminate education of them far beyond their fixed condition are sufficient reasons for us to oppose this scheme.

Translation: The "coloreds" are too inferior to learn and those who might learn something will become uppity.

On the free coloreds as a burden:

The District of Columbia contains about three thousand six hundred slaves and ten thousand free colored persons. This latter class embraces very many most worthy members who contribute to the wealth of the community but the necessities of a large portion of them impose an onerous tax upon the public revenue and upon private charity. This condition of things does not arise exclusively from their own demerits: they have been gradually and to a very considerable extent ousted by the increase of white labor from the positions formerly filled by them as domestics and laborers.

Translation: We have enough of those free "coloreds" to deal with, so why build something that would attract more of them? Especially when we have poor whites who will do menial work.

On Miner and the Republican conspiracy:

A misguided philanthropy inflamed by political demagogism would readily supply the means and the agents to execute its designs; an incendiary press in our midst will soon follow and with all these varied and active agencies stimulated by the presence of adherents in Congress, in constant operation our District will be converted into the headquarters of "slavery agitation" from which it may deal forth in every direction its treasonable blows. It is unnecessary to depict the fatal consequences to ourselves and to our country.

Translation: Don't let outsiders change our way of life. This is nothing but trouble. Big time.

And to those who might donate money:

> With justice we can say to the advocates of this measure, you are not competent to decide this question; your habits of thought, your ignorance of our true relations to the colored population, prevent you from making a full and candid examination of its merits and above all the temper of the public mind is inauspicious even for its consideration. If your humanity demands this particular sphere for its action, and if, to use your own language, prejudice would brand them at your Northern schools, establish separate institutions in the free States, dispense your money there abundantly as your charity will supply, draw to them the unfortunate at your own door, or from abroad and in all respects gratify the largest impulses of your philanthropy; but do not seek to impose upon us a system contrary to our wishes and interests, and for the further reason that by so doing you injure the cause of those whom you express a wish to serve.

Translation: Things were fine here before you abolitionists showed up. You have no idea about this town. If you are hell bent on doing this, go do it up North. Don't *make* us hurt you.

The letter succeeded in killing the drive for a secondary school. Miner's fundraising efforts were wholly unsuccessful. Her health declined, and she stepped away from the school, which closed for a year while she sought treatment in California. While there, she was in a carriage accident, which injured her in such a way that she never fully regained good health.

Miner was forty-nine when she died, but her dream did not. Within the first seven years of her school's existence, six of her former students had set up their own schools.[28] Based on Miner's success, and with the 1862 congressional mandate to create public schools for colored students in Washington, Congress voted to incorporate Myrtilla Miner's school in 1863. It would be named the Institution for the Education of Colored Youth founded by Myrtilla Miner.

Fifteen years later the school became part of the District's public school system. It was renamed the Miner Normal School. A candidate for the two-year course could be either male or female, must be at least sixteen years old and of good moral character, and would be required to pass exams in reading, writing, arithmetic, geography, and grammar.[29] The Miner Normal School, which became Miner Teachers College in 1929, trained a legion of black teachers who went back into the black school system well into the 1940s.

Myrtilla Miner accomplished her primary goal: teaching colored people to teach higher education. Now it would be up to someone else to create a school where that teaching could be done.

3 | THE LAW GIVETH AND THE LAW TAKETH AWAY

THINK ABOUT THE CIVIL rights breakthroughs that occurred in the 1960s and what they meant to the United States. Freedom riders. The March on Washington. The Voting Rights Act of 1965. Thurgood Marshall's appointment to the Supreme Court. *Loving v. Virginia*. Something or someone you encountered today was likely affected by the events of that decade.

Now rewind a century and imagine those changes magnified exponentially when slavery gave way after the "Great Unpleasantness" ended. Any vestigial legalized racism was supposedly excised by the Thirteenth and Fourteenth Amendments to the US Constitution. The argument could be made that an American living in the late nineteenth century experienced mind-blowing societal shifts whose magnitude would not be felt again for another one hundred years. These shifts began in the '60s—the 1860s.

In 1867, less than two decades removed from the active Washington, DC, slave trade, colored Washingtonians gained the right to vote. And vote they did. By the end of the decade, seven colored men had been elected to the District's city council. The laws began to change. The council passed an ordinance that declared that "any quiet and orderly person" who was "well behaved and respectable" should be welcome in establishments, taverns, restaurants, shops, and concerts in the District regardless of race—and all people should be treated the same. In reality this didn't happen, but for a time these laws were on the books.[1] In the same moment, the city elected Mayor Sayles J. Bowen, the most radical of Republicans, a white man who believed wholeheartedly in integration.

So did the crusading senator from Massachusetts, Charles Sumner, who shared Bowen's view, especially when it came to schools. The arrogant and brilliant Senator Sumner was almost delusional about the country's willingness to accept civil rights for colored people. He repeatedly proposed legislation for equal pay, equal housing opportunity, and integrated transportation. And he hated slavery and anyone who liked it.

Once during a debate on the Senate floor, Senator Sumner said a pro-slavery South Carolina senator, Andrew Butler, had "chosen a mistress to whom he has made his vows, and who though ugly to others is always lovely to him, though polluted in the sight of the world is chaste in his sight: I mean the harlot Slavery."[2] The suggestion that the good gentleman from South Carolina was cavorting with a whore, metaphorical or otherwise, was astounding.

Senator Sumner never saw the blunt object aimed at his head. He was at his desk when he felt a blow to his skull. Two days after Sumner's speech, Congressman Preston Brooks of South Carolina, a relative of the harlot-lover, struck Senator Sumner on the head with a metal-topped cane. Repeatedly. Witnesses described the attack in detail: "Sumner rose and lurched blindly about the chamber futilely, attempting to protect himself bleeding profusely." Two other lawmakers rushed to his aid, but by then Sumner had ripped the desk from its floor bolts to protect himself. Congressman Brooks beat Senator Sumner senseless. As the unconscious senator was carried away, Brooks walked calmly out of the chamber without being detained.[3] Sumner was incapacitated for many months.

The reaction was much less dramatic when Senator Sumner pushed legislation that promoted integration in schools. He was simply defeated. However, though one door had closed, another opened. Rather than agree to the insane idea of the races learning together, Congress opted for separate public schools in DC. There would be a "double headed school authority" in Washington. Congress would regulate the white schools through city councils, a board of education, a superintendent, and a board of trustees. The colored-school flow chart was a little more streamlined. The colored schools would be overseen by a board of trustees appointed and governed by the secretary of the interior. Until the board was established, a white superintendent would oversee the schools.

In 1862, the *first* piece of legislation was passed authorizing the use of 10 percent of taxes collected from colored residents for primary schooling. Given how few colored citizens actually owned land at the time, this was not nearly enough money to start a whole new system, which some speculate was the point. Two years later the act had to be fortified to create a pool of money for all children that would be appropriated based on the percentage of white and colored children in the system. Allocating funds by percentage presented another problem. The number of free blacks in the late 1860s obviously exceed the number before Emancipation Day. Yet the percentages were based on the number of free colored children in DC in 1860. It was simple math. The funding act was revised again to address this problem, but there was another concern. The money had to actually be dispensed to the newly established colored trustees put in charge of the creating the colored public school system. The financial pipeline was sluggish at best. In 1864 only $628 of the $25,000 set aside made it to the trustees.[4] In response, Congress put in place a third act as of July 23, 1866, that required funds be handed over to the colored trustees in a timely manner or the DC commissioners would be penalized. Ultimately the funds would go directly to the independent board of trustees for colored schools.[5] At the time, "independent" meant "not our problem"—but to a few wise colored men it meant "our turn."

William Syphax seized the moment. It was no surprise when, in 1868, this "well known and intelligent colored citizen of Washington" was appointed the chairman and president of the District of Columbia Board of Trustees of the Colored Public Schools.[6] He was praised for "fidelity and excellent judgment as the Chairman of the Board."[7] Initially Syphax had supported Senator Sumner in his push for integration, both men believing it was the best way to get the best schools for colored children. Senator Sumner once told him, "Mr. Syphax, I want your child to study out of the same book, at the same desk, and under the same teacher as mine; for I am sure that the white man will always provide for his child a good education."[8]

Syphax realized that, while Sumner's assessment may have been correct, it wasn't going to happen. Syphax knew that he had to act quickly to establish a separate secondary school for colored students while the political winds were at his back and the coffers were open. Where Myrtilla

Miner's efforts to create an institution of higher learning were affected by her gender, northern support system, and maybe even her race, William Syphax had the advantage of his family status and local history. His grandmother had been Martha Washington's maid, and according to local legend and some Syphax family historians, William may have been a descendant of Mrs. Washington as well as a relative of Robert E. Lee, by marriage.[9]

Syphax's enslaved father had been owned by the man who owned Arlington, Virginia—all of it. William had grown up hearing tales from his father about meeting George Washington and Thomas Jefferson when they came to visit the rich landowner for whom he worked. Syphax's mother, Maria, was the colored daughter of the landowner and the aforementioned maid.[10] When the landowner died, he left a large piece of land to Maria Syphax, where her family lived for decades—that is, until the government attempted to seize it through a post–Civil War tax loophole.

William Syphax was a big man, over six feet tall, with a strong, sharp nose and a prominent forehead. He had been educated in a private school in Arlington and had forged a career as a messenger and clerk in the Department of the Interior. He was smart and persuasive, and used both these traits, and his commanding presence, when he boldly and successfully petitioned Congress to pass a bill that returned the fifteen acres of land to his family.[11] President Andrew Johnson signed it. If William Syphax could wrestle land from the government, he could surely build a congressionally sanctioned colored school system. But first Syphax would need the help of the community. Schools required pupils.

The population of Washington had changed after the end of the war. Between 1860 and 1867, the number of colored people in Washington increased 200 percent as former slaves found their way north.[12] Manual laborers with little or no education, many of them newly emancipated, became a part of what was known as alley life in Washington. Off main streets, these small interior courtyards were lined with back-to-back wooden shacks. Sanitation was minimal at best, but this was the only housing available to some of the new arrivals.

Many middle-class working blacks, Irish, and Italians lived in these areas too.[13] Some became functional communities; others suffered from disease and crime. The alleys were not sequestered in one part of town;

they were woven throughout the District. Their existence was impossible to ignore, which contributed to the hostility from many whites and some of the original free blacks, who saw the alley dwellers as a threat to the city, or at least their comfortable way of life.[14]

Many alley children had to work to help their families survive, so school was not an option. Others did not see the point. Here's a poem from a child questioning the wisdom of spending his days in a classroom. Lost on him is that while sitting in a classroom, he learned to write.[15]

School
Is, Such, a Funny, Place,
I, Don't, See, Why, We, Go
But, Yet and, Still, We Have,
To, Go, Each and Every Day,

But, yet, And, Still, We, Have
To, Go, It, Really, Don't Make
Sence, For, I, Just, Hate, To
Go, To, School, And I, Know
That, You, Will, Agree

For, School, is Just A
Place, For, Fools, and Fools
Don't only, Go, I Go,
And I, Am, not, a Fool

To combat these attitudes and to create a supply of students for the new colored schools, Syphax appealed to clergy to encourage their congregants to send their children to the new schools. In a letter dated September 10, 1868, Syphax wrote:

Dear Sir: The Trustees of the Colored Schools for Washington and Georgetown earnestly desire to enlist your valuable cooperation with them in efforts to render these schools as efficient as possible . . . by often holding up before the people of your charge the absolute necessity of education, in order to fit their children for the new duties of freedom and civil equality and to enable them to take and worthily fill positions of honor and responsibility. If educated they can do this; if ignorant they never can. . . . Carefully instruct the people in the importance of sending their children regularly and punctually to school . . . by advising the parents to always sustain the regulation and the good discipline of the schools . . . by urging the parents to visit the school, make the acquaintance of the teachers of their children, see how the schools are conducted and to show the teachers that they take an interest in their children's progress. . . . The children of the people of color, for the most part, can attend school for but a few years, when they must seek employment by which to obtain a livelihood; it is, therefore, of the highest importance that they should make the most of their brief time in school.

Brief for now.

Many of the small grammar schools were stuffed into old abandoned buildings with the children practically sitting on top of one another. The white schools had been around for sixty years and had built up something of a curriculum. The colored schools were lucky to get an old army barracks and

William Syphax (1825–1891), president of the board of trustees of the colored schools of Washington and Georgetown.

The Historical Society of Washington, DC

a few desks. Clearly, all the schools would be separate but certainly not equal. But at the time, not equal seemed better than nonexistent. To build better structures, Syphax and his colleagues used the funds raised from taxes and appropriated to the Freedmen's Bureau, a department created to help ease the country's postwar transition. In 1864 there was only one colored public school. By 1872 there would be seventy-five.[16] The system started with seven teachers; the number grew to eighty in eight years. The colored board of trustees named the schools after their greatest supporters, such as Senator Charles Sumner and his partner Representative

Thaddeus Stevens. Flattering white supporters in this way was a helpful tactic and a reflection of the cleverness and political savvy employed by Syphax and his compatriots. Sumner and Stevens fought for the Freedmen's Bureau and saw to it the that hospitals and infrastructure would be built to support the newly freed colored population. This included helping to establish Howard University, which for the next hundred years would act as a big brother to the District's colored academic high school.

George F. T. Cook, from one of the richest colored families in the District, became the first superintendent of the colored schools. William Wormley, another colored board trustee, was a successful hotel owner. The trustees worked together to improve education for those children who wanted and needed it. They fiercely fought off saboteurs who regularly tried to reduce the power of their positions. At one point Syphax, Cook, and Wormley battled back an attempted coup by the evolving white board of education that would have folded the colored trustees under the trustees for the white schools and made the colored trustees subordinate. It was in the hands of the president before Syphax and his colleagues realized that a law to abolish the colored board of trustees was almost a reality. It wouldn't be the last time this fight would be fought.

Syphax and Cook and Wormley were part of a group of Washingtonians referred to by the colored newspaper the *Washington Bee* as the "Colored 400" and often described as "aristocracy" and "black dynasties."[17] These families, actually about one hundred of them, could afford to create their own small, private schools or church schools long before public education became available. Many were like Syphax, not only of African descent but also related to the people who had *owned* their families during slavery, which is why many of their ancestors could read. These free blacks had been in Washington, DC, as long as there had been a Washington, DC.

Because they had political savvy, tentative white connections, and in some cases money, Washingtonians like Syphax, Cook, and others were able to use the new laws to finally establish a secondary school for colored teenagers, the school that would one day become Dunbar. Over time the argument would be made that the school was only for *some* colored children—their children, original free Washingtonians. The newcomers and children of the alleys were barely represented in the early school system. Only about one-third of colored children eligible for schooling at this time attended some kind of school.[18] Many resented the class distinctions, a result of color phobia among whites and some colored Washingtonians. The elite social status of these men and their friends, as well as their ancestry, embedded what has become a longstanding, incendiary dispute about color in the history of Dunbar.

With public money and a little private financial help from the estate of Myrtilla Miner, the Preparatory High School for Colored Youth held its first classes on November 4, 1870, in the basement of the Fifteenth Street Presbyterian Church. Its mission was to provide students with "incentive to higher aim and education."[19] At first there were four students: Rosetta Coakley, John Nalle, Mary Nalle, and Caroline Parke. The number soon grew to eleven and by the end of the first year to forty-five; by the end of the fourth year the student body stood at 103.[20]

The school's beginnings were humble. At first, the field of study was, as described by historian Henry Robinson, "hardly more than an advanced grammar school laboring under the disadvantages of an inadequate faculty, overcrowding, and drop outs. But gradually the high school's curriculum improved through the efforts of principals."

A white abolitionist from New Hampshire, Emma J. Hutchins, had been teaching grammar school and was recruited to head the new high school, which was more like a single class. There were no formal graduations in these early days because many of the older students studied only a few years before their roles morphed into that of teachers. Caroline Parke started high school in 1870 and two years later was employed as an assistant teacher at the Preparatory High School with an annual salary of $700.

After Hutchins returned north, she was succeeded by Mary J. Patterson, the first black woman in the United States to earn a college degree. She had graduated from Oberlin in 1862. Patterson, remembered as a forceful woman, served as principal for nearly twelve years and is credited with laying the foundation for a strong and rigorous course of study. The students were required to master arithmetic, algebra, grammar, German or Latin, geography, history, physics, and geometry before they could graduate. For example, a physics test question posed to students at the colored high school was "What is the distinction between cohesion and adhesion?" A sample task from geography class was " Name in order the bodies of water through which you would sail going from Chicago to Halifax."[21]

The first real graduation took place on June 7, 1877. The graduates were Mary L. Beason, James C. Craig, Cornelia Pinckney, James B. Wright, Carrie E. Taylor, John H. Parker, Dora F. Barker, Fannie E. McCoy, Julia C. Grant, Mary E. Thomas, and Fannie M. Costin. All eleven graduating students participated at the commencement. James Wright gave a speech about the "Elements of Success."

For years the high school existed as an entity but did not have a physical, permanent location. After a year in a church basement, the colored high school moved to the Thaddeus Stevens Elementary School for one year. Overcrowding became an issue as growing teenagers were packed into the grammar school building serving smaller, younger students. The school was moved again, briefly using the Myrtilla Miner School, but perhaps the relocation to the new Charles Sumner School was a harbinger of things to come.

The Sumner School, named for the crusading senator, was beautiful. Although it was an elementary school, it was designed by one of the most important architects in DC's history, a German-born Marxist named Adolf Cluss. Washington was Cluss's adopted home, but he did not take on any of the bigotry associated with the town. When he designed a school, be it for colored or white students, his goal was to build a structure that promoted dignity for the teaching profession and inspiration for the students. The Sumner School would also serve as the office for the superintendent and the board of trustees of the colored schools of Washington and Georgetown.

At its opening in 1872, the chairman of the building committee called the Sumner School "a house that none need be ashamed to enter, and from which none shall be turned away while there is room to accommodate, be they white or black, high or low, rich or poor. If they seek for education, they shall be welcome."[22] But for the local commissioners the growing number of colored children moving through the grades would not be ignored for much longer.

Financing schools for colored children was not a priority for Congress. The political climate had cooled to civil rights. For most of the colored population in the United States, the last two decades of the nineteenth century were a bleak period. By the 1880s, Reconstruction was a thing of the past, replaced by the Redemption. Southern Democrats, many still angry that their people had not been compensated for their slaves, regained power and used the judicial process to erase the gains of the 1860s and early 1870s. The Republicans who had led so much of the advancement of the colored man were voted out of office. That included the presidency in 1876. President Rutherford B. Hayes was nicknamed "Rutherfraud" because he was awarded the office by agreeing to abandon Reconstruction.

The legislation of the next decade unraveled the work of the prior two.[23] The new balance in Congress continued to roll back the legal clock by choosing not to renew or codify civil rights legislation. So, for example, it once again became legal for private businesses to refuse colored customers. An overwhelming number of Supreme Court decisions during this time obliterated colored rights.[24] In 1883 the court overturned the Civil Rights Act of 1875, which had barred discrimination in public places and transportation in the states. As the historian Rayford Logan wrote, "The last decade of the nineteenth century and the opening of the twentieth century marked the nadir of the Negro's status in American society."

In the nation's capital, however, a growing and increasingly educated colored population would not be denied. Those who could afford to and had enough foundation in reading, writing, and arithmetic took advantage of the system. The percentage of colored students in the District enrolled in public school was higher than that of whites. While 16 percent of school-age white children went to the public schools, 18 percent percent of colored kids were enrolled. The average colored attendance was 97 percent. Some students traveled up to two hours to get to high school, and the teachers worked zealously. Superintendent Cook reported he needed more space and more faculty. He told the city's commissioners, "The degree of success attended to the school was large due to an expenditure of energy and labor on the part of its teachers that cannot long be maintained without serious injury to health." It seemed that almost monthly the *Washington Bee* would make the case for "a respectable high school" given that "our present [colored] school system is the best in the country."[25] And once a grand high school for white students was established, the colored citizenry put on the pressure. In 1892, the same year in which lynching in the South climbed to an all-time high, Washington, DC, would finally open one of the first academic colored high schools using public funds.[26]

"Well equipped" and "roomy" was how ninety-two-year-old Robert Mattingly remembered his alma mater in the last years of his life. The façade of the three-floor building, designed by the head of the office of the building inspector, Thomas Entwistle, boasted red Philadelphia pressed brick. The footprint of the building was 147 feet long and 80 feet deep and featured one central entrance flanked by two wings on each side. The $112,000 budget, about $2.7 million today, had been appropriated by the US Congress. The gables on the front were a decorative terra cotta, and at the very top of the central entrance are the letters *H* and *S*, for high school. *H* and *S*—two letters that so many had waited so long for were right there, carved in stone.

When young Robert Mattingly approached 128 M Street, he arrived with his eighth-grade promotion card in hand. He would find his way to the small gym in the basement, the labs at the rear of the first floor, and the large study hall on the second floor. He also would soon learn the ways of life in high school. There were cliques. One, called the Ravens, claimed devotees of the philosophy of Edgar Allen Poe and seemed "jovial" but "pompous."

As a high school student, Robert's options were to bring lunch from home, eat in the small cafeteria, or visit Mrs. Seely's lunch cart stationed at the front of the building. He discovered those who could afford a treat went to Mr. Landry's lunchroom, where for ten cents you could down a glass of milk and one of three pies: apple, peach, or sweet potato. But most importantly, he would have to decide on a course of study. Built to hold 450 students, the school had three tracks: academic, science, and business. He could study French, German, biology, and political economy, as well as the required four years of English, history, and Latin, two of math, and one of physics or chemistry.[27] Robert elected to pursue science.

"My section teacher was Miss Elizabeth Hunter, a teacher of German. Her control appeared to be somewhat spotty." After watching some students disrupt the class, Robert went to the principal and asked for a transfer to the academic track. At the time he didn't know he would one day be a principal in the DC school system. Matting returned to his hometown after graduating Phi Beta Kappa at Amherst College. He was the first of twenty-seven M Street/Dunbar graduates to attend Amherst in the following sixty years.

On that day, the principal was Dr. Winfield S. Montgomery, the fourth to run the M Street school. Born into slavery, Montgomery graduated Phi Beta Kappa from Dartmouth and earned his medical degree from Howard. If his academic résumé seems extraordinary for a high school principal, it was—but not for an M Street principal. The school's

My Section Teacher at Armstrong, first, second, third, fourth years

My Mathematics Teacher, third and fourth years

My First Principal at Francis, Feb. 1927 to June 1928

My Classmate at Columbia University, Summer of 1929

And a loyal, staunch friend through the years

Mr. Robert N. Mattingly

Phi Beta Kappa from Amherst College

Robert Mattingly, as described by his former student and and longtime friend, Madison Tignor. Tignor went on to become a beloved teacher at Dunbar High School.

Courtesy of the Tignor family

lead educators were Ivy League and honors graduates, some of whom had studied abroad and many of whom had graduate degrees. Richard T. Greener, the first black graduate of Harvard, was principal in 1873. F. L. Cardozo Sr., who had been born a slave, was principal from 1884 to 1896, and earned degrees from Glasgow University and the London School of Theology. At the end of the decade and century, Robert Terrell, another Harvard graduate and a lawyer, led the school.

Why would men and women with medical and legal degrees not pursue careers in their chosen fields? Two words: Jim Crow. Many of these men and women simply would not be hired at universities, hospitals, and law offices. While life for many blacks in DC was better than it would have been in the Deep South, it was hardly a social nirvana. The District of Columbia was still a city struggling with its postwar identity.

One place this dynamic presented itself was within the school system. The colored high school was doing well—very well. In 1899, several colored students outscored white students in statewide test. This did not please many people. One year later, in 1900, the entire education system would be upended when reorganization left colored leaders no longer in charge of their schools. Since the school system's inception, there had always been a colored superintendent of schools leading the way and making the decisions for the colored grade schools and high school. In 1900 the position was downsized to assistant superintendent of colored schools, and that position would now report to one *white* public school authority. George F. T. Cook, a proud man who had led the colored school system for nearly thirty years, resigned.

The colored community was concerned, with good reason. In this political era, would the new superintendent and board of education care for the colored schools at all? Would neglect destroy what had been built? Would they be told what books to use and how many water fountains each school could have? The new struggle for control played out in a dramatic showdown between the white authorities and one of the most memorable and controversial principals of M Street, Mrs. Anna Julia Cooper.

4 | IT'S THE PRINCIPAL

NIGHT AFTER NIGHT, THE principal of the colored high school was publicly accused of being ineffective, insubordinate, and disloyal. And night after night, her supporters testified to her strong moral character and academic abilities. Rumors of smoking and drinking at M Street High School, as well as rumblings about illicit romantic liaisons, had festered over time.

For almost two years, the newly configured and predominately white board of education had been avoiding the thorny question: What to do about Anna Julia Cooper? Someone wanted her gone. It could have been any number of white Washingtonians concerned about her independent streak. Mrs. Cooper also had colored enemies, mainly proponents of the vocational education model. They found her "academics first" philosophy threatening. And she was a colored woman at the turn of the century who had no children but did have two college degrees. She was that rare sort of soul who didn't seem to answer to anyone or anything but her own moral compass.

This potent combination ignited a protracted inquisition of Anna Julia Cooper, the emerging powerhouse principal of the M Street High School. She had come a long way from being a newly married girl of nineteen turned widow at twenty-one.

Anna Julia Haywood was born into slavery in 1858. Of her mother, Hannah, she wrote, "[She] was a slave and the finest woman I have ever known. Though untutored, she could read the Bible and write a little."[1]

Anna did not feel the same about her father, however, whom she barely knew: "I owe nothing to my white father beyond the initial act of procreation. My mother's self-sacrificing toil to give me advantages she had never enjoyed is worthy the highest praise and undying gratitude." The central advantage was education.

Precocious Annie Haywood decided at five years old she would be a teacher.[2] She learned to read and write a bit, something her two brothers did not. In her hometown of Raleigh, North Carolina, her intellectual gifts did not go unnoticed. The founder of the Saint Augustine's Normal and Collegiate Institute, Dr. J. Brinton Smith, extended a scholarship to the bright young colored girl. By the age of nine she was tutoring other students as a "pupil teacher."[3]

Annie Haywood was constantly in search of new academic challenges, easily mastering what was made available to her as a girl. She recalled in her writings, "Well, I found after a while that I had a good deal of time on my hands. I had devoured what was put before me, and like Oliver Twist, was looking around for more. I constantly felt as I suppose as many an ambitious girl has felt, a thumping from within unanswered by any beckoning from without."

Annie wanted to join the young men in their more rigorous course of study. She pushed and pushed until she was allowed to take Greek, Latin, and mathematics along with the fellows. The eager teenage girl in a room full of boys was something of an amusement to her dear old principal.[4] "[He] looked over from the vacant countenances of his sleepy old class of boys for an answer, over to where I sat, to get off his solitary pun—his never failing pleasantry, especially in hot weather—which was to, as he called out 'Any one?' to the effect that 'any one' to them meant 'Annie one!' " She was always ready with an answer.

She stayed at the school nearly fourteen years and fulfilled her childhood dream of teaching. There she met her future husband, another teacher, George Cooper, an Episcopal clergyman seventeen years her senior.

Married only two years when her husband died, Annie found herself unexpectedly alone. She could continue to teach at a meager salary. For a lesser mind, that would have sufficed, but the same instinct that had led Cooper to demand equal coursework in school led her to the only possible conclusion for a woman with her brain: she set her sights on college, even though those around her believed it was a fantasy for a poor young woman from North Carolina. She wrote, "When at last that same girl announced her desire and intention to go to college it was received with about the same incredulity and dismay."[5]

Despite the lack of support, she gathered up all her energy and asked a few believers to write to Oberlin College on her behalf. Oberlin was founded in the 1830s with an extraordinary philosophy for the time: according to its charter, students were received "irrespective of color." And that included young Anna Julia Cooper. The year Cooper received her undergraduate degree after completing the "gentleman's course," she stayed on to get another degree in mathematics.

She was teaching in her home state of North Carolina when the call came from Washington. The colored superintendent of schools, George F. T. Cook, wanted to recruit his fellow Oberlin alum to teach at DC's colored high school. Cook had contacted Oberlin to ask if there were any graduates he should meet and it recommended Cooper; she was the perfect fit. In 1887 she came to the District, moved in with a prominent family, and began teaching math and Latin at M Street for an annual salary of $750.[6]

Also teaching at the high school at the time was one of Cooper's Oberlin classmates, Mary Church, the daughter of well-off colored real estate developer who had begun life as a slave. Since only unmarried women could teach, the single Miss Church had to leave her post when she married another M Street teacher, Robert H. Terrell, who eventually became principal of the school. Terrell, a lawyer by training, once joked he preferred teaching to the law because "I do so like the consistency of the paycheck."

The Terrells became legends of Washington, DC—a true power couple. They both were socially and politically prominent in their efforts to "advance the race." She became the first black woman appointed to the board of education and was instrumental later in life as a political activist, leading the charge to integrate restaurants in the capital. After leaving his post as principal of M Street, her husband became the first colored municipal judge in Washington, DC.

But how was it that a high school principal came to the attention of the president of the United States and be appointed a judge? Terrell came with the highest recommendation from Booker T. Washington, a confidant of President Theodore Roosevelt.

Terrell's exit from the school was both an opportunity and the beginning of deeper trouble for Mrs. Cooper. By the time she became principal, Anna Julia Cooper had accomplished fifteen years of teaching, scholarship, and charitable activity in local community organizations. She was a respected woman who understood the bigger picture. She knew it was her time to shape the future, not only for the school, but also for a generation of colored men and, perhaps more importantly to her, colored women. About education she would often say, "Not the boys less, but the girls more."

With a few exceptions at the turn of the century, education for colored students was basic and minimal. What Anna Julia Cooper wanted to do in DC was radical. Her goal was to build a solid classical curriculum that would be rigorous, challenging, *and* on par with the courses of study at white schools in the District.

The timing was right for Cooper's plan. The year she assumed the principal's post was the year the business curriculum was officially moved out of the M Street school and into a new colored school, Armstrong. For years it had irked some that former principal Francis Cardozo had introduced a two-year, noncollegiate business curriculum into the academic high school. The local paper often accused him of being more of a politician than an educator because he was once the South Carolina state treasurer. Academic purists were thrilled when Congress gave the nod for a colored trade school.

Armstrong High School opened in 1902, giving colored teenagers two options for secondary education: academic and technical. At M Street, Cooper was now free to amp up the curriculum to include all the courses a student—white or colored—would need to be considered for the finest colleges in the country: physics, chemistry, Latin, algebra, history, English, Greek, German, Spanish, trigonometry, and something called "political economy." She also believed in the arts as a way to shape students. She was an accomplished musician herself and encouraged extracurricular activities like dramatics. Cooper believed "dramatic action enables the pupil to vitalize the thoughts and ideas he has studied, to take them into his own life, to make them through imagination a part of his own real self. . . . Dramatics in the schools will help realize the body as the perfected tool of the soul."[7]

Cooper also had an ample supply of well-trained teachers and better-prepared students. The seeds planted by Myrtilla Miner had sprouted and grown. Miner's small teachers' school had been incorporated into the public school system. In its earliest years, graduates of the Miner Normal School, then a colored teachers' college, were guaranteed a job in the DC school system. By the time Cooper needed highly qualified teachers, Miner had produced a few hundred graduates, mostly women. About 45 percent of them stayed in the District and taught in lower schools.[8]

Her faculty included the Miner School valedictorian for the class of 1904, E. B. Henderson, who was also an M Street alum. He was the gym teacher for M Street and spent three summers studying physical education at Harvard. It was there he learned a game called basketball, created by a Canadian athlete. Henderson saw its potential for young colored men and he brought it back to Washington. He established the first-ever colored basketball league. He was also a civil rights activist his whole life and saw to it his students used sports as a means to an end.

Though physically small, Anna Julia Cooper was commanding. Presiding over a classroom from behind a giant wooden desk, her steady gaze and perfect posture demanded attention, and the whiteness of her high-necked blouse against the darkness of her skin echoed the white chalk rows of perfectly written words on the blackboard behind her. Addressing her students she was clear but firm, compassionate, and often sympathetic to those students whose grammar school educations had left them a bit behind. This style left her open to criticism. She didn't care, however, because her students ultimately did well on college entrance tests, even if there were struggles along the way. Cooper had a more diverse student body than her predecessors. Her students were the children of laborers, farmers, book binders, porters, nurses, coal dealers, clerks, watchmen, and bricklayers. Some of the children had to work part time or would drop in and out of school. She was committed to helping them. In her first year as principal, Cooper had under her supervision just over five hundred students, by some counts four hundred girls and 130 boys.[9]

The second part of Cooper's plan was to think about the future that lay beyond M Street for those five hundred kids. She spent hours writing letters to admissions officers at all the best colleges and universities, alerting them to the fine Negro candidates she could offer. She, like many race leaders, often used the word "Negro" instead of "colored." She assured the colleges that her students could pass any entrance exam, but that taking such tests probably wasn't even necessary. According to legend, some of her students had outscored their white peers on citywide tests. Her scholars were ready.

While she was principal, M Street graduates William Richard, French Tyson, and Hugh Francis all matriculated at Harvard. Others followed them to Cambridge; still more went north to New Haven to attend Yale, Providence to attend Brown, and Hanover to attend Dartmouth. In four years she placed twenty-two students in Ivy League schools, as well as at Amherst and Rutgers, and many others went on to Howard University and the Miner Normal School.[10] It was a remarkable record, given the era.

Those college admissions officers knew they were not dealing with an ordinary secondary school teacher. By the time she became a high school principal, Cooper was one of the country's leading feminist intellectuals. She was also considered one of the great community leaders in the District, having helped establish civic organizations such as the Colored Women's League. She was the only woman ever to be elected to the American Negro Academy, an influential think tank whose members included W. E. B. Du Bois and Arturo Schomburg. Her seminal work, *A Voice from the South*, a collection of essays about race, gender, and their intersection, was published in 1892, the same year M Street opened its doors. The book's success clearly established her as a change agent.

One of Cooper's well-known essays reveals why she believed so fervently in education. "What Are We Worth?" asks the title question of coloreds and women living in the late nineteenth century. These two segments of society would have to fight for recognition of their worth, but how? Cooper knew in her heart the answer was education. She believed that "education then, is the safest and richest investment possible to man. It pays the largest dividends and gives the grandest possible product to the world—a man." A man (or woman!), a full being with rights and expectations of liberty. Manhood, womanhood, personhood meant worth. She reasoned education would lead to worth. Education affected home and hearth. Education could even mean the difference between life and death.

Cooper was keenly aware of the mortality rates among colored Washingtonians, especially those facing the unsanitary conditions of the alleys. Cooper had vowed she would "teach the most neglected."[11] She worked with organizations around the District to try to create stability for those in need. Her efforts were part of the unspoken social contract of the times. She was engaging in what was called "racial uplift," and Cooper exercised it in her private life as well. She raised seven foster children, some of whom attended M Street.

Invitations arrived from around the world asking the passionate educator to share her message. In 1900 she addressed the Pan African Congress in London along with W. E. B. Du Bois, a kindred spirit. Du Bois, an educator, sociologist, and writer, believed "the Negro race is going to be saved by its exceptional men." He was convinced that "the black boys need education as well as the white boys." Of course, Cooper would have added "women" and "girls" to those statements.

While their philosophies weren't in lockstep, a profound belief in education as the way toward equality linked Cooper and Du Bois. Their relationship was cordial and professional. As principal, she extended an invitation to speak to the children—one of her first—to Du Bois. In the winter of 1902, Du Bois was pointed in his remarks at M Street. He explained that a movement in the country sought to limit the education of the Negro.[12] He was invited back to speak to all the principals of the colored schools. He gave a lecture titled "Heredity and the Public Schools." His use of heredity referred to the environment in which Negro boys and girls were taught. He warned against those who believed Negroes were inferior but acknowledged that there were conditions that could lead to the appearance of inferiority. He cautioned the District's teachers to beware of those conditions. One couldn't say whether his speech was prescient or a catalyst for things to come. But something was brewing in the office of the superintendent of schools that would almost wreck Anna Julia Cooper's life and endanger the future of M Street.

In the parallel universe of the District's white school system, Percy Hughes was the mirror image of Anna Julia Cooper. Mr. Hughes, who favored bow ties and sported a slight comb-over, became a teacher in the same year as Cooper. His social position was such that his marriage made the local paper and he served on presidential inaugural committees. At just about the same time Cooper took over at M Street, he too got a promotion. While running the grandest of the white high schools in the

District, Central High, he was tapped for a bigger role, and this is where their similarities ended. Hughes was named the director of schools in June 1902, something that could never have happened to Mrs. Cooper.[13] Hughes was seen as the obvious choice: white, male, and the senior principal in service who was known for his "efficient work as the head of the largest school."[14]

Hughes wasted no time making his first reports to his direct superior, the superintendent of schools. Under the new structure, Hughes had jurisdiction over all of the District's schools; his power now extended not just to the white schools, but to the colored schools as well, due to the Jim Crow-style change in law. Shortly after taking office, Hughes became very interested in some charges of disorderly conduct at the M Street School.

"A demoralizing state of affairs at M Street high School!" complained a member of the Women's Christian Temperance Union, a ladies' organization that promoted total alcoholic abstinence as a core value of a civilized society.[15] These especially temperate ladies alleged that some uncivilized behavior was going on at the colored high school. The accusation was there had been nothing done about some male students who had allegedly been found drinking and smoking on campus. Corroborating the account was a handsome, conservative colored doctor, Oliver M. Atwood.[16] He claimed to have counseled one of the boys in question, an orphan with little parental guidance.[17]

While they had no official capacity within the school system, Dr. Atwood and six or seven other gentlemen of color made it their unofficial duty to look after the concerns of *their* high school. Atwood was nearing the end of a lucrative career in the District and had his eye on a seat on the board of education. An allopath serving Washington's colored community since 1873, he advertised that he "guaranteed to cure all comers."[18] He was a presence in a certain Washington, DC, colored social circle. His name would appear in the paper time and time again at this party or that event. He would address civic organizations on weighty social issues like "Prohibition in Politics" or how to improve the lives of the colored community in Washington. He believed in personal responsibility. He said, "In laying stress about race pride the community is apt to lose sight of individual development."[19]

The development of colored youth into good citizens was his main concern with respect to the M Street accusations. This charge of drunkenness was troubling and he wanted answers. Dr. Atwood claimed that one of the delinquents confessed to consuming twenty-five-cents worth of whiskey and a beer. The teenager said he was part of a group of boys who drank off campus before coming to school.[20] What Dr. Atwood didn't realize at the time was that as a colored critic of the colored high school principal, he would provide the perfect cover for an attack on Cooper by the white establishment.

Mrs. Cooper had written to the board in response to the accusation and thought her strongly worded denial of the presence of any inebriated students on campus would be the end of the issue. She didn't see a need to appear in person to defend herself. She believed the "confessor" was a child who was upset about being expelled for putting talcum powder down a classmate's shirt.[21] The charges represented an annoyance for a woman of Cooper's intellect. At the time, she believed she had more important things to do. Anna Julia Cooper would often describe her approach to academic design this way: "We are not just educating heads and hands, we are educating the men and women of a race."

But rather than quashing the incident, Cooper's attitude became an invitation for the aggressive new director of schools to look closely at her work. Director Hughes didn't stick with just the discipline issue, however. He submitted a report to his superiors that recommended minimizing M Street High School's algebra and English curricula. He maintained that the M Street students were not accomplishing the same work in the same amount of time as white students. He began to say publicly that students at M Street might not be able to handle the same curriculum as students at the white schools and that perhaps the work should be adjusted to a more manageable course of study. Hughes told his professional peers:

> When I first became director I looked into the question of the work of the M Street High School, being pretty well acquainted at that time with the work in the white high schools because I had been principal of the Central School for several years. We gave a test in algebra early in the year and the results of the test in the colored high schools as compared with the results of the same test in the white high schools were such that I felt it wise, after consultation with the head of the department of mathematics, to have the pupils

in the colored high school remain longer in the elementary work, i.e. in reviewing the work which had been done in the graded schools. As a result of this, the white high schools finished the subject of factoring about the first of November, but the colored high school was not ready to leave that subject until nearly the middle of December being almost six weeks longer upon it. The same results in character came in other tests, both in English and Latin, and such other tests as were given. The result of this was that after conference with the superintendent of schools, I felt it wise to hold the High School down to the principle of doing thoroughly the work they were doing without any attempt to keep pace with the white schools.

Cooper may have been the first opponent of "teaching to the test." She allowed her teachers to take as much time as they needed to make sure the students understood thoroughly. Hughes's assumption that Cooper's students couldn't do the work was what Cooper referred to as the "Where am dat handkerchief Desdemona?" moment.[22] It is the moment when ignorance is assumed based on race. In Act III, scene IV, of Shakespeare's *Othello*, the Moor actually asks of his wife, Desdemona, "Lend me thy handkerchief . . . that which I gave you." Yet certain listeners hear, "Where am dat handkerchief?" because the words come from an African's mouth. As one of Cooper's student's later recalled, "It was pure heresy to think that a colored child could do what a white child could."[23]

Civic leaders were outraged at what they saw as Hughes's assault on the school. The same had happened in other communities with sad results. Just a few years earlier, in 1899, the US Supreme Court had supported the decision by the Richmond, Georgia, board of education to close down the town's only colored high school while maintaining white high schools. The locals said there weren't enough viable colored students to warrant the school.[24] Cooper and her allies knew the academic reputation of M Street was critical to its existence. M Street's good name had to be protected.

Complaints were lodged. Howard-educated lawyer Shelby Davidson led the charge with a letter of protest to the board of education. The response to Davidson's communication—rather than to the actual issue he raised—came almost immediately from the white superintendent. It was entered into the board's minutes.

M Street's curriculum is identical to those in other high schools. The Director can raise the standard of scholarship by adapting the teaching to the needs of the individual pupils or classes of pupils. Deficiencies that are apparent in the work of many of the pupils of this school are not in the opinion of the Board due wholly whether to lack of preparation in the graded schools or to unskillful teaching in the high school or to the fact that some pupils attempt high school work who are incompetent to perform it, but to all of these causes combined. . . . It is far from the purpose of the board to deprive any pupil whose intelligence, industry, and moral worth so entitle him of any opportunity whatsoever for preparing himself for future advancement in learning and usefulness in life. It is however manifestly the duty of those interested in education of the young to insist upon reasonable standards of efficacy on the part of the pupils. Deficiencies in the work of pupil are found in all high schools to a greater or lesser degrees and must be dealt with in each as local condition seem to demand.[25]

The superintendent adroitly showed his support for Hughes without directly attacking M Street. What the school's founders had feared was coming true: the colored citizens were losing control of their schools.

Cooper was not deterred. On occasion the principal simply defied the director. She, too, believed that she could "raise the standard of scholarship by adapting the teaching to the needs of the individual pupils or classes of pupil." For example, when her students were given new, less complex sets of textbooks, she simply returned to using the original volumes without consulting anyone.

At other times, Cooper tried to engage Hughes. In June 1903, Cooper called on the director to discuss two of her most earnest students. They were scheduled to graduate that month, but there seemed to be an issue with the completion of one or two courses.

"Director Hughes, two of my pupils have conditions from back in the second year, one in algebra and one in geometry. You may remember Miss Banion?" she asked, likely knowing the white director had no knowledge of the colored teenager.

The director's response was short and direct. "Well, have the girl review the material and take an examination upon it to complete her coursework." Mrs. Cooper was to report back with the results. She did so, at his home, on a Sunday just before graduation.

"Director, my Miss Banion has taken the examination and is not quite up to the passing point, but she has done her best. She is a hardworking student."

"What mark has been made?

"Sixty-five percent. We must realize the girl had not been studying the subject for the past two years and when she had it, she was under some disadvantages. She is just ten points off of passing clearly. Given her earnest desire to learn, I would recommend graduation, Mr. Hughes."

"Do you believe the girl had done the best she could?"

"Yes, I think so. "

"If these are the circumstances, then you have my approval."

Hughes would later claim that the Miss Banion had only made 45 percent on her examination and that Cooper had given him "wrong information."[26] Hughes told people Principal Cooper was in denial. He said that perhaps her knowledge of the conditions at M Street as compared with those in the white high schools was not sufficient to enable her to make the comparison very clearly. The thinly disguised implication was that Anna Julia Cooper was in some way incompetent or inferior to her counterparts.

The following year, around the time of graduation, Director Hughes went on the offensive. He contacted the M Street principal. "Mrs. Cooper, I've been made aware of four students who teachers said were unprepared to go one to the next grade. Mrs. Cooper, you are to send those students back after a conference with their parents." It was a clear, nonnegotiable position: hold the students back one year.

Hughes later told a congressional committee that Cooper agreed but then appealed to one of the two colored members of the board of education to help her secure diplomas for the students. They in turn appealed to the colored assistant superintendent, who considered the students' records and character. The colored assistant superintendent agreed to graduate the students, but the white superintendent countered that the assistant was not authorized to do so. The colored chain of command did not matter. A few months later, formal charges were brought against Anna Julia Cooper, accusing her of impudence and "inefficiency and ability to maintain good conduct and decorum."[27]

"There is a concerted movement to persecute Mrs. Cooper," claimed Reverend Francis Grimké, a Princeton Theological Seminary graduate who preached at the Fifteenth Street Presbyterian Church, where the high school had humbly begun. He voiced much of what colored Washington believed. "There is a plot for the undoing of Mrs. Cooper." It was man versus woman. White versus colored. Belief in racial inferiority versus race pride. Who would win?

In the segregated capital of the country, the answer was the person with the most power or access to it.

As the principal of the country's premier academic high school for Negroes, a word Cooper and other intellectuals often used, she was more philosophically aligned with W. E. B. Du Bois than Booker T. Washington. Her career was in jeopardy because of a wider philosophical and political argument about what was better for Negroes—the Du Bois model of intellectual advancement or the vocational/industrial method promoted by the other great race leader of the time, Booker T. Washington.

The two men desired the same thing: a better existence for their people. One thought the road to equity would be achieved by using the mind; the other believed it would come through the work of the hands. Their positions reflected their backgrounds. Du Bois was born a free man; Washington was born a slave. Washington was greatly admired for developing and transforming the Tuskegee Institute into an excellent school that promoted self-reliance through practical skills. Washington believed economic advancement would come through self-determination and that challenges to racial segregation and disenfranchisement weren't the immediate priority. That view put him at odds with other Negro intellectuals.

On September 18, 1895, Washington took to the podium at the Atlanta Cotton States and International Exposition and delivered the speech that would define him, which became known as the Atlanta Compromise.

Of those of my race who depend on bettering their condition in a foreign land or who underestimate the importance of cultivating friendly relations with the Southern white man, who is their next-door neighbor, I would say: "Cast down your bucket where you are"—cast it down in making friends in every manly way of the people of all races by whom we are surrounded. . . .

Cast it down in agriculture, in mechanics, in commerce, in domestic service, and in the professions. And in this connection it is well to bear in mind that whatever other sins the South may be called to bear, when it comes to business, pure and simple, it is in the South that the Negro is given a man's chance in the commercial world. . . .

Our greatest danger is that in the great leap from slavery to freedom we may overlook the fact that the masses of us are to live by the productions of our hands, and fail to keep in mind that we shall prosper in proportion as we learn to dignify and glorify common labor, and put brains and skill into the common occupations of life; shall prosper in proportion as we learn to draw the line between the superficial and the substantial, the ornamental gewgaws of life and the useful. No race can prosper till it learns that there is as much dignity in tilling a field as in writing a poem. It is at the bottom of life we must begin, and not at the top. Nor should we permit our grievances to overshadow our opportunities. . . .

To those of the white race who look to the incoming of those of foreign birth and strange tongue and habits for the prosperity of the South, were I permitted I would repeat what I say to my own race, "Cast down your bucket where you are." Cast it down among the eight millions of Negroes whose habits you know, whose fidelity and love you have tested in days when to have proved treacherous meant the ruin of your firesides. Cast down your bucket among these people who have, without strikes and labor wars, tilled your fields, cleared your forests, built your railroads and cities, and brought forth treasures from the bowels of the earth, and helped make possible this magnificent representation of the progress of the South. . . .

While doing this, you can be sure in the future, as in the past, that you and your families will be surrounded by the most patient, faithful, law-abiding, and unresentful people that the world has seen. As we have proved our loyalty to you in the past, in nursing your children, watching by the sick-bed of your mothers and fathers, and often following them with tear-dimmed eyes to their graves, so in the future, in our humble way, we shall stand by you with a devotion that no foreigner can approach, ready to lay down our lives, if need be, in defense of yours, interlacing our industrial, commercial, civil, and religious life with yours in a way that shall make the interests of both races one. In all things that are purely social, we can be as separate as the fingers, yet one as the hand in all things essential to mutual progress.

The wisest among my race understand that the agitation of questions of social equality is the extremist folly, and that progress in the enjoyment of all the privileges that will come to us must be the result of severe and constant struggle rather than of artificial forcing. No race that has anything to contribute to the markets of the world is long in any degree ostracized. It is important and right that all privileges of the law be ours, but it is vastly more important that we be prepared for the exercise of these privileges. The opportunity to earn a dollar in a factory just now is worth infinitely more than the opportunity to spend a dollar in an opera-house.

His message was not what many Negroes wanted to hear, and exactly what many whites did. Men like the superintendent and director of high schools in Washington, DC, thought vocational training should be integrated back into the M Street curriculum and that the school's current all-academic program was not serving all Negro students.

Booker T. Washington was called both respectfully and pejoratively the "Great Accommodator" and the "Good Negro." A skilled politician, he attracted and cultivated relationships with white political and business leaders like Andrew Carnegie. He became a power broker, making and breaking careers, as he had with Judge Terrell in Washington. He was a colored man who summered next to President Roosevelt and was the first colored person invited to eat in the White House with him, in 1901.

The acceptance that met Washington's message and his power deeply disturbed those pushing for integration and equality. Du Bois considered Washington "shrewd and tactful" and did admire his sincerity. However, Du Bois, along with other DC intellectuals like Kelly Miller and Archibald Grimké, believed Booker T. Washington's method would lead to "industrial slavery and civic death." Du Bois, in his book *The Souls of Black Folk*, wrote in chapter three (called "On Booker T. Washington and Others"):

There is among the educated and thoughtful colored men in all parts of the land a feeling of deep regret, sorrow, and apprehension at the wide currency and ascendancy which some of Mr. Washington's theories have gained.

Mr. Washington distinctly asks that black people give up at least for the present three things—

First, political power.

Second, insistence on civil rights.

Third, higher education of Negro youth.

The triple paradox:

He is striving nobly to make Negro artisans businessmen and property-owners; but it is utterly impossible under modern competitive methods for workingmen and property-owners to defend their rights and exist without the right of suffrage.

He insists on thrift and self respect but at the same time counsels a silent submission to visit inferiority such as is bound to sap the manhood of any race in the long run.

Even though Washington appeared as a commencement speaker at M Street in 1904, Anna Cooper was in danger of being run over by the Tuskegee Machine, as his political clique was known. But her beliefs were truly a hybrid of the Tuskegee sensibility and the more intellectually focused aspirations of Du Bois. She celebrated the dignity of hard, manual work in her essay "The Ethics of the Negro Question."

The American Negro is capable of contributing not only of his brawn and sinew but also from brain and character a much-needed element in American civilization; and here is his home. . . . His blood has mingled with the bluest and the truest on every battlefield that checkers his country's history. His sweat and his toil have, more than any other's, felled its forests, drained its swamps, plowed its fields, and opened up its roads and waterways.

In the same essay she explained the pitfalls of labor with suffrage.

The Negro under free labor and cutthroat competition today has to vindicate his fitness to survive against a color-phobia that heeds neither reason nor religion and a prejudice that shows no quarter and admits no mitigating circumstance. . . . The condition of the male laborer . . . is even more hopeless. Receiving 50 cents a day for unskilled but laborious toil, from which wage he boards himself and is expected to keep a family in something better than a "one room cabin" the Negro workman receives neither sympathy nor recognitions from his white fellow laborers.

The answer was clear: education first.

Anna Julia Cooper, 1892.
Documenting the American South, University of North Carolina at Chapel Hill Libraries

————— ✺ —————

In September 1905, the work, conduct, philosophy, and personal integrity of Anna Julia Cooper would be judged by the District of Columbia Board of Education: seven white citizens and two colored, one of the latter in professional debt to Booker T. Washington.[28]

Friday, September 22, 1905. The school board officially announced it would consider the charges against Anna Julia Cooper. Director Hughes's statement, in which he contended that the students of M Street were "incapable of taking the same studies" as the students in the city, was presented.[29]

Tuesday, September 26, 1905. A local white businessman and Atwood sympathizer, T. S. Leisenring, was allowed to testify and claimed that Cooper's record as a teacher in North Carolina was not as glorious as reported. He called on the board to inquire with a local congressman to confirm his allegations.

Thursday, September 28, 1905. North Carolina Representative George White, who was black, testified. He was expected to malign Mrs. Cooper but instead offered robust support, which was entered into the minutes.

> Mrs. Cooper was a splendid woman and she was greatly respected in the State from which she came. She taught in the Raleigh institution after she married Mr. Cooper and continued to do so after his death and until she went to Oberlin College. She then came here when she was first assistant principal of the M Street School and then principal. The colored people of Washington thoroughly resent the persecution of her in this matter and if the board should decide against her they are willing to appeal to a higher tribunal.

Friday morning, September 29, 1905. A headline in the *Washington Post* read, COLORED PEOPLE AROUSED OVER HIGH SCHOOL INQUIRY. Apparently Congressman White had been made to wait two hours while the board conducted other business until 10:00 PM. The delay tactics left time for only two witnesses, including White, to speak for a total of thirty minutes. Others who had come out to voice their support were not allowed to address the board.

Friday evening, September 29, 1905. Cooper's accusers, T. S. Leisenring and Dr. O. M. Atwood, were asked to return to the Franklin Building to meet with the board. Mr. Leisenring was discredited by Congressman White's pro-Cooper statement.

Wednesday, October 4, 1905. The board took five days to respond to the congressman's assertion that Cooper was being persecuted. In the only official public statement to the press, board member Charles Needham spoke on the record to the *Washington Post*:

> I've always stood for the use of the same text books in the colored schools as in the white schools. The question however concerns the curriculum and in that too I believe there should be an equality of studies all the way through. I do not think the charges of drunkenness against the pupil and the non-reporting by the principal have been sustained. I think the matter should not have been allowed to run along so long.

At the time Needham's word meant something. Years later, he had to resign as president of George Washington University after depleting GWU's endowment from $200,000 to $16,000 by signing a promissory note that listed his house as security. The home was worth $8,000 at the time.[30]

Thursday, October 5, 1905. Only one witness appeared before the board. Director Percy M. Hughes was called to testify. He never wavered from his position. The charges remained the same: colored pupils could not complete the same courses in the same time as white students. He said four English teachers at M Street had told him that their students were incompetent in English. Cooper pushed certain students ahead for collegiate honors, competing with whites for scholarships. Cooper refused to hold students back, and when directly ordered to do so, she "disobeyed" him. There was no mention of drunkenness in the record.

Tuesday, October 17, 1905. Anna Julia Cooper had been prepared to present her case on October 16, 1905; however, three committees arrived that day demanding the opportunity to defend her. One group represented the parents; another represented the civic-minded colored women of the District. Mr. Jesse Lawson, a Howard-educated lawyer, said he had "evidence" to prove Cooper's administration was satisfactory to the majority. It was a bold move for Lawson. He too had benefited from the help of Booker T. Washington, but in 1870 his wife, Rosetta, had been one of the first four pupils to attend the Preparatory High School for Colored Youth in the basement of the Fifteenth Street church. This was personal. Cooper would have to wait one more day.

Wednesday, October 18, 1905. Finally, almost two years after the accusations had first been made, Anna Julia Cooper had her say. Cooper presented her enhanced scholarships, the increased reputation of the school, and the impressive placement of graduates as evidence of her dedication and success as an educator. She took the opportunity to testify that her school should not be discriminated against by being forced to teach a lower curriculum, nor should any other colored schools. She told the board she was defending a bigger issue, that of race efficacy.

Cooper and her Washington allies were fighting for something more serious than just what textbook to use. They knew they were in a rare position to change things for others. Ninety percent of colored people still lived in the South under harsh Jim Crow laws. Ninety-five percent of all colored people couldn't read or could barely read. Even within the confines of Washington, those colored citizens who were poor and uneducated lived in desperate conditions. The students of M Street, at this point mostly working- and middle-class sons and daughters of domestic workers and clerks, could help themselves and one day would help their race heal from the scars of slavery and move on to prosperity.

Not only were her life's work and professional reputation on trial, so was Cooper's reputation. Leading up to the proceedings, rumors spread about the widowed principal having a romantic relationship with a man named John Love, one of her teachers. If that allegation was not damaging enough on its own, what made it worse was that John Love and his sister Lula were two of the foster children Cooper had taken in years earlier. They continued to live with her as young adults, as did four other teachers. Her champions constantly referred to her character and Christian values in a likely effort to neutralize all the rumblings. And while these charges never appeared in any official board of education notes, the rumors had circulated around town. Her credibility had been compromised.

With all the testimony—rumors, facts, and otherwise—in the ether, the board of education returned its verdict after twelve days of deliberation.

Monday, October 30, 1905. The Board of Education of the District of Columbia came to its decision. Present that evening were board members Mr. Gordon, Dr. Kingsman, Mrs. West, Mrs. Francis, Mr. Bundy, Mr. Parker, and Dr. Needham. The report read as follows:

From the Board of Education of the District of Columbia,

The committee of the whole Board, having heard the testimony of many witnesses regarding the condition in the M Street High School reports as follows:

1. Bearing in mind that it has been and is the policy of the Board of Education to maintain the M Street High School for colored children at the same grade and with the same standards in every particular as prevail in the other high schools of the District, the committee has examined officers, teachers, and records to ascertain whether this requirement of the Board has been observed. We find that in one instance where a text book on English history had been adopted by the board for all high schools, some of the faculty of the M Street High School, with the consent of the principal, requested and secured a change of this text book and resorted the use of a former one on the ground that it was easier for their students. This was in violation of the action and policy of the Board and should not have been permitted.

2. We also find that in the year 1903–04 a rule of practice which had prevailed for some time in the Central, Eastern, and Western High Schools, of examining the first year students at about the end of the first quarter to ascertain their qualifications and fitness to continue high school work was put in force in the M Street High School and the same examination required in the other high schools was held. The result of this examination by the teacher of the M Street High School found that about sixteen students were deficient or weak, and that four students were entirely unqualified for the work. Upon this report, the Director of High Schools, with the approval of the Superintendent issued an order which was sent to the principal of the M Street High School in the same form as to the principals of the other high schools, directing the four unqualified pupils be sent back to the grades for further preparation. The principal acknowledged receipt of this communication

and replied that she would follow the order, but, on the contrary, she immediately appealed to the colored Assistant Superintendent and to the colored representatives on this board, to have this order revoked on the ground it was a new procedure in the M Street High School and that the parents would be offended to have their children sent back. In response to the appeal, the Superintendent directed that the order be revoked, thus excepting the M Street High School from the operation of a wholesome practice prevailing in the other high schools. We find, first, that the action of the principal in this matter was irregular, improper, and not conductive [sic] to the policy of maintaining the high standard of education work in this school required by the Board; and secondly, that this order to return these four pupils to the grades should not have been revoked; on the contrary, the principal should have promptly put the order in force.

3. We further find that too large a number of pupils have been kept in the M Street High School who are not qualified to do the work and we cannot agree with the principal in what she terms "sympathetic" methods and conduct on the part of the teachers to enable unqualified pupils to purse studies in the High School. These methods have resulted in too many and too frequent reexaminations of weak students in order to enable them to pass from one grade to another and to graduate, while in a few instances conditions have not been passed as required. We do not believe that this conduct is conducive to the best interest of the child and the race for which the school is maintained. We believe that a fewer number of well qualified students, able to pursue the courses in high school, and a fewer number of well educated graduates, will do more for the reputation of this school and also the race than will a larger number of students and graduates with a considerable portion of the unqualified students among them. We therefore insist that the officers of the Board and the faculty of the M Street High School maintain a proper standard of work, a thorough and discriminating system of grading the students, with no attempt to force students beyond their ability to do the work, and that the practice of frequent reexaminations of students without proper intervals in which to make up their deficiencies be discontinued.

4. Evidence was presented, showing that on a single occasion two students were presented to the principal for discipline who had been drinking intoxicating liquors and who showed some effects of the intoxicants at the time. These students were disciplined for misconduct in being absent from the school. Later the principal was called upon for a report as to whether there were any drinking habits among the pupils. She reported that she had not been able to find any evidence that such practices prevailed. While it clearly appears that these two students had been drinking, yet we are satisfied that it was a single instance and that there is no ground for the general charge that has been made that there has been drinking among the pupils of this high school; on the contrary, it appears that the students are generally well-behaved, orderly, and studious.

5. While we criticize the work as set forth, we believe that the principal, Mrs. A. J. Cooper, is a woman of good intellectual attainment, of high moral character, and of excellent reputation among her people. The errors complained of are a result mainly of her too sympathetic feeling or the weak pupils under her care; and while this sentiment may be commended in itself and prevail to some extent in the grades, we are clearly of the opinion that it should not prevail to the prejudice of proper standards of work in a high school. We find that the principal has not maintained that proper official relation, that strict loyalty to the director of high schools that should prevail in a well organized system.

6. We further find that here is not a proper spirit of unity and loyalty to the work among all the members of the faculty of the M Street High School that should prevail. This want of unity has manifested itself in exaggerated and unfriendly criticism in the interest of and also against the principal. Some teachers have been guilty of writing and instigating articles for the public press tending to create dissatisfaction and disorganization in the work. This disorganization has been extended to the student body and produced some improper conduct on the part of the students.

7. We further find that as a result of the disinclination of the faculty and officers of the M Street School to enforce the same methods and standards prevailing in the other high schools, the Director and superintendent have yielded in a few instances to these

demands, we do not approve of this action. We believe that the Director should continue to keep a close and careful observation of the work in this high school, and strictly maintain the regular standard of work; that the Superintendent should call the faculty and present the conclusion of this report and insist upon unity of effort, loyalty to superiors, and a maintenance of the standards of work prevailing in the other high schools.

8. The Committee expresses its full confidence in the integrity and conscientious purpose of Mr. Percy M. Hughes, director of high schools, and believe that in all matters pertaining to the M Street High School he has been guided by a sense of his high responsibility as director and with the object of securing the best scholarship and discipline in the school; that the superintendent, Mr. Alexander T. Stuart, and the director are in hearty accord with the Board of Education in its policy to maintain the same standards, curriculum, text books, and education work in the M Street High School that prevail in the other three high schools in the District, and we are pleased to say that all the representatives of the colored race who have appeared before the committee concur and have expressed their strong desire that the same standard of work and ratings prevails in the M Street High School that prevail in the other high schools.

9. In view of all the facts and conclusions and the very strong desire by a large proportion of the colored race in the District to have Mrs. Cooper retained as principal, we recommend her retention with the express direction however that the standard work, the grading of students, and the recommendation of students for graduation be conducted distinctly in accordance with the policy of the Board of Education and the conclusion of this report, and that in her official conduct she shall recognize the authority of her superior officer, the Director of the High Schools, and conform in her office conduct in all respects to the rules of the Board of Education

10. In conclusion the committee recommends that a strict observance be made of the work in the M Street High School with a view of maintaining the standard of work herein set forth, preventing any improper conduct on the part of the teacher and student to create disaffection, securing a strict observance of that discipline, official recognition of superior officers, and conduct essential to

the best and highest education results in this important school, and that stated reports of these observations be made to the Board for proper actions.

On Motion the Board adjourned to meet on Wednesday, November 8, 1905.

Safe, but not sound. Anna Julia Cooper kept her job but was put on notice that she would be watched closely. The board of education failed to realize that it too had been watched through this process by both the white and colored communities. Neither group liked what it saw. Cooper's status didn't change, but the board's would.

Four months later, the same cast of characters—Director Hughes, Superintendent Stuart, Dr. Atwood, and Professor Miller—testified about Cooper and the board of education, only this time they did so in front of a congressional committee. The subject was ostensibly the reorganization of school oversight in light of the havoc that had surrounded the Cooper inquiry. But the discussion returned again and again to M Street. The proceeding was a de facto retrial of Anna Julia Cooper. This time Director Hughes had an audience with more power: congressional representatives who were not from Washington. And his testimony featured a bombshell about the board, its colored members, and Mrs. Cooper.

MR. HUGHES: Just before the time of graduation last year about middle of June the high school committee one night had laid, I think by Mr. Bundy, a request for a graduation of two whose records were not clear, a Miss Grace Daniels and a boy the name of Jackson. His first name I have forgotten. The committee was ready at that time before it had received full information in the matter to recommend that the diplomas be granted. I suggested that the teachers who had these pupils should be asked as to their records in the subjects taken and the committee determined on that course. The matter was referred to Doctor Montgomery, the colored assistant superintendent of schools. Officially under the rules it should come to me as director of high schools. Doctor Montgomery looked into the matter and then called up over the phone and asked whether the pupils ought to be graduated. I told him I did not think that they should be graduated; that their records were not clear; that the marks were marks showing the judgment of teachers who knew the pupils and that no superior officer or the board of education itself could properly set aside a mark which meant the judgment of the teacher upon the work done. Montgomery nevertheless recommended the graduation of pupils and they were graduated. I at that time protested to superintendent against my having to sign the diplomas which I knew were not earned.

REP. MORRELL (R-PA): Was that protest made in writing?

MR. HUGHES: No, not at that time. I finally turned over to the M Street School the unsigned the diplomas. They were given to the graduates the night of graduation in June and after the event they were gotten from the graduates by Mrs. Cooper. . . . The parents of the students came to the principal of the school who stated to them that the papers did not have all of the signatures upon them and she would secure them. They were left at the Franklin School and I had notice from one of the clerks there that the papers were there awaiting my signature. I told him that I had protested that matter and did not feel I ought to sign those diplomas knowing that they had not been earned. The matter went on until about the 24th or 25th of July I received a statement saying that Mr. Daniel was anxious to secure the diploma of his daughter who had been graduated in the M Street High School and that the board of education ordered that I sign those diplomas. It was then I called upon Mr. Gordon, president of the board of education, and talked the matter over with him and immediately afterwards called upon Mr. Stuart, the superintendent.

REP. MORRELL: One minute—in what manner were these directions of the board conveyed to you, in writing?

MR. HUGHES: Yes, sir.

REP. MORRELL: Have you a copy of that?

MR. HUGHES: Yes, I have a copy of it.

REP. MORRELL: Do you mean to tell me that these two pupils whose diplomas you refused to sign stood up or whatever the ceremony is with the other pupils whose diplomas you did sign and were to go through the form, whatever it may be, of graduation? What form have you?

MR. HUGHES: The graduation last summer took the form of a concerted graduation of the high and normal and manual. The exercises consisted of music, an introductory address by Mr. Washington, and I think presentation of scholarships came in; and then the pupils by schools came up and received their diplomas.

REP. MORRELL: Whom did they receive those from?

MR. HUGHES: I am not sure; I think one of the commissioners presented the diplomas.

REP. MORRELL: Do you mean to say that two unsigned diplomas were, with the knowledge of the board of education and the superintendent of schools, handed to two pupils and by that form they were graduated from the high school?

MR. HUGHES: Not with the knowledge of the board so far as at that time Mr. Stuart the superintendent was aware of it. I had given up the diplomas without the signatures after conference with him. His position was—

REP. MORRELL: How long before graduation did you refuse to sign diplomas?

MR. HUGHES: I think perhaps three or four days.

REP. MORRELL: Three or four days.

MR. HUGHES: I think perhaps that time elapsed between my talking with Mr. Stuart and the time they were graduated.

REP. MORRELL [addressing Superintendent Stuart]: Mr. Stuart, I would like to ask you after the conversation you had with Mr. Hughes. Did you immediately notify the school board?

MR. STUART: Do you refer to Mr. Hughes's protest?

REP. MORRELL: Yes.

MR. STUART: That of course I transmitted.

REP. MORRELL: You transmitted that at once?

MR. STUART: At once, oh yes.

REP. MORRELL: Then the board must have been aware that those pupils did not have signed certificates if they knew that those pupils were to go through the form of graduation and you transmitted that information to them at once.

MR. STUART: Yes, sir.

REP. MORRELL: There is no other conclusion that I can see. May I ask that connection by whose orders those pupils who did not receive signed certificates took their place among the other pupils who were properly graduated?

MR. HUGHES: I presume that Mrs. Cooper simply assumed they were to have the diplomas. They were properly in line with others.

REP. MORRELL: How could she assume that was so?

MR. HUGHES: She knew the board of education had acted upon and granted these diplomas.

REP. MORRELL: In spite of . . .

MR. HUGHES: Not in spite of my official protest at that time for it had not come to me it had passed through the hands of Dr. Montgomery. I was passed over and Doctor Montgomery was given the whole case to investigate and report upon and he reported with the recommendation that these pupils should graduate.

It became clear that Hughes's crushing description of an inept board and a sneaky group of colored educators would go unchallenged in the permanent government record. Cooper's supporters tried to course correct. Even Dr. O. M. Atwood came around and realized that colored schools and their educators were treated inequitably. He tried to engage a congressman on the issue.

MR. GREENE: You claim there is discrimination against the colored people?

DR. ATWOOD: I do not claim that.

MR. GREENE: What do you mean then?

DR. ATWOOD: I mean simply that whenever there are any evils in the white schools, they get to them immediately but not so with the colored schools.

MR. GREENE: Then you mean to say there is discrimination against colored schools?

DR. ATWOOD: If you desire to put it that way.

MR. GREENE: I ask you that.

DR. ATWOOD: It seems the disposition of the board of education to refer all these matters in the colored schools to the colored trustees and they make their report and then they let it go and that is end of it.

MR. GREENE: Why should not that be a fair proposition? Do you to have those matters sent to the white trustees?

DR. ATWOOD: I think the entire board should consider them. I told the commissioners. I said we do not want any two-sevenths of the people as represented by the board to govern the colored schools. We want the whole seven-sevenths to give their management control of the colored schools. No two-sevenths is sufficient. They are not put there for that purpose.

When Professor Kelly Miller was allowed to speak, he also questioned the wisdom of the current structure, under which the colored superintendent could not oversee the schools. Professor Miller also used the opportunity to call out Director Hughes as no one had before. He told the committee, "The director of high schools made certain broad statements offensive to the colored pupil." In just a few years, the colored schools were at the mercy of a power structure that did not believe in the students. Hughes would go onto to write a letter directly the congressmen repeating that the M Street students were "not ready" for the same curriculum and books as the white high school. He said that "weakness was clearly shown" and that M Street "purported" to have the same standards. He did not mention that at the time the District spent forty-one dollars per pupil at M Street and sixty-five dollars per pupil at its white counterpart, Central High School.

Just as Anna Julia Cooper wrapped up her fourth year as principal, the composition of the District's board of education would change yet again. The seven-member board would be expanded to nine members, three of whom would be women. Three members (one woman and two men) would be colored.[31] In an effort to assure independence, the new legislation made judges of the Supreme Court of DC responsible for the board of education appointments. The director of schools position was eliminated, and a new superintendent would be appointed: Percy Hughes.

Late that summer the newly constituted board of education took over. Representing colored Washington were new member Dr. O. M. Atwood and returning member Mary Church Terrell. Would Terrell, a well-known, politically connected civil rights advocate, be an ally of Cooper's? They'd been at Oberlin together, and Cooper had succeeded Terrell's husband as the principal of M Street.

Among the board's first assignments was reviewing all of the teachers in the system and making recommendations. In late August the board of education appointed 1,475 teachers, both black and white. Only four educators were not invited to return to their posts: John Love, a teacher at M Street School and Cooper's foster son; C. J. B. Clarke, M Street's assistant principal; Mary Nalle, one of the first four students at the original high school in 1870; and Anna Julia Cooper.

After leaving M Street, Cooper founded a small college/night school for working-class colored adults in Washington, continuing her great fight to teach the most neglected. She and Mary Church Terrell both continued their activism, but they ceased to be close after Cooper lost her job while Terrell was on the board.[32]

Cooper left DC for a time and went on to earn her PhD at the Sorbonne in Paris. At one point she even returned to M Street once again to teach Latin. She penned a dramatic poem in honor of the school that referred to it as a "radiant star" that taught, "truth, brotherhood, and temperance" to all. Later in her life she would recall the events surrounding her leadership at M Street as "the Washington School upheaval of 1906. . . . The legal experts of D.C. found it expedient to promulgate a new doctrine, that reorganization of the school system involved the reappointment of all teachers—a thousand in a day. Thus it happened that the principal of M Street High School and several others were 'overlooked'—not put out but left out of the shuffle, so to speak, just a simple little matter of 'move along Joe!' "[33]

In 2009 after her 105 years on this earth and 45 years after her death, Anna Julia Cooper was honored on a postage stamp for her lifetime achievements—and if you look on pages twenty-six and twenty-seven of the most recent US passport, you will see a quote from Cooper. She is the only woman quoted and her message is as true today as it was the day she said it: "The cause of freedom is not the cause of a race or a sect, a party or a class—it is the cause of humankind, the very birthright of humanity."

5 | BRICKS AND MORTARBOARDS

IN THE FALL OF 1906, the newly configured board of education had a problem on its hands: overcrowding. White students from the academic high schools were being farmed out to the technical and business schools. M Street's building had been over capacity for a decade. The situation was just as some whites had feared it would be: ambitious colored Americans were finding their way to DC, dreaming of government jobs and a better-than-decent public education system. As a result, the overcrowded school system was becoming the norm, but conditions were getting dangerous.

The student body at M Street was nearly 50 percent larger than the building's stated capacity. At its peak there were 983 students in a school meant to accommodate 450 to 500 bodies.[1] M Street teachers sometimes taught two classes at once to get the job done.[2] It had been a problem for years. Before resigning, Superintendent Cook told the city commissioners that at M Street, "the degree of success attended to the school was largely due to an expenditure of energy and labor on the part of its teachers that cannot long be maintained without serious injury to health."[3] The building hadn't aged well and was too antiquated to support an extension. M Street also suffered from an inferior campus. It did not have a gym or a yard or a real cafeteria like its white counterparts Eastern High, Western High, and Central High.

Plessy who?

Within four months of taking office the new board of education president, Captain James F. Oyster, walked into the House appropriations hearings, run by the DC commissioners, and said he needed money.

> I am on the committee for building and repairs and I certainly appeal to you, gentlemen, to be as liberal to us in view of those conditions as you possibly can. If you could make a tour or inspection of the difficulties we have to encounter in locating rooms and buildings for the accommodation of scholars, I think you gentlemen would have empathy for us.[4]

Oyster was always addressed as "Captain," a title from his days as a commander of the National Rifles, a white DC militia company is which he was considered a pretty good shot.[5] The Oysters of Washington were a family of means, so prominent that, when the captain's seventy-six-year-old brother, George, died four months after his wedding to a twenty-six-year-old woman who then sued for a sixth of the estate, the story made the *New York Times*.[6] George Oyster was an art collector, a horse breeder, and DC's dairy and eggs commissioner.[7] That was fortunate for the Oyster family because they were big in butter—the best-known butter merchants in the city, according to the *Washington Bee*—and their advertisements insisted their product was a "Diamond Brand," strictly pure and delicious, not to mention lucrative.

Captain James F. Oyster, one of five Oyster siblings, was the businessman in the family. He helped establish Washington's first chamber of commerce and served as its first vice president. He was the commissioner for the board of trade for a time. But most often his name appeared in the paper during his tenure as the president of the board of education.

Clearly a man so busy needed an escape, a quiet place in the country. When he and his wife bought a lovely plot of land in Maryland, they commissioned a prominent architect, Appleton P. Clark Jr., to create their little haven away from the city. With a thirty-five-foot-wide hall that spanned the entire width of the mansion, a foundation of white quartz, a formal portico, and nine bedrooms, the Oyster's vacation house was described as "one of the handsomest summer homes near Washington . . . a 'conspicuous ornament' to the landscape."[8] It still stands today as the Mansion at Strathmore, a home to the arts with an event space interested parties can rent for about $1,000 an hour.

The captain, a big barrel-chested man with a substantial mustache, a man who expected the best of, well, everything, took it upon himself to tour the District schools when he assumed office. He did not like what he saw. The captain publicly pointed out what he believed were problems with fireproofing, rubbish disposal, coal consumption—you name it. Looking after the city's buildings, including the schools, was the job of Snowden Ashford. His title, city building inspector, described his duties perfectly. Buildings were *his* business, not that of the president of the board of education, although Captain James Oyster thought otherwise.

Oyster was fifteen years older and at least fifteen pounds heavier than Ashford, although they were equals in the facial-hair department. Ashford was also a native Washingtonian, a trained civil engineer, and an architect. When a local reporter asked Ashford about the board president's visits, he said: "Education would no doubt be served much better if the board of education were to devote its entire attention to education and leave the matter of buildings to those whose training has made them authorities on the subject."[9]

It was the beginning of a fractious relationship that would have a direct impact on the new colored high school. While Oyster and Ashford were marking their territory, the DC commissioners had successfully made the case for money to build two new high schools. Congress, which held the purse strings for the District, commissioned a study that found what locals already knew. According to the report, the District's public schools needed to be larger, and manual training schools, playgrounds, and gymnasiums were needed.[10] The Congressional report also stressed that the neighborhood school model was the way to go—for the white students at least.[11] Every effort should be made so that white students could walk to a well-equipped local school and socialize with their neighbors.

For the colored students it was a different story. When it came to high school, colored kids had to get from wherever they lived to the academic M Street or its neighbor up the road, the technical/trade school Armstrong. As a colored student, if you wanted to go to high school, you had to travel. Unintentionally, the formation of the colored system, which was not set up to be advantageous, created two magnet schools.

Congress set the budgets for the District's two new high schools. M Street, the colored high school, would get $550,000 for a new building. The white high school, Central, was allocated $1.2 million. The white high school would get an athletic field and a stadium, but when M Street's extracurriculars came up during the appropriations meeting, the commissioners balked.[12]

> COMMISSIONER JUDSON: On page 137 in line 14, I see that there was included the item for the construction of the new M Street High School the words, "The construction of an athletic field and the construction of a stadium." I ask that those words be stricken out. The school board inserted those words.
>
> REPRESENTATIVE TAYLOR (R-OH): That language is carried in both of the items there.
>
> COMMISSIONER JUDSON: Yes but it should be included only in the item for the Central High School.

That one line item, that one decision, would have serious repercussions sixty years later. At the time the lack of athletic accommodations was an injustice; in the future it would lead to a dramatic turn in education in the District.

The municipal architect's office would have—should have—worked closely with the board of education to help plan the new schools. And that might have been the case if the new municipal architect had not been Snowden Ashford. Ashford had been elected to this new position, an important one, and he would oversee all the building designs in the District. A group of assembled government officials voted unanimously for Ashford to get the post. Well, almost unanimously. There was one hold out: Captain James Frederick Oyster. Simply put, Oyster did not like Ashford's attitude.

During Ashford's nomination process, Oyster wrote letters to the US Army Corps of Engineers and accused Ashford and his colleagues at the building inspector's office of "falsifying themselves in their official capacity in order to cover up defective work for which they were responsible."[13] The letter was so nasty that the head of the US Corps of Engineers wrote back immediately to the entire board and said he "bitterly resented" the implications and "malicious" insinuations.[14] Oyster clarified his position: he really didn't have a problem with the Corps, just Ashford. It was on.

"It is nothing personal," Oyster told the press when he displayed his disappointment at Ashford's nomination, "but in the Board of Education's view a better man could be named."[15] Oyster promoted the idea of hiring someone well known, with a high-end aesthetic. First he suggested Appleton P. Clark Jr., but there was not enough money in it for Clark. He declined the nomination, saying he couldn't afford to give up his lucrative private business designing, among other things, summer homes for wealthy businessmen.

When Oyster couldn't stop Ashford from getting the municipal architect's post, Oyster tried to make it go away with a little help from his friends. Six months after Ashford was in place, a friend of the Oysters (who happened to be a congressional representative) introduced a bill that would create a new position: Superintendency of Buildings and Supplies [sic]. The legislation proposed that the new position would be filled by the board of education and would oversee the physical needs of the schools. It would essentially eliminate the need for a municipal architect. Although he never fully admitted to or denied the rumor that he helped author the legislation, Captain Oyster acknowledged that he believed it would "have great benefit." The *Washington Herald* described the move as a "new turn to an old feud."[16] The bill did not pass.

Both men could be prickly. They were quick to challenge each other at commissioners' meetings. Ashford often answered questions with questions, no matter who was asking. Oyster once asked that the room be cleared of all onlookers, only to be informed that the proceedings in progress were public hearings. The tension escalated, reaching its height in 1911, just as the final decisions were being made—or not being made—about the new colored high school.

For almost two years the men sparred publicly, using the local press as their boxing ring. The subject matter could be trivial. Oyster called for Ashford's dismissal because of the kinds of desks he had purchased. The move was not successful, as the headline from the February 2, 1911, *Washington Herald* trumpeted: NO EVIDENCE TO SUSTAIN CHARGES. About two months later, Ashford tried a passive-aggressive tactic to taunt Oyster: failing to inform the board of education when he temporarily shuttered two schools for structural problems. The *Washington Times* titled its account of that skirmish BOARD OF EDUCATION AND ENGINEERING DEPARTMENT CLASH AGAIN.

"Absolute folly!" Oyster was unequivocal in responding to Ashford's decision to remove furnaces from two schools without first consulting the board. Ashford also called for and got an investigation into the board's duties charging "that irregularities and gross carelessness marked the conduct of the local schools."[17] The board was ultimately vindicated.

Ashford intimated more than once that Oyster's business pals were getting kickbacks on things like coal sales. At one point he told a congressional committee that he thought the board of education should be suspended and a new organizational flow created—one that would give the municipal architect more autonomy, of course.[18]

In his acceptance remarks following his election to a fifth term as president of the board, Oyster charged Ashford with "inexcusable and expensive blunders," claiming to have found $39,000 in unnecessary expenses. He promised to pursue the issue all summer. On August 17, 1911, the *Washington Times* devoted three columns to the rift with the headline, CAPT. J. F. OYSTER SCORES ARCHITECT. The next day, the paper ran another two columns of copy on the subject, capped with the headline, ASHFORD REPLIES, "I DID MY DUTY." The atmosphere was so poisonous the *Washington Times* editorial page took both men to task in the summer of 1911.

But Oyster had another card to play: the race card. The design of the new colored high school, the one with the national reputation for churning out scholars, was still unclear. Oyster had a good relationship with the colored citizens of the District. Given the uncomfortable relationship between the education-seeking colored community and the white leaders in charge of the schools' curriculum over the past decade, a reception was held in Oyster's honor at M Street in appreciation of his support for improving the colored grammar schools and high schools. How could he cement his position as the colored intellectuals' friend?

Oyster had an idea. He decided the new colored high school should be designed by *the* prominent educational architect of the time, not just a local. Oyster announced at a board of education meeting in November 1912 that he would pursue William B. Ittner of Saint Louis, Missouri. Ittner was considered a visionary, and he transformed the way schools were built. The Ittner Plan shunned block-like brick warehouses with little light and instead introduced expansive, naturally lit, well-ventilated structures.[19] He was one of the first people to connect environment with the ability to learn. From 1898 to 1915, Ittner designed fifty public schools, for both blacks and whites, in Saint Louis.[20] He earned international attention when the World's Fair was held in Saint Louis and people from all over saw the innovative work he was doing.

Oyster tried to convince the board to sign on to Ittner's service for the colored high school, claiming the design would bring with it the "the promise of unparalleled excellence."[21] And perhaps the best thing about William Ittner, at least from Oyster's position, was that he was *not* Snowden Ashford. Oyster wrote to Ittner on November 6, 1912. He heard back almost immediately, but had to report to his colleagues that "it was improbable to secure Mr. Ittner."[22] Ittner was building eight schools in the country at the time. He had already signed on to design the new white high school in DC, the one with twice the budget allotted for the colored high school. The two schools were slated to open at the same time, separate and the colored school one-half as equal.

With the clock running out on financing and the colored board members wanting a new school soon, it became clear Ashford would lead the project. Oyster resigned from the board of education before construction even began.

The one thing Oyster and Ashford seemed to have in common was a professional desire to be fair to the colored students. During his tenure, Ashford was adamant that all the money appropriated for the colored schools went to the colored schools.[23] Ashford had designed the Alexander Crummell School, a colored elementary school, and oversaw improvements at the Congress Heights School.

For this new school, Ashford would have to raise his game. The stated goal was to create a "dignified brain factory."[24] Everyone would be watching: colored Washington, white Washington, Congress, and who knows who else in the forty-eight states. After his fierce public battle with Oyster, this was a chance to erase any doubt about his skill or intention. The first plans Ashford presented were deemed "too ambitious."[25] His second plan was accepted in March 1914. The design was regal, truly. The building was fashioned after London's grand Hampton Court Palace, once the home of Henry VIII. The plans called for tapestry brick for the main structure and limestone and terra-cotta for the trimmings. According to projections, the school would hold twelve hundred students. The timeline was to start construction in the fall of 1914 and complete construction by the spring of 1916, however the contractor's bid was not accepted until early 1915. As seems to be the case with all construction, the project started late.

The new school was an opportunity to hit a restart button for M Street. The Anna Cooper episode had aired some dirty laundry that had been piling up in the colored school system, which was a magnified version of some of the internal struggles at M Street. A teaching position at the school was a prestigious job for a colored woman and even for a colored man. And prestige is often accompanied by politics. For years the colored paper, the *Washington Bee*, charged that friends of friends were given the best assignments at M Street. Jealousies festered over promotions and appointments often thought to be based on political affiliations rather than merit. At times there were out-and-out feuds. A teacher once received a letter warning him that another educator had publicly called him "a sneak, a menace, . . . ungrateful and despicable." The informant described the display as a "most unmanly, ungenerous, and malicious assault upon you, your character, and your record." But a new high school could erase old drama.

Identifying the new location of the M Street School presented two challenges. The first was where to put the new larger school. The commissioners and members of Congress wanted to put the new colored high school on Howard University's campus. Maybe the idea was to keep "them" all together and avoid spending any money to purchase land for the new building. But the Howard location was far from the majority of the colored population, and parents did not want their young teenagers so close to young adults attending college. The colored community fought this with a "flood of protests." The response was "the strongest protests against a school site ever made in the city."[26] At the last minute, the commissioners agreed to purchase for $44,000 a narrow strip of land on First Street NW between N and O Streets.

Since the school wasn't going to be on M Street anymore, the second challenge was that it would need a new name, but that was a tricky prospect. A Du Bois School or a Booker T. Washington High School would incite one sort of protest or another. The names Syphax, Sumner, and Stevens were already assigned to grammar schools. The commissioners considered naming the school after James M. Gregory, the first colored citizen to be presented as a candidate for West Point in 1867 but who was denied by President Johnson. He went on to become one of the earliest graduates of Howard University. John R. Francis was another possible namesake. He was a doctor and educator who set up the first private hospital for Negroes in Washington.

Ultimately the school would be named for a nonpolitical figure who exemplified all the hopes and dreams of the colored community and who had somehow lived a life that showed education and excellence were key steps in the path to equality. The choice was not a native Washingtonian. He was not someone who had attended M Street School. He was not even alive at the time of the school's construction.

At eighteen years old, Paul Laurence Dunbar went to the Callahan Building at the corner of Third and Main in Dayton, Ohio, to apply for a job as an elevator operator. He longed to be a writer but the reality was he needed money to support his dear mother, who had worked all her life as a washerwoman. His father, who had fought in the Civil War, left the family home when Paul was two and died when he was twelve, so over time Paul and his mother, Matilda, developed a strong bond. It was Matilda who wanted him to be named Paul after the prolific New Testament author; perhaps she had preordained her son's fate. She certainly encouraged him to read and write poetry.

Both of Dunbar's parents had been born into slavery in Kentucky, and neither learned to read until adulthood. Matilda recalled to her son that her kindly master had allowed her into the house where, if she was quiet, she could sit and listen to poems being read. Matilda passed along her lifelong love of literature and encouraged her young boy to write poems, something he started to do at age six.

In school he developed good friendships, even with white youngsters. One of his best buddies was a rascal named Orville, the son of the family for whom his mother sometimes worked.[27] Though Dayton had its share of racial conflict, coloreds and whites sometimes lived in the same areas. Ohio was a nonslave state that had hosted frequent stops on the Underground Railroad. By the time Paul reached his teenage years, the law in Dayton deemed colored students could attend whatever schools were in the districts in which they lived. Paul went to a neighborhood school but was the only colored person in his class. Yet he was class president and editor of the newspaper and yearbook. His pal Orville was an average student more interested in tinkering away at projects; he built a printing press at sixteen.

Paul wanted to make a living as a writer but was turned down for a job at the *Dayton Herald*.[28] Life was not like school—after graduation, his skin color mattered more. He knew he would have to make his own way. When his buddy Orville and his brother Wilbur opened their own printing business, Wright & Wright Printers, Paul asked them to help him start a paper for colored citizens.

On December 13, 1890, the *Dayton Tattler* debuted with Paul as editor and Orville as publisher.[29] He wrote this greeting to his readers:

> Dayton with her sixty thousand inhabitants, among which five thousand colored people, has for a long time demanded a paper, representative of the energy and enterprise of our citizens. It is this long-felt want which the *Tattler* now aspires to fill. Her mission shall be to encourage and assist the enterprises of the city, to give our young people a field in which to exercise their literary talents, to champion the cause of right, and to espouse the principles of honest republicanism. The desire which is the guiding star of our existence is that some word may be dropped in our columns, which shall reach the hearts of our colored voters and snatch them form the brink of that yawing chasm-paid democracy.

The *Dayton Tattler* folded after printing just three issues. Dunbar had a hard time finding advertisers, and the Wrights could not extend him any more credit. But it was a very happy and productive six weeks for Paul and he appreciated his dear friends' help. He wrote a poem about Orville, which in a moment of pique and fondness he scribbled on a wall in their shop.

> Orville Wright is out of sight
> In the printing business.
> No other mind is half so bright
> As his'n is.[30]

Dunbar continued to pursue his dream as he ferried businessmen up and down in the elevator by day. By night he performed poetry readings around Dayton. The Wrights printed up his flyers and programs. He became known about town as the "elevator poet." When the Western Association of Writers held its annual meeting in Dayton, one of Paul's former teachers arranged for him to read some of his work to those attending. It was a huge opportunity to take the stage in front of so many influential scribes.

His appearance at the event was a success, but Dunbar wasn't able to capitalize on the goodwill because he wasn't officially published. There was no work to sell or promote. So the young man making four dollars a week borrowed $125, more than half his annual salary, to pay a publishing house to release his first book. It was called *Oak and Ivy* and was dedicated to his mother, Matilda Dunbar:

TO HER
WHO HAS EVER BEEN,
MY GUIDE, TEACHER AND INSPIRATION
MY MOTHER
THIS LITTLE VOLUME IS
AFFECTIONATELY INSCRIBED

If a person got onto an elevator run by Paul Laurence Dunbar, that person likely got off the elevator owning a copy of Dunbar's book. He had figured a way to pay back his debt: sell copies of his book to the people trapped in the elevator with him for a few minutes. It worked, and it helped Paul's work go viral, insofar as things went viral in the nineteenth century.

With hopes of selling some books and finding creative work, he quit his job and headed to Chicago, host to the World's Fair in the summer of 1893. He found work as a washroom attendant and floor sweeper. He made friends, including a young man named Joseph, a great classical violinist. One day Joseph revealed he was the grandson of Frederick Douglass. After introductions were made, Dunbar was soon working as a clerk for the elder Douglass. August 25 was "Colored American Day" at the World's Fair, and Douglass was set to speak. It turned out to be the day he gave his famous speech addressing the "Negro problem."

Men talk of the Negro problem. There is no Negro problem. The problem is whether the American people have loyalty enough, honor enough, patriotism enough, to live up to their own Constitution. . . . We Negroes love our country. We fought for it. We ask only that we be treated as well as those who fought against it.

When Douglass finished speaking, he invited the twenty-one-year-old Paul up on stage to recite a poem. Douglass declared Paul Laurence Dunbar "the most promising young colored man in America."[31]

Paul Laurence Dunbar.
Courtesy of Ohio Historical Society

Even though the "elevator poet" was now fielding paid invitations to read out of state, the offers weren't enough for survival. He returned to Dayton and to the elevator job and to writing on his Remington typewriter. He had pieces published here and there. But his dream to make a living as a writer wasn't realized until his second work, *Majors and Minors*, was financially backed by two white patrons enamored with his work. Influential literary critic William Dean Howells reviewed *Majors and Minors* in *Harper's Weekly* on June 27, 1894, Dunbar's twenty-fourth birthday. His life changed immediately.

By the turn of the century Dunbar's work had appeared in the *New York Times* and the *Saturday Evening Post*. He traveled across the country and to Europe, reading to both white and colored audiences. He rode his horse Old Sukey in President William McKinley's inaugural parade in 1901. He spent one year in Washington, DC, living among the educated colored citizens of the time and working in the Library of Congress, which was segregated at the time, even for a well-known poet. He didn't like the position and returned home to Ohio a famous man. By this time Dunbar had earned enough money to take a mortgage on a house for his mother in Dayton.

Dunbar was usually photographed wearing a dark topcoat and starched white shirt and sometimes a white tie. His expression often looked both serene and sad, as if he were thinking about something he truly loved but couldn't have. Perhaps it was a wife, as he was divorced after four years of marriage. Perhaps it was his health. He survived one bout with tuberculosis but sometimes lost himself to the lure of liquor. The stoic expression he wore in portraits was not unlike the subject of one his poems, "We Wear the Mask":

We wear the mask that grins and lies,
It hides our cheeks and shades our eyes,—
This debt we pay to human guile;
With torn and bleeding hearts we smile,
And mouth with myriad subtleties.

Why should the world be over-wise
In counting all our tears and sighs?
Nay, let them only see us, while
    We wear the mask.

> We smile, but, O great Christ, our cries
> To thee from tortured souls arise.
> We sing, but oh the clay is vile
> Beneath our feet, and long the mile;
> But let the world dream otherwise,
>   We wear the mask!

His work was unique for the time: the emotions and thoughts of a colored man presented artfully and articulated with truth. This was something that most whites were never privy to nor cared to seek out but which colored people identified with and took comfort in reading.

Dunbar grasped all strata of colored America circa 1900. He easily moved back and forth between writing his poetry in Standard English and in what has been called a "Negro Dialect." "We Wear the Mask" is an example of the former while the first stanza of the poem "Temptation" is a good example of the latter:

> I dun got 'uligion, honey,
> an' I's happy ez a keing,
> Evahthing I see erbout me's
> jes' lak sunshine in the de spring

It's not hard to guess which style of his poetry was more popular in the mainstream in the early 1900s.

A literary review of Dunbar's work changed his life and ruined it to some extent. Critiquing Dunbar's work, Howells wrote that he much preferred Dunbar's "Negro Dialect" poems, as he believed them to be a real reflection of colored life. Howells set the tone for all other critics, who agreed with him about Dunbar's work. When Howells wrote the introduction for Dunbar's third work, *Lyrics of Lowly Life*, he could not have said it more plainly:

> I felt, that however gifted his race had proven itself in music, in oratory, in several of the other arts, here was the first instance of an American Negro who had evinced innate distinction in literature.... Yet it appeared to me then, and it appears to me now, that there is a precious difference of temperament between the races which it

would be a great pity ever to lose, and that this is best preserved and most charmingly suggested by Mr. Dunbar in those pieces of his where he studies the moods and traits of his race in its own accent of our English. We call such pieces dialect pieces for want of some closer phrase, but they are really not dialect so much as delightful personal attempts and failures for the written and spoken language. In nothing is his essentially refined and delicate art so well shown as in these pieces, which, as I ventured to say, describe the range between appetite and emotion, with certain lifts far beyond and above it, which is the range of the race. He reveals in these a finely ironical perception of the Negro's limitations, with tenderness for them, which I think so very rare as to be almost quite new.

This view haunted and angered Dunbar his whole career, but he wore the mask.

Paul Laurence Dunbar was an intelligent and gifted man who, despite his original station as the son of slaves, persevered and became the best and the first of his kind in his field. He represented what the founders of the colored high school dreamed for their own children and their race: success through determination and hard work. Not only would the new colored high school in Washington be named after Dunbar, it would also take on one of his poems as its core value, its guiding principle, its mantra, and its official motto. On page eight of his very first book, *Oak and Ivy*—the one he self-financed through elevator sales—is a poem called "Keep A-Pluggin' Away" that begins:

I've a humble little motto
That is homely, though it's true,—
Keep a-pluggin' away.
It's a thing when I've an object
That I always try to do,—
Keep a-pluggin' away.
When you've rising storms to quell,
When opposing waters swell,
It will never fail to tell,—
Keep a-pluggin' away.

If the hills are high before
And the paths are hard to climb,
Keep a-pluggin' away.
And remember that successes
Come to him who bides his time,—
Keep a-pluggin' away.
From the greatest to the least,
None are from the rule released.
Be thou toiler, poet, priest,
Keep a-pluggin' away.

. . .

To this day, ninety-year-old Dunbar graduates can recite those lines by heart.

Paul Laurence Dunbar never reached his nineties. Dunbar could not escape reoccurring tuberculosis and died at age thirty-three in the parlor room of the home he bought for his mother. It was ten years before the school bearing his name in Washington would open its doors.

On October 2, 1916, Paul Laurence Dunbar High School welcomed 1,117 students and thirty-five teachers, a month later than expected.[32] It almost didn't open at all. The last payment was made to contractors on July 22, and the building was deemed complete enough, even though plumbing and electrical work were needed well into August. Unfortunately that payment was the last of the money from the previous fiscal year. Congress was about to adjourn without passing a new appropriations bill to free up the funds to finish up the school and, more important, pay for all the maintenance. The school district was short the $10,000 to pay the twenty-nine workers, janitors, and electricians at the colored school. In addition, it seems that in Ashford's zeal to create an incredible facility, he spent all the money on the school building and left little else for desks, lockers, and the like. Dunbar High School needed more money for some of the basics. In a rush measure, on September 1, President Wilson signed a compromise that would get money into the system again, but colored Washington would have to wait one more month.

The new Dunbar High School lived up to the original plans. Snowden Ashford had done it—the school was majestic. It was a brick-and-stone-trimmed building measuring 401 feet by 150 feet. It sat only about ten feet back from the street. A parapet ran across the top of the building leading to an entrance that was reminiscent of a castle; the two notched towers looked like giant chess rooks, complete with merlons. On the towers were embrasures in the shape of a cross, and between them hung the American flag. There were three floors, and each level had nearly story-high windows, twelve panes each, which allowed as much natural light as possible. Two stone staircases, with balustrades, led up to a landing at the front door and into the heart of the school: the armory. The architecture seemed to be a mash-up of Elizabethan and Collegiate Gothic, although the city commissioners officially referred to it as Tudor.[33]

There were 110 rooms total: 35 classrooms, a library that could hold 1,400 volumes and accommodate 125 students at a time, a printing press valued at $4,000, a small cafeteria, and a greenhouse. The auditorium could seat 1,500 and featured an enormous pipe organ. In the basement were chemistry and biology labs, a pool, boys' and girls' gyms, a cafeteria with a working kitchen, and a rifle range.

Principal Garnet C. Wilkinson (M Street, 1898; Oberlin; Howard Law School) presided over the official dedication of the school. It took so long to plan that it didn't happen until the following year. The celebration was elaborate, a weeklong event from Monday, January 15, to Friday, January 19, 1917. The events lasted from morning until night. Daylong exhibitions featured sports and military drills. The students presented organ and recital pieces by Schubert and Schumann. In attendance at the nightly assemblies were both white and colored Washingtonians—judges, politicians, and local activists among them. W. E. B Du Bois was slated to speak but canceled at the last minute due to health issues. Taking up the mantle of the moral and intellectual conscience during this week of pageantry was civil rights leader Nannie Helen Burroughs, who had graduated from M Street with honors in 1896. The religious leader and educator who founded a training school for women and girls told the audience,

> Lift up the race until it touches the sunlight of Almighty God, building a service and civilization for God and humanity. . . . The world would lull to sleep if it could. I urge teachers and preachers to work

to keep awake the manhood and womanhood of the Negro. . . .
In my judgment you have a fine opportunity for the education of
your children as is afforded in the breadth and length of this land
whether they be white, colored, or any other race.

But the real star of the event was none other than seventy-eight-year-old
Matilda Dunbar, the beloved mother of the famous poet, who reminded
everyone of how the school had come to be.[34] Colored Washingtonians
kept plugging away until they got their own full-fledged high school.

When the mainstream *Washington Times* covered the opening day of
Dunbar High School, the headline read NEW DUNBAR SCHOOL: UNIQUE
INSTITUTION—THE LARGEST AND MOST UP TO DATE FOR COLORED
PEOPLE IN THE UNITED STATES. The NAACP magazine, *The Crisis*, ran
the story with a caption that proclaimed Dunbar THE GREATEST NEGRO
HIGH SCHOOL IN THE WORLD.

Dunbar High School.
Courtesy of Charles Sumner School Museum and Archives

6 | OLD SCHOOL

IT BECAME TRADITION TO usher incoming students into the auditorium on the first day of classes for a formal welcome to Dunbar High School. The returning upperclassmen took their place in the balcony to get a good vantage point to check out the newbies. The freshmen arrived having heard rumors of initiations—nothing too evil, just upperclassmen giving the young ones wrong directions and a verbal lick here and there. As one young boy scribbled in his yearbook, "It will only be a few weeks of torture, but next year we will be the torturers."[1]

Few qualifications determined who could attend Dunbar: a student had to live in the District, could not have a communicable disease, and had to pass the eighth-grade exit exam. In order to enroll from outside the District, students had to pass a high school entrance exam.[2] It was a fairly democratic process, but the democracy ended at the door of Dunbar. Inside Dunbar, the ground rules and expectations were laid out the first day. Principal Walter Smith, who led Dunbar for twenty-two years, was known to look over his little round glasses, which were as smooth and round as his pate, as he spoke.[3] He laid down the law the first week.

The contribution which DUNBAR will make to your development will be in furthering your progress along the lines already started, and aid in the opening up of new fields for new powers and aspirations which will be awakened with the coming years. Here you will learn to live in accord with one another in a large community, doing your part well that all may be well. You will learn to know that the good leader is he who first was a good follower. You will learn that the good of all is the highest good, superior to the good of one or a few. Happy will you be if you seek always to do your part, great or small, in the best way you can. You will be trained in much that the world counts as worthwhile. Yours will meet with many of the world's best minds, and receive inspiration and growth by contact. If you have improved your opportunities while here, while here you will go forth strengthened in mind, morals, and body, well prepared to do that part of the world's work which will be your share.

As for the students transferring in, part of the surge of Great Migration and those who moved expressly to DC to take advantage of Dunbar, the school administration had this advice:

There are many things which will seem strange to you here at Dunbar. . . . May you find here the greatest aid and encouragement in your efforts and may you know the happiness that comes from doing your best in your lessons and in your behavior. . . . You must have a desire to live up to the highest and best ideals of Dunbar scholarship and deportment.[4]

The message was that Dunbar stood for something. Dunbar proved that Negroes were able to do anything that anybody else could do, and do it as well or better.

Every moment of the first school day was choreographed. Students were given instructions on exactly how to exit the auditorium. Students were to go through the doors immediately, emptying seats from the rear three rows at a time (not two—three!), keep to the right in the halls, and move rapidly. Students were instructed to walk along halls and up and down stairs two abreast at all times (not three—two!), and students were not to walk arm in arm or with arms around one another. Students were not to loiter, but were not to rush either. Instead, they were instructed to keep a "military cadence."

The students who could afford to and didn't have to work every day after school were encouraged to join clubs. There was the glee club and

The Dunbar sports teams were originally the Poets;
they later became the Crimson Tide.

Courtesy of the Historical Society of Washington, DC

the debating society. There were academic clubs, such as the biological club, which was devoted to nature and the sciences. There were social clubs like the Fleur De Lis Club, established in 1904, which focused on literary works and school spirit. The Rex Club—*rex* meaning "king" in Latin—was a young men's group devoted to being manly. The club soon took on the job of helping to patrol the halls and keep the overcrowded facility in order.

And there were sports. The fairly good-sized football and basketball teams went by the moniker the Poets, a name that seemed especially unfortunate when one considered that their main rivals were called the

Generals. Students were encouraged to cheer on their players, and even some of their team-spirit chants were about academic prowess.

> It's D-U-N-B-A-R H-I-G-H High!
> It used to be so hard to spell
> It almost made me cry
> But since I came to Dunbar High
> It's just like pumpkin pie
> It's D-U-N-B-A-R H-I-G-H High!

First and foremost, Dunbar was about academic rigor. The all-classical pedagogy focused on English, mathematics, the sciences, ancient history, Negro history, military drill, physical education, music, drawing, domestic science, Latin, Spanish, French, and German.

At one point, the Dunbar workload was so heavy the board of education had to get involved after a parent appealed to the members to do something. During an investigation, one student reported that she woke up at 5:00 AM every day just to finish the work. One student had begged his teacher not to assign a test because he had to answer 150 questions for another class. The teachers agreed to decrease the workload to one hour per night for each major subject.[5]

The school's difficulty was causing a serious attrition rate in the mid-1920s. Dunbar began losing students for three reasons. Most were students who failed out, followed by students who transferred to technical schools, and then students who had to leave in order to work.[6] The Dunbar position was a bit unforgiving. In a detailed report presented to the principal, the head of the history and English department reported that "thirty-seven left the first semester, the majority of these being self-supporting pupils who lacked the courage and finance to continue the work."

It was clear that boys left school more easily and earlier than girls. Often they were offered jobs, but the boys would eventually return. The girls stayed in school as long as possible because it was a social marker to make it through Dunbar. As the author of the report, Professor Otelia Cromwell, wrote, "Often only a brick wall of insurmountable Ds makes a girl stop."

The report suggested the failure rates were the result of a change in the student population. By the 1920s, ten times as many students enrolled in high school than in the 1890s. The Dunbar faculty felt that students who belonged in vocational schools, business schools, or possibly in the job market were all coming to Dunbar—and perhaps they shouldn't. Cromwell wrote, "The pupils entering the high school are not as selective a group as they were thirty years ago. The schools universally are going deeper down the scale socially, economically, and also intellectually."

The solution was early intervention during the first year. Dunbar would track students by ability groups to cater to their needs, identify students who perhaps should transfer to vocational schools, and then facilitate that transition. In the 1920s a new Negro business high school, Cardozo, opened in the old Central High School building, so students who wanted secretarial or business skills could go there. Phelps was a vocational school for those seeking specific training. And for those who needed to get jobs, the new Dunbar model was to keep them in school until they were academically competent enough to stand a chance in the world. Right or wrong, the faculty felt the way to preserve Dunbar was to keep the academic bar astronomically high. The school was not a democracy but a meritocracy or a dictatorship, with academic expectation as the undeniable, unchallenged boss.

Being a Dunbar student was a way of life. The strong program was a given and was the reason why students went to Dunbar. And *would* excel, period. The school adopted a crest and a Latin motto, *Adveris Major, Par Secundis* (Greater in Adversity, Equal in Prosperity). The words formed a halo around a woman in a robe with a book on her lap and it was embossed on every yearbook. New students were informed that to be at Dunbar they had to have "a serious purpose to succeed." To achieve those ends, students were counseled about what to eat and wear and how to behave. All students were given a small handbook and asked to read it and consult it regularly. The handbook went far beyond the classroom. It would make a libertarian uncomfortable. The student handbook instructed students not to gossip and to have good manners. It suggested sleeping eight hours a day "with the windows open." There were even guidelines on how to pick friends: "Girls and boys who fail in lessons, who are unsatisfactory in deportment or careless in their habits, should not be chosen as companions."

The way the administration saw it, when a student chose to come to Dunbar, and if a student was lucky enough to stay there, he or she was a

Dunbar students of the Virgil Class of 1927, devoted to the
study of literature.

Courtesy of the Historical Society of Washington

representative of Dunbar wherever that student went. Two pages of the
student handbook were devoted to how to act in public.

On walking on the street:

> Avoid loud talking, boisterous laughter or familiar actions. If you
> desire to converse with a friend walk with her a little way but don't
> loiter.
>
> Leave the street corners for traffic. [7]

For conduct at social affairs, students were told to:

> Always greet your hosts and hostesses upon entering the hall. If the
> function is a dance remember the following suggestions:
>
> Boys ask the girls to dance.
>
> Boys, after dancing thank your partner and escort her back to
> her seat. Do not leave her in the middle of the floor.
>
> Girls, remove all wraps before dancing.

Do not accept an invitation to dance with anyone with whom
you are not acquainted.

Gum chewing is in bad taste. Avoid it.

Some of the advice was practical and had to do with safety. Racial tensions were high in Washington following World War I. There had been riots in the summer of 1919. Negro citizens had been beaten by mobs of whites egged on by incendiary headlines about colored marauders. The Ku Klux Klan marched right down Pennsylvania Avenue on a spring day in 1925. The handbook advised students who rode streetcars, which were integrated, to speak in soft tones, not to yell, and to move quickly and quietly to their seats. The advice was as much about survival as manners.

The assistant principal and dean of girls was Julia Evangeline Brooks. She was an impeccably groomed, handsome woman. In stature and carriage she resembled a very good-looking black version of Eleanor Roosevelt. She told her girls to keep their suits cleaned, pressed, and mended. The use of cosmetics should be avoided. "The superfluous use of powder is condemned," advised the student handbook, and girls were told to "use your powder puff at home or in the dressing room or locker room, not in the classroom corridor or on the street." Clothes should be "appropriate" materials—ginghams, percales, and dimities—so that they could be washed frequently. As for other fabrics: "Silks, chiffons, Georgettes, satins have no place in your wardrobe. Do not buy them."

The boys' rules were not as precise, but the rules for all students had one consistent theme: cleanliness. Take baths daily. Brush teeth thoroughly three times a day. Form a habit of 100 percent neatness. "Be unwilling to wear soiled garments," and "Keep your shoes shined and mended. Don't be 'at the heel.' Let your habits proclaim that you are a true lady or gentleman."[8] There was a near obsession with hygiene in the Dunbar rulebook. It was known as "The Gospel of the Toothbrush," as preached by Booker T. Washington.[9] At the Tuskegee Institute he made hygiene an integral part of the curriculum, and reportedly, no student was allowed to stay who did not use a toothbrush. It was a form of civilization in Washington's opinion.

Cleanliness was the American way for the upper and middle classes, and striving Negroes knew appearing immaculate was key to their acceptance and future prosperity. It was also a way to distinguish oneself from the European immigrants and poorer southerners, white and black, who were moving into the cities. Some were unfamiliar with the basics of hygiene that were necessary in big cities where, in close quarters, disease could easily spread. Some of the new arrivals couldn't afford luxuries such as running water and soap. And while poor whites and middle-class whites were distinguishable to some, in the eyes of the law and the eyes of many Washingtonians, colored was colored.

Here is a true story. A clerk in a southern store was once unwilling to accept a coat returned by a Negro because she said it was no longer considered clean. When the manager made her take it, she whispered to another clerk, "We can't put that coat back in stock. Who wants to buy a nigger coat? Some little white girl will probably come in and buy it and not know it is a nigger coat."[10] Being exceptionally clean and neat was at least one thing a Dunbar student could control to knock down assumptions about his or her hygiene that were based on skin color.

There was a price to pay for not living up to Dunbar standards. Students who weren't true ladies or gentlemen would find themselves on the bench outside Miss Brooks's office. Nobody wanted that. As one graduate said, Bin Laden would have been frightened of Miss Brooks.

An M Street graduate herself, Miss Brooks was one of the Twenty Pearls, the women who founded the first Negro sorority, Alpha Kappa Alpha. She was keen on ritual and tradition. She maintained discipline and decorum at Dunbar for twenty-six years, working right up until her sudden death from a heart attack suffered at home after a full day of work at the school.[11]

It was a running joke among the students that as a year-end present someone should give Miss Brooks planks of wood so she could lengthen the bench outside her office. This would accommodate the growing number of students who found themselves parked there for breaking the rules. A student who was absent more than three consecutive days had to reregister to get back in. If a student disobeyed one of the lunch monitors, he or she would end up sitting on the bench. Miss Brooks was known to line up young men outside her office and stare them down, finally remarking, "You don't look like the criminal type to me!" At dances she would walk around with a ruler to ensure that at least six inches separated boys and girls. Principal Smith didn't care for dances at all. "Well, he was Bulldog Smith," recalled the valedictorian of the class of 1935. "He hated to hear the kind of music that we had then. You know the kind of music in 1940, I mean, 1935. It wasn't that much, but it was like swing music. We never—we didn't have dances at our school like they did at Armstrong. They had a dance every month or something. But Mr. Smith didn't like to hear that music. So, we only had dances once every now and then."

Each teacher was known for his or her individual style of discipline.

"What are you here for, young man?" Principal Smith would ask.

"I will flunk your grandma!" said Mr. Allen, a Latin teacher.

"Go back and get your excuse," was a regular line from French teacher Mrs. Brewer.

"All the ladies and gentlemen will be quiet" was all Miss Brooks had to say to hush a room. If Miss Brooks herself didn't catch you breaking the rules, she had ways of finding out about infractions nonetheless. Class cutters were a special pet peeve of her boss and co-disciplinarian, Principal Smith, and she had spies around the city. The man who owned the candy store on the corner would pick up the phone if he spotted unusual activity in his store during school hours. If Miss Brooks noticed that a certain group of Dunbar students was not at school and, say, the singing group the Ink Spots was in town, she would head right over to the Howard Theater and ask the manager to flip on the lights. Then she would escort AWOL students back to class—and activate the grapevine. Their mothers knew what had happened before the kids got home.

Students could not avoid Dunbar teachers if they tried. One could be a fellow member at church, in Miss Brooks's case the Nineteenth Street Baptist Church, where her father was a pastor for many years. A teacher could live next door. And in the early days, each student was assigned a section teacher he or she would see three times a day: in the morning, at recess, and again at the close of school. The section teacher would track the students' attendance and performance, and guide and mentor them along the way. "It was an attitudinal institution," said Carol Miller, class of 1925. "You got support not just from your teachers but from your classmates. If you got sick, they took care of you."[12] Or if a student was in trouble, a teacher might intervene. Geneoa Rhodes was working every day, running an elevator from 4:00 PM to 11:00 PM in a apartment for forty dollars a month. Her teacher, Miss Juanita Howard, tried to find Geneoa another job with better hours so that the girl could put more time and energy into her schoolwork. Miss Howard reported to the principal and guidance committee: "She has a stepmother whom she helps; the father of no help to either. Is a well-behaved and earnest pupil."[13] During the Great Depression the school stepped in and started a child welfare group to help children in need.

The Dunbar difference has been attributed to the teachers and what it meant to be a teacher there. They were highly educated. For example, Julia Brooks had three degrees. And she was not unusual in the stable of teachers Dunbar attracted. Many Dunbar teachers had graduate and master's degrees. They should have been teaching at the collegiate level or practicing in their field of study, perhaps medicine or law. Practically speaking, however, these men and women could not and would not be accepted for jobs—even at some of the universities from which they graduated. Some could not get jobs in their professions. One Dunbar principal was a medical doctor. Two were lawyers. "We had teachers who attended the best schools, like Harvard and Yale. They were motivated, and they motivated us to excel." The teachers also found at Dunbar a level of autonomy and very decent paychecks. The teachers in the Negro schools were always paid on par with the teachers in the white schools. There was a standard pay scale because both the white and Negro system were overseen by the same entity. The good and fair salary attracted talent.

Each year Dunbar had an academic dream team, including:

Jessie Redmon Fauset, Phi Beta Kappa from Cornell. She taught Latin and French at M Street/Dunbar for fourteen years before Du Bois asked her to become the literary editor of the NAACP's magazine, *The Crisis.*[14]

Dr. Carter G. Woodson taught Spanish, French, and history at M Street/Dunbar for nine years. While he was teaching at M Street, he earned his PhD from Harvard, the second African American to do so—the first being W. E. B. Du Bois. He is the father of Black History Month. Dr. Woodson believed "if a race had no recorded history, its achievements would be forgotten and, in time, claimed by other groups."

Haley Douglass, the grandson of Frederick Douglass, taught science.

Otelia Cromwell was the first black graduate of Smith College and the head of the English and history departments at Dunbar.

Teachers and students were often interconnected. For example, Dunbar teacher Angelina Grimké wrote the play *Rachel*, which is considered the first full-length drama production with a black playwright, director, producer, and cast. One of her favorite students went on to become the most widely published woman playwright of the Harlem Renaissance, May Miller. May was the daughter of Kelly Miller, the lawyer who had testified before Congress and fought so hard to maintain M Street's academic standing early on.[15]

The first three Negro women to get PhDs were all connected to Dunbar: Dr. Sadie Tanner graduated from there in 1915, Dr. Georgiana Simpson taught there, and Dr. Eva Dykes was both a Dunbar graduate and teacher. Dr. Tanner received the first doctorate of the three—but how that came to be is a bit of a funny story. Dr. Tanner was first because the University of Chicago held its ceremony in the morning. Dr. Simpson got hers the same day from the University of Pennsylvania, but in the afternoon. Yet Dr. Dykes was actually the first of the three to complete all the requirements and earn the distinction—Radcliffe simply had its official ceremony a few weeks later.

Eva Dykes was able to get through Radcliffe on five different scholarships of $500 each and help from her uncle. Her personal life motto was "to do my best in any undertaking whether I like it or not. The satisfaction of doing my best brings a greater reward than the actual accomplishment of my aim."[16] Dykes was a virtuoso

Eva Dykes earned her PhD at Radcliffe in June 1921. An M Street Class of 1910 alum, she taught Latin and English at Dunbar.

Courtesy of the Special Collections and University Archives, W. E. B. Du Bois Library, University of Massachusetts Amherst

pianist by the age of eight. She undertook graduate work at Radcliffe and managed to complete her 644-page thesis despite the fact that she was turned away from research libraries because she was black.[17]

At Dunbar, Dr. Dykes earned a reputation for being both good and hard. Repeatedly in her evaluations by Dunbar's principal, she was given an "ES," which stood for eminently superior. She was a tough presence despite having a dazzling smile and standing all of five feet two. One story goes that Dr. Dykes had a student who would repeatedly stomp into class. He had been in the military. She ignored his behavior for a bit, but then one day told the young man to come back to her classroom at the close of school. She made him practice entering the classroom repeatedly until he could do so silently.[18] She knew what it took to be a Dunbar student: she had graduated from M Street.

Dykes and Tanner had both returned to teach a new generation. For some, this work was a matter of helping to build an institution dedicated to excellent education for Negro children. Many of the teachers stayed at the school for years and saw the fruits of their labor. In the school's first decade in the new building, despite Jim Crow and all its obstacles, Dunbar did something unprecedented and rather remarkable: it continued to send many Negro students to some of the best northern schools, including Harvard, Yale, Brown, Syracuse, Amherst, Williams, the University of Illinois, Pratt, Dartmouth, Boston College, Wellesley, Wesleyan, Rutgers, Smith, Morgan, Lincoln, the University of Southern California, the University of Colorado, Wilberforce, the University of Michigan, Bryn Mawr, and Colgate.

Some graduates simply could not afford to leave the District, but a quality education could be had at home. Almost all of these students went on to Howard or Miner's Teachers College, blocks away from where they had attended high school. Class after class of well-educated Negroes built the economic foundation for a self-sustaining black middle class in DC. Not everyone would be a doctor or a lawyer, but to have a good life in DC they didn't have to. Dunbar graduates became electricians, messengers, typists, lunchroom assistants, clerks, stenographers, elevator operators, beauty shop owners, firemen, insurance agents, ministers, postal workers, drugstore owners, and teachers—so many teachers, almost a quarter of each class.[19] Teaching was an excellent job for a woman, and after the repeal of Rule 45, women no longer had to be unmarried to teach. And then there was Washington's major employer: the federal government. Working as a clerk or assistant was a pretty good job for a Negro—until Woodrow Wilson came to town.

Woodrow Wilson resegregated government offices almost immediately after becoming president. Within a year of his taking office, applicants were required to submit their photos when applying for any federal civil-service job. Dividing screens were installed in offices, and separate lunchrooms and bathrooms were established. Negroes who held high-level jobs were demoted. This new layer of disrespect and disruption was something the valedictorian of the Dunbar class of 1920 knew about personally, and it would motivate him to spend his adult life trying to achieve equality for his people.

On June 17, 1920, the first class of students to spend all four years in the new building received their diplomas. The commencement ceremony featured speeches by two best friends, class president W. Mercer Cook and valedictorian W. Allison Davis. Both young men were headed to Williams College, where their buddy Sterling Brown had been for the past two years. Davis had received a full scholarship to the college due to an arrangement the college had with Dunbar: Williams paid the tuition of Dunbar's top graduate. Cook didn't need the help as much. His father was a rather famous musician and composer, Will Marion Cook; and his grandfather, John Hartwell Cook, had been one of the first Negro lawyers to practice in Washington and was dean of Howard University Law School from 1876 to 1878.[20]

The three friends would go onto great things in life. Cook was appointed the US ambassador to Senegal. Sterling Brown rose to prominence as a poet and educator. Allison Davis would one day grace a US postage stamp commemorating his groundbreaking work in anthropology.[21] But back in the early 1920s, they were three young men just starting to make their way in an inhospitable world. For Davis, the scholarship was important. Money was not as abundant in his household as it once had been, thanks to President Wilson.

It began with his father John Davis. After returning home from his service in the Spanish-American War, John Davis suffered a huge loss—his wife died of scarlet fever. He was fortunate to remarry and build a life that included three children, Dorothy, John Jr., and William Allison Boyd Davis. Although John Sr. didn't go to college, he was extremely smart and worked hard. He was enamored with Teddy Roosevelt and affected a similar look, including the pince-nez spectacles and full mustache.

Government jobs were available to colored Amercians during the first decade of the twentieth century, and a person could do well. Some open-minded whites in Washington could see that working with the colored population was a win-win. For example, the official in charge of the Government Printing Office, a Roosevelt appointee, once said this of his thousand or so employees:

> There are 400 Negro employees in the Government Printing Office. Colored persons work in the various departments side-by-side with other employees in harmony and with great efficiency. I wish to declare with all emphasis that any employee of this department who tries to precipitate the devilish stricture of race prejudice will be immediately dismissed and will not again be employed![22]

John Davis Sr. worked his way up through the GPO and became the director of a large office with twelve men reporting to him, almost all of them white. His situation was palatable in some ways because he was well known in Washington. He was a big landowner, having inherited a great deal of property from his mother. She had been a cleaning woman with the kind of relationship with her white abolitionist employer that had prompted him to leave her a large part of his estate in his will. She in turn left it to their son, John Davis.

In his own life, Davis professed "total commitment" to being a good father and enjoyed giving his family luxuries big and small.[23] For Christmas 1901, he presented his wife with special engraved liquor glasses made for the occasion. Even though John Davis had wanted nothing to do with his own father, he enjoyed his inheritance and the fact that it made him one the largest property owners in Prince William County, Virginia. At one point, he owned two laundries and six small houses.

But perhaps most of all, John Davis loved his farm in Nokesville, Virginia. It was big enough to require staff and farmhands to look after the cows, calves, Berkshire sows, and pigs. Staff looked after the children, Allison, John, and Dorothy. On Sundays, family members put on their best clothes. Father Davis favored a straw boater and bow tie. The women wore high-necked and low-hemmed dresses. The children wore knickers and button-down shirts, their hair combed, even if only for that moment. The farm was where, as a small child, Allison Davis could ride his Irish Mail toy car to his heart's delight.

After John Davis's hero Roosevelt left office and one-termer Taft exited the White House, the nation elected Woodrow Wilson, and Davis's world fell apart. Under the new racist rules, he lost his position and was demoted to a menial post in the same office he had once helped run. His salary was adjusted accordingly; as a result, he literally lost the farm. By April 1, 1914, Davis was auctioning off all his animals and farm equipment. He wasn't able to reclaim his former position and ultimately lost all his property in order to ensure that his children—including his valedictorian son, Allison Davis—had the best education.

Handsome and smart as a whip, Allison Davis graduated Phi Beta Kappa and summa cum laude from Williams with a degree in English. He had ambitions of writing poetry or novels, so he continued his studies at Harvard, earning a master's degree in English in 1925.

"After Harvard, then there was a job open, a junior professor at Williams, and they wouldn't hire him," his son Gordon Davis explained during a conversation at his law firm, Dewey & LeBoeuf.[24] The view from his high-rise office was obscured by clouds on that gray March day in 2010. "They wouldn't hire him. It was a very embittering moment. Just a few years before, he was the star to the faculty, and now they wouldn't hire him because he was black." Still, his father remained focused. "He was . . . dignified. It was almost his first name. He carried himself with a great deal of dignity and restraint. . . . We had a sense of his importance."

The same could be said of his youngest son, who is hard to miss. To call Gordon Davis a dandy is far too twee a description for a man who stands nearly six feet six. Today he is very much a New Yorker after four decades in Manhattan, a man who is not afraid to don a velvet blazer or a persimmon-colored tie. For a big and slightly imposing person with piercing green-gray-blue eyes, he speaks with great softness about his father. His office is a three-dimensional scrapbook showcasing small pieces of memorabilia, clippings, photos, and plaques that mark key moments of his life.

Gordon Davis was the superstar commissioner of parks and recreation for New York City who restored Central Park in the 1980s. He was the president of Lincoln Center and is currently on the board of the Kennedy Center for Performing Arts. He was a running buddy of the late *60 Minutes* journalist Ed Bradley. He is quick to show you pictures of his family. His father, of course, but also of his uncle, John Davis, who attended Dunbar and went on to become a well-known civil rights advocate. Like his father, Gordon Davis went to Williams and, also like his father, went to graduate school at Harvard.

After the elder Davis left Cambridge and was rejected by Williams, he went on to teach at a historically black college in the South that had a mostly agrarian course of study but was introducing a few humanities courses. Davis was moved and saddened by how academically unprepared his students were. A friend had warned him about what to expect.

According to his son, "After three years of trying to teach these country people Shakespeare, he said, 'There is something wrong here.'" Davis was witnessing the limiting effect of race and class on educational opportunities in the South. This experience would send him toward the social sciences, specifically anthropology. He went back to Harvard to get his master's and then earned another from the London School of Economics. He wanted to investigate the source of the belief among all classes of southern whites that Negroes were inherently inferior. The only way to do this was to embed himself in the world of the Deep South. He packed up and moved to Natchez, Mississippi.

Davis and his wife, Elizabeth, along with a white anthropologist and his wife, Burleigh and Mary Gardner, infiltrated the southern community to study what the two anthropologists referred to as a "southern American caste system." For almost two years, the Gardners lived among the white locals and the Davises lived among the Negroes. The class distinctions were so acute among these southern Negroes that at one point the Davises had to hire a young apprentice to live with the deeply uneducated in place of him and his wife because the Harvard-trained Davises couldn't assimilate realistically in that particular neighborhood. The anthropologists, who made themselves a human control group, would meet in the cornfields at night to share information. They had to maintain their distance in public because, as they found, there would be no way for an educated Negro and an educated white to ever meet.

Their findings revealed two completely different "caste" systems, each with its own judgments about its own race and other races. In all cases when whites and blacks were seen as one community in "Old City," as it was called in the book, whites were always considered superior. An unemployed poor white was superior to a Negro doctor. When the groups were considering each other separately, a Negro doctor would never been seen as on par with a white doctor, though he would be thought superior to a poor white by both whites and Negroes. But this Negro doctor would still have to be kept in his place because "uppity" Negroes were the biggest threat to "the correct Negro-white relationship."

The castes created a code of behavior. The anthropologists found that the whole system of assumed inferiority perpetuated real inferiority. Negroes could only get housing in the worst, dirtiest, most undesirable areas, a sign of inferiority to whites. In citizens' minds, this was not a sign of racism—it was just the proper order of things. But in this belief, Davis found the answer to his question about why the college students he had taught had a hard time understanding Shakespeare. In the Deep South, the unequal distribution of school funds based on Negroes' "mental inferiority" was one way the caste system maintained itself through the generations. "Inferior" students got inferior schools, but truly, it was the inferior schools that created the inferior students. The two years of study resulted in the book *Deep South*, a seminal book in modern anthropology.

Davis had a long career examining how race issues affect our societal roles and opportunities. He used his studies to help change thinking about who could learn and who couldn't. He is perhaps most well known for debunking the IQ test as a measure of intelligence. His work describes a system in which the IQ test merely measured whether or not a student was middle class. "This study had the most practical effect of any of my work," Davis recalled later. "It led to the abolition of the use of intelligence tests in New York, Chicago, Detroit, San Francisco, and other cities. This was one time I got what I wanted: a direct effect on society from social science research."[25] His work was cited during the historic *Brown v. Board of Education* case and was also used in the formation of Head Start.

According to Gordon Davis, "He was an extraordinary scholar, but did not seek the limelight the way some public intellectuals do now." For example, when the elder Davis accepted a position at the University of Chicago, he was breaking ground—yet he remained stoic. "When my father attained tenure in 1948, he was the first black to obtain tenure at any white institution—college—state or private." But it wasn't simple. He was the first black professor at the University of Chicago, a deeply segregated city.

"They voted him on the faculty committee, but the debate was whether or not he would be able to teach. So he was on the faculty, but the issue was, *Could he teach?*" recalled Davis's son and namesake, Allison Davis, sitting in an office on South State Street in a building that had once been the headquarters for the Overton Hygienic Company. In the 1920s the ornate space had housed black businesses and banks and one of the largest producers of African American cosmetics. As time passed,

The Allison Davis stamp was issued on February 1, 1994
by the USPS.

the city built one of the worst housing projects across the street, and the Overton building was abandoned for forty years until it was later redeveloped. (Perhaps this is why my cabdriver insisted I take his card and call him when I needed to leave and then waited for me to get inside the building before he pulled away.) The building is part of Davis's portfolio; in addition to being a former civil rights advocate and lawyer, he is now an über-connected real estate developer about whom many have an opinion. This area, Bronzeville, was on its way up before the crash of 2008.

Allison Davis is also well known for having an eye for talent. Subtle clues around the office remind visitors that he was Barack Obama's first boss out of law school. "He came and saw us after his junior year, second year of law school. We all had lunch. It was not just a meeting. I mean he was something special." Davis went on to become one of Obama's biggest fund-raisers. "The next year, he came back and said he was going to work for Sidley, which is a huge law firm, which is where Michelle had worked. But I think he must have been there a week or two before they probably asked him to write a memo as to why their client was not culpable in an employment discrimination case, and he said, 'Can I come over there?' The only condition was we had to pay for his bar review course."

Davis and his brother grew up in Chicago. Because of their race, they did not live where the other professors and their families did. They lived on the west side of Cottage Grove Avenue, a strict dividing line between white and black Chicago. "Growing up, we lived with that ambiguity, that funny trick race plays on you in America. If we went to one side of Cottage Grove, the white kids beat us up. On the black side, that wasn't our neighborhood, the black kids would beat us up," Gordon revealed.

Both of Davis's sons are so light skinned that for those unfamiliar with very fair black people, they could easily be mistaken for white, and often are. Both self-identify as black and always have their whole lives. Gordon Davis recalled to a *New York* magazine writer that when he was playing basketball for Williams, one day he was trying to get a ride to a game. A car full of upperclassmen pulled up, and he hopped in. One said to him, "I hear we have a pretty good nigger on the freshman team." His response: "Yes, that's me."

It was a strange twist in their lives that their father's work revealed so much about the power of skin color and its effects on educational and life opportunities. It is an irony not lost on either son. Allison Davis was a consultant for and made a cameo appearance in the movie *The Human Stain*, which is about a black professor who pretends to be white for much of his life. In the movie, Davis is on screen for about two minutes portraying a racist railroad car diner, a white man who is so rude and demanding he causes the heart attack of a Negro waiter. The scene is a flashback to an earlier event in the main character's life. The colored waiter was actually a Negro doctor by day who was moonlighting for money to help his family, including his son, the passing-for-white protagonist in the film. "That's when I kill the father." Davis chuckled, "There are so many ironies in the movie. The college scenes are in fact shot at Williams. The first scene with Nicole Kidman is really the Williamstown post office. There's a plaque honoring the issue of the [Allison Davis] stamp in the background. And . . . I'm an irony." The irony was this: a real black man plays a fictional white racist who causes the death of a black man who is the father of a black son who passes as white.

The issue of color within the black community is as complicated as that last sentence.

7 | CHROMATICS

THE FOLLOWING EXCHANGE HAPPENED during a recent cab ride from Union Station after giving the driver the address 1301 New Jersey Avenue NW:

"Oh, you're going to Dunbar High School. You know, you had to be light-skinned to get in there."

"Oh, yeah? How do you know that? Did you grow up in DC?"

"No, I'm from Long Island. That's just what I heard."

If something is said long enough it becomes part of the mythology of a place. The specter of intra-racism stalks Dunbar's reputation: Dunbar High School only allowed light-skinned blacks to attend. Only the children of black doctors, lawyers, and elites could go to Dunbar. Neither is quite accurate, but there is truthiness at the source of those claims.

There was never a paper bag taped to the front door of Dunbar High and used as a basis for turning away anyone darker than the tan sack. Unless dark-skinned students only showed up on the days when pictures were taken, then there are thirty-one years' worth of yearbooks offering visual proof that all of Dunbar students were not "light, bright, and damn near white." And files full of parental contact sheets dispel the myth that all Dunbar parents were affluent doctors and lawyers. Plenty of parents had indeed done well financially and professionally, but many others held several jobs just to make ends meet.

"Dunbar wasn't a school for the elite," maintains West Point graduate and one-time deputy assistant secretary of defense H. Minton Francis,

Dunbar 1941. "Students from all economic classes and parts of the city went there. Brains were recognized, not money."[1]

Still, conversations with Dunbar graduates almost always touch upon color. A good portion of the alums downplay any such classist or color-struck behavior, or at least say they didn't partake in it. One member of the class of 1935 put it this way:

> Anybody could go. We had students whose parents worked as domestics in rich people's homes. It made no difference. But, everybody—anybody—could go. And then school was compulsory until you were sixteen, so we were all going to school. You know, we've done ourselves a whole lot of disservice because we put a lot of emphasis on color and hair. Like, one will say, "There's no bad hair. If you got hair at all, it's good hair." I had a big argument with a lady, and when they do that, I get my yearbook. I said, "Now look at these pictures."

But it was quite a different reality for Dunbar students who experienced something profoundly unpleasant—or felt thoroughly unwanted—because of their looks or where they lived. The depth of the hurt was made very public by Pulitzer Prize–winning columnist Colbert King (Dunbar 1957), in a piece he wrote for the *Washington Post* Magazine, "The Kings of Foggy Bottom."

> I remember my first day at Dunbar like it was yesterday. The class was biology. Our teacher, a very proper, fair-skinned woman, asked us to state our names and identify the junior high schools we had attended. Many of my new classmates had come from Banneker Junior High, the school for folks on the Hill situated across the street from Howard University. The teacher seemed to recognize several of the students as sons and daughters of men and women in her social circle. When those students identified themselves, she nodded approvingly.
>
> My turn. "Colbert King from Francis Junior High." She looked as though she had encountered a bad odor. After class, I compared notes with Benjamin Riley, another student enrolling in Dunbar from nearby Terrell Junior High. He thought he had received the same snub.

It is not that the light-skinned elite at Dunbar openly ridiculed those of us who dared to try to make it or that our efforts went unrecognized by the teachers. But for the most part, they weren't going to invite us into their social swirl.

King's piece points out an important part of high school that has nothing to do with official school policy or academics: social roles. It is well documented that for a long time black Washington high society was color- and status-conscious. Your test scores at Dunbar, no matter how fantastic, might not have translated into invitations to parties. A teacher might have shown another student more interest because of his or her ties to an old colored Washington family that had been in the District for decades. Sam Lacy, the great sportswriter, hated his time at Dunbar. He considered himself "one of the masses," and Dunbar a club for the privileged. He left Dunbar his sophomore year to go to Armstrong. where most of his friends were enrolled.[2]

College English professor Leroy Giles (Dunbar 1947), said of the issue, "It was legend in the ghettos where I came from: the dark-skinned Negroes were separated from light-skinned ones at Dunbar High School. Such was not true literally, but symbolically it was true, for professionals tended to be light skinned and their children hung out together."

Some graduates remember being turned away from outside social functions because of their skin tones. Floyd Robinson, a former star football player at Dunbar, adores his alma mater. He is handsome in his old age, and his white hair stands out against his dark skin. "We had a lot of clubs, and these clubs discriminated. There were some people they wouldn't let in these clubs, and it's just the way it was. Some of the discrimination wasn't all based on color."

"No, it wasn't," his wife, Lonise, chimed in. She also went to Dunbar and is active in a class alumni group. "It had to do with the kind of social thing—"

"It was both. It was both," insisted Floyd. "There were some girls who could just get away with things."

"I think that, you know, while that was so, it goes back to slavery."

It is an old truth. Slaves and servants who worked in the fields did not get the same treatment as those who worked indoors. Luxuries such as learning to read were often reserved for those often lighter-skinned people who worked in the house. And those who worked in the house were often the offspring and/or lovers of the white plantation owners or employers, some of whom saw to it they were educated, even a little bit.

Once emancipation arrived, the newly freed light-skinned servants and slaves had a long head start on education and all its advantages. The founding fathers of Dunbar were all free colored men who had some white ancestry and as a result had been afforded education. Their education and connections gave them the ability to negotiate the establishment of the Preparatory High School for Colored Youth, Dunbar's "grandfather" institution.

It is most likely that the earliest students at the Preparatory School were descended from mixed parentage and prominent families. The academic rigors of the school required that students be able to read, and at the time, those students were children who had received some elementary schooling. In certain circles in the late nineteenth century, skin color meant access. It was an outgrowth of colorphobia that was normal among whites at the time. Take the case of Anita Hemmings, who was technically the first black graduate from Vassar College. Only Vassar did not know her race until days before her graduation in 1897. While most in her class thought she was just a "pronounced brunette," as one person described Anita, her roommate had suspicions. The girl's father hired a private investigator who discovered the truth. After she begged, the school chose to let her graduate—but Vassar did not admit another black woman for more than forty years. Truthfully it hadn't thought it admitted a black woman in the first place. And that is why people chose to pass. It was a sad and often self-hating way to get a better job, a better home, or a better education.

However, in the eyes of the law what you looked like did not matter. If you had "one drop of Negro blood in you," that was enough. The fancy name for the one-drop rule is hypodescent, and at the turn of the century it was the legal measure. In Alabama, Georgia, Tennessee, and Virginia, a Negro was defined as a person with "any Negro blood however remote the strain." In Arkansas the definition was a little more descriptive: a Negro was "defined in relation to carriers visible and distinct admixture and concubinage." While in Florida and Mississippi a Negro would be "all persons with 1/8th or more Negro Blood and teachers and pupils must be the same race."[3] When Homer Plessy tried to ride in a Louisiana train car designated for white riders, arguing that he was by his calculation only one-eighth Negro, he was arrested. The Supreme Court case that bears his name, *Plessy v. Ferguson*, sealed the deal that blacks and whites were to be kept separate all the time, no matter what shade a person might be.

Still, there were those who were color struck. The 1926 novel *When Washington Was in Vogue* cleverly reveals how much attention was paid to color within the black community. The book's love story is told through a series of letters from a man newly arrived in Washington. The author, E. C. Williams, was the principal of M Street from 1909 to 1916, right up until the new Dunbar High School building opened. Throughout his tale, the book's main character describes the various women he meets along the way.

> Now you will want to know about the belle of this particular set. Well she is a "peach" and no doubt. She has a handsome face, a fine color, pretty hair, a striking figure and vivacity plus. For sheer physical beauty, Tommie Dawson is quite her match, though you could not get many people in that crowd to admit it, for Tommie's undisguised brownness would disqualify her at once.[4]
>
> Miss Clay was quite as stylish as Caroline. She would be a pretty brown girl if she would stop trying to be white. She was bleached several shades lighter as far as her face was concerned. I noticed first that her neck was very dark brown.[5]

Manufacturers took advantage of some people's desire to appear lighter skinned by marketing creams that would ostensibly do the trick. Negro newspapers often ran advertisements for Dr. Palmer's Skin Lightening Cream, featuring the tag line CHOOSE YOUR OWN COMPLEXION. The skin cream, called ARTRA, promised "a lovelier lighter skin tone for you."

Many very, very fair-skinned blacks—people with green eyes or red hair—self-identify as black. The head of the NAACP from 1931 to 1955 was Walter White, a black man who looked white. He was so fair that when someone once asked him his race and he said Negro, the person answered, "Are you sure?"[6] Walter White experienced the destruction that any kind of racism causes. In his autobiography he recalls when his own father, also fair skinned, was critically wounded in a car wreck and taken to a hospital. The whole family rushed to the scene. White's darker-skinned brother-in-law, the first to reach the hospital, identified the man on the stretcher as family. The attending hospital workers were shocked at their own mistake. "Have we put a nigger in the white ward?" one asked.[7] The hurt man was then taken out of the nicely appointed and well equipped facility and wheeled across the street to a dilapidated building for colored patients. Had Walter White arrived at the hospital first, instead of his brother-in-law, the ignorance of the hospital attendees might have worked to their family's advantage. Walter White's father died two weeks later.

White could have passed for white. Many people chose to do so in search of easier lives, better places to live, steady jobs, or more desirable schools. The DC Board of Education regularly received complaints of colored students trying to pass as white. In the fall of 1904, representatives of the Kenilworth Citizens Association asked the board to attend to the following four items:[8]

1. Providing water for the building before school opened.
2. Completing a fence around the yard.
3. Providing a teacher for the 7th and 8th grade.
4. The children of John Colvin, a colored man, have been attending the Benning School, a white school, and should be transferred to a colored school.

The first two were referred to the Committee on Building, Repairs, and Sanitation. The other two were kicked up to the superintendent, who in turn kicked item four back to the board. When the board asked Mr. Colvin for a response, Colvin maintained that he was white, his children were white, and they could attend that school. The board put the burden of proof on the Citizens Association, which quickly presented affidavits from people who swore they knew that Mr. Colvin was colored. Colvin demanded to see the papers and wrote this response to the board:

I most respectfully state that I am a white man and married to a white woman. It is true that I have some Indian blood in my veins, but none of the African. I have never associated to any extent with colored people, or been known as a colored person. The names of the person who have signed letters and made affidavits in this matter are entirely unknown to me, except as to one. I further most respectfully state that I am willing, if the Board desires to produce affidavits or letters as to my wife's, my children's, and my associates, and also as to the nationality of my wife and myself.

With that the board closed the matter but informed the principal in the school that it was his duty to transfer out any colored student enrolled in his school. The Colvins eventually had to take their children out of school and move because of harassment.

The Colvins may or may not have been passing. It is possible John Colvin may not have known whether he was black. A popular story among the Dunbar set tells of a woman in Connecticut who didn't know her father was black until after his death, when she found his Dunbar yearbook.

Five years after the Colvin investigation, a more infamous case involved a little girl named Isabel who was barred from elementary school because someone informed a teacher she was "colored." Seven-year-old Isabel had blonde hair and blue eyes. Unlike the Colvins, Isabel's father didn't completely deny any African ancestry. As a younger man, after all of his family had died or left Washington, he had simply moved to a white section of town and assumed life as a white Washingtonian.[9] He married a white woman, and they sent their daughter to a white school. However, because he kept his name and his job with the Government Printing Office, people in other parts of DC knew of his earlier life. When confronted by the school principal and the board of education, he explained that his daughter was the fifth descendant of the marriage between a white man and an octoroon, and she was white as far as the family was concerned. As the *New York Times* put it when they covered this story, CHILD 128TH NEGRO BARRED FROM WHITE SCHOOL BY AUTHORITIES.[10]

One Dunbar/M Street graduate thought colors lines were a farce, making him "post-racial" long before it became the buzzword of the twenty-first century. Jean Toomer became a well-known writer and philosopher who was part of the Harlem Renaissance. As a child he had lived a racially multilayered life in the nation's capital. He lived with his grandfather P. S. B. Pinchback who, when he was in Louisiana, had been the first colored governor in the United States. In DC they lived in a white neighborhood, but Toomer always attended black schools, including M Street.

When Toomer graduated from high school in 1914, he traveled across the United States, attending different colleges. He taught in a Negro school in the South. As an adult he decided to renounce the idea of confining racial labels. Sometimes on legal documents he is referred to as Negro, other times he is listed as white. Was he passing? Was he unaware of some of the designations? Did he even care about racial identification? At some point he stopped racially identifying himself at all. He said he was an American. He wrote of his choice:

> I wrote a poem called "The First American," the idea of which was that here in America we are in the process of forming a new race, that I was one of the first conscious members of this race. . . . I had seen the divisions, the separatisms and antagonisms . . . [yet] a new type of man was arising in this country—not European, not African, not Asiatic—but American. And in this American I saw the divisions mended, the differences reconciled—saw that (1) we would in truth be a united people existing in the United States, saw that (2) we would in truth be once again members of a united human race.[11]

8 | COMING OF AGE

THE CLASS OF 1946 had a special theme for its yearbook. The book included the standard letter from the editor, but this one looked a little bit different. It was part of a black-and-white pen illustration of a parchment scroll placed in front of a treasure chest dripping with gems. The title of the introductory essay was "Glimpses of the Jewel."

> Open the lid. Behold! Among the jewels of the world, The Diamond Dunbar. Over seventy-five years ago, this jewel came into being in the nation's capital. The keepers of this jewel during these years have polished it so that now its brilliance is widely known. Many have sought and found this gem; others will continue to seek it.

The diamond metaphor is as an apt one. Diamonds are the hardest known natural material. They start as rough carbon that changes structure after long periods of intense pressure and high temperatures. Those rough diamonds are pushed and pulled to the surface where they can be cut and finished into sparkling jewels. It sounds not unlike the educational process at Dunbar. Seventy-five years after that first class met in a rough church basement, through hard times, hard work, and a lot of pressure—both self-imposed and societal—Dunbar was a true gem.

The class of 1946 has an active alumni group. Throughout the year, newsletters are mailed out full of updates and whereabouts, with sweet bits about travels and sad bits about classmates who have passed. Each year, those who are able meet for a mini-reunion lunch, but the sad truth is that the number of attendees gets smaller and smaller. While the class-mates all share similar recollections of daily life at Dunbar—challenging classes, high expectations, motivating teachers, crowded rooms, race pride—the details of their personal lives are incredibly different. The funny thing is, many of them still live up to their earned class superlatives from a yearbook list stating the class's best, biggest, and most of something or another.

During a recent gathering, James Grigsby, who was voted "Most Loquacious," said grace over the buffet luncheon: "Serious thanks, Heavenly Father, for your goodness and for your mercy. We are thankful, Dear Lord, for your goodness to us and for your mercy, help us to do a good job in whatever we say and do. Help us to be pleasing in your sight. Now, Lord, we ask to bless the food that has been prepared for nourishment, help it to strengthen us so that we can serve you in a greater way. We would not forget those who are less fortunate, bless them, for we pray these prayers in your name. Amen." Grigsby, who is known to friends as Buddy, is quick with a laugh and always has a friendly word. He lived up to his loquacious attribution in the kindest way when he approached a classmate sitting in a wheelchair. Wearing a white guayabera shirt and a big smile, he leaned down to kiss his classmate and exclaimed, "You sure do look pretty!" She had suffered a severe stroke, and Buddy continued to hold her hand and talk to her even though she could not say anything back.

Wilma Welch was voted the "Most Popular" girl in her class and still has the lovely manner of a southern lady who makes everyone feel welcome. She puts together the class newsletter and is always eager to make sure everyone has a chance to share a story. She married James Wood, voted the "Most Popular" boy, but they divorced long ago. She spent her adult life as an elementary school teacher in the District. Her love of Dunbar has not waned in sixty-five years: "I really cried when I graduated because I really didn't want to leave. It was just a wonderful experience, and you didn't have any fear. Any problems like that. You were happy to report to school every day."

Wilma's father was a Dunbar graduate in the 1920s, but died when she was a baby. Her mother raised her alone, so Wilma learned to be fairly self-sufficient. She took the streetcar to school every day, and when operators went on strike, it was no matter—she walked the whole way.

"When I got to Dunbar, it was just like, 'Ahhh . . .'" Wood said as she exhaled, not dramatically, but with Zen-like composure. She just wanted to get to school, to be with her friends in the armory, to be in class.

"The armory was the best place in the world," Wilma recalled. "That's where the cadets practiced. But lunchtime, that's where everybody came. That's the place to meet." When asked if she remembered how Dunbar compared to the white schools in the District, Wilma replied, "I never gave it a thought."

Vashti Atkins, editor in chief of the yearbook, was voted "Busiest." In one photograph, an action shot of her correcting copy, she looks pensive. As she stares off into space, the expression on her round face is that of someone who really does not want her picture taken. "I was just more serious because I was older, and I've been through so much."

Vashti chose not to attend the most recent class of 1946 get-together. She is still quiet and likes being home with her husband, Stewart. Slowly, over a lunch of pizza and ice tea, she revealed why her high school years were not full of dances and dates. By the time the picture was taken for the yearbook, Vashti was twenty years old. Her first day at Dunbar was seven years before she graduated. "I entered Dunbar in 1939. I finished the freshman year . . . started sophomore year; that was the fall of 1940. In December 1940, I was diagnosed with tuberculosis. I was put in the hospital, of course, which was the Glendale Hospital. At that time all—[it] had all tuberculosis patients. I was in the hospital three years and eight months."

Glendale was a tuberculosis sanatorium in Maryland where patients and potential carriers were quarantined and put on long-term bed rest. According to Vashti, her condition wasn't serious, but her treatment was invasive.

At that time there was no medication for tuberculosis. It was bed rest or—I've forgotten the name of the thing—but air was pushed into your lungs so that your lungs rest and it gave the chance to heal.

Yeah, I was put on bed rest for some time. I can't remember that well now, but for some time, and it didn't heal. So then they gave me an operation which was what they call a phrenic, and we were told there was a phrenic nerve, right, that will be in some place which would make the lung rest. So they tried the phrenic nerve operation and—well, over time, that took a lot of time. That didn't work. So, finally they gave me this pneumothorax. That's what is what it is called.

Surgery to move a nerve that controls the diaphragm, artificial inflation of the lungs, and isolation was a lot for one teenage girl. She was the youngest of nine children, but by her high school years it was just Vashti and her mom on their own.

One day at the hospital she looked up and saw that her new room-mate was a girl who had been in her homeroom that first year at Dunbar. They bonded over their shared experience and remained friends when they were both allowed to return to school, older and wiser than most of their classmates.

"Vivian Stark. Vivian was my best friend and we ate outside sometimes on the front [steps]. I don't remember the cafeteria because you know, I took my lunches. All those poor kids did take their lunch. I remember eating outside on good days. Me and my good friend Vicky." Vashti went to college because of someone's profound generosity. Somebody—to this day, she doesn't know who—arranged a scholarship for her to go to college. She was the only one of her nine siblings who did so.

Vernon Tancil was voted "Most Sophisticated." He went on to travel the world and then settled on the West Coast to become a park ranger. James Bruce was voted "Most Energetic," which still fits to this day. Over breakfast at the ornate Palmer House in Chicago, where they know his order, he told me of his amazing life in Japan. Enid Tucker was the "Most Pleasant" girl in the class and true to form, likes to discuss family and friends. Jeannine Smith (Clark) was voted "Most Attractive." In her eighties she can still turn heads driving her zippy little Mercedes over to the Cosmos Club for crab cakes and a little political discussion ("I tell you, that man, Mr. Obama, is not a real black American!").

Back at this particular small class lunch, the friends made jokes and swapped the kind of stories that begin, "Girl, you got that Benjamin Buttons thing going on . . . you look good." They shared stories about old times, but not many of them included Jo-Jo Stewart, a tall member of the track team. He'd been close to only a few classmates, including Louis Campbell, voted "Biggest Jiver," and Leon Ransom, "Most Witty" and "Noisiest." Jo-Jo wasn't on the list. Most said he was a nice fella, but they didn't know him

HER MAJESTY — THE QUEEN

HOMECOMING QUEEN AND ATTENDANTS

Left to right: LaVerne Clark, Joyce Meadows, Mary Dixon-Queen, Helen
Saunders, and Dolores Collins.

Dunbar High School Yearbook, 1946

well. Smart. Graduated midyear. But one man offered his unvarnished
opinion of Jo-Jo: "Joe Stewart, aw . . . he thought he was white."

Joe Stewart thought he was from New York City. He *knew* he was from
New York City. Home for him was 143rd Street with his pals Val and Rudy.
"All we needed was a nickel, a jar of Vaseline, a towel, and a comb . . ."
In the last weeks of his life, he recalled his earliest memories of life in

NYC. The nickel was to get on the subway to Coney Island, the Vaseline was to put on their bodies so they wouldn't get cold jumping in the water, the towel was to dry off, and the comb was get their hair looking right so they would look good on the way back uptown. Jo-Jo and his friends ran around the streets of Harlem and Washington Heights and explored Brooklyn and Queens. He lived in a melting pot of Irish, Italian, Jewish, and Negro New Yorkers.

By 1943, the United States had survived the Depression but was deeply involved in World War II. Jo-Jo's future did not look bright. This was largely because Jo-Jo was bright—but highly unmotivated. He was not old enough to enlist, and he had only an intermittent interest in school. He got As in the classes he liked, and Ds in the classes that bored him. He described his young self this way: "Getting me to study was like putting cooked spaghetti through a keyhole."

It wasn't that his mother didn't try. Education on all levels was valued in his home. Edna Pride graduated from Scotia Women's College in Concord, North Carolina, one the first colleges established for Negro women after the civil war. Edna worked as a schoolteacher in North Carolina. When she became a stay-at-home mom, she was still always learning new things. One day Jo-Jo came home and found that the southern food of his youth would be prepared for special occasions only. Edna had taken a course on nutrition and wanted a healthier lifestyle for the family. That didn't keep Jo-Jo from enjoying the chocolate cake she made every week. He would come home, make two parallel cuts across the circular cake, about an inch apart and then lift the large rectangular chunk of cake straight up from the center of the round. He would place the long rectangular slice of cake on a plate for immediate consumption. But before digging in, he would gently press the two sides of the cake together and doctor up the icing a bit, thereby reducing a ten-inch diameter cake to a nine-inch cake.

Jo-Jo's people were of tough stock. His paternal grandfather, Samuel Banks Pride, was a professor of mathematics at Biddle University in North Carolina, now the HBCU Johnson C. Smith University (The acronym HBCU refers to historically black colleges and universities). His wife, Jessie Houston Pride, was an elementary school teacher. Professor Pride was also known to stay up all night on the family porch because some local KKK members let it be known that they did not appreciate the fact that he and some like-minded individuals helped establish a high school for colored children in Charlotte. Second Ward High School stood until the mid-1960s.

Originally from DC, Jo-Jo's father, Joseph Turner Stewart Sr., was a song-and-dance man at heart. That's how he had ended up in New York, where he met Edna. She'd gone to Manhattan for a vacation and wound up with a husband. Joe Sr. was employed by the post office and had worked his way up to clerk. His son was noticeably impressed one day when he accompanied his father to work and saw his dad strap on a .45 pistol. In those days, if you supervised the shipping deck, even for mail, you were armed.

As far as he was concerned, Jo-Jo had a pretty good life in New York City. He attended a public elementary school, then entered George Washington High School. It was a good school—the alma mater of Henry Kissinger and Alan Greenspan—but Jo-Jo Stewart was slipping through the cracks. Keeping him in school was a battle, and as he remembered it, the school didn't really help. "People were not interested in African American kids being in academic classes, and I didn't pay attention, so the combination was not good."

In the early 1940s, Edna Stewart pointed out to her husband that no one was saying Jo-Jo Stewart and college in the same sentence, and asked what were they going to do. Joe Sr. had a good job for a Negro in NYC, but Joe Jr. was on the edge, an especially dangerous place for a smart kid with a fast mouth. The answer became clear: send Jo-Jo to the same high school his father had graduated from on June 23, 1915—M Street School, now Dunbar.

The Stewarts' new homestead was with Ma and Pa Stewart in Southeast Washington. Joe Sr. would stay in New York. He repeatedly tried for a transfer, but a job in Washington never materialized, so his parents took in his son and wife. But that didn't mean he was absent from his son's life.

"Pop used to chew on my ear by telephone and when he came down. He would be down about every other week. As you may remember," my father said to me, "your grandfather was relatively small, but he weighed ten tons when he stood on your chest."

Ma Stewart and Pa Stewart were both short and stout in old age. Together they resembled a salt and pepper set, in that order. Walter Colfax Stewart—Pa Stewart—was a deacon in the Episcopal Church, fond of opera and a taste of liquor now and again. An average Saturday afternoon went like this: Pa Stewart would sit down at the table. He'd call over his grandson. "Ah, Jody," he would say. "Go get me my forty drops." Jo-Jo, whom he called Jody, would fetch a glass and a bottle of whiskey and bring it to Walter. Ma Stewart—Lillian—would sit at the other end of the table with her hands folded, lips pursed and growing tighter because she was horrified that her grandson was carrying liquor. Ma would stay quiet until she could take it no more.

"Walter, that boy should not—"

"Aw . . . woman!" was Pa's response. He'd have his drink, it would be over, and then it would happen again the next week.

Once Jo-Jo moved to Washington and was ready to enroll midyear at Dunbar, he realized something strange. He was passing three high schools every day to get to the one high school where he could go. "Funniest thing about it, I don't think anyone ever mentioned to me it was a segregated high school." He had been to Washington many times but just to see family. "Washington was a segregated city, but it wasn't southern Alabama, for example. There wasn't segregating on public transportation, but we knew we weren't going to go downtown to the movies. I was the new kid in town, so I went along with the flow. But I remember being truly offended by the idea that you had that kind of system in the capital of the land of the free and the home of the brave, and I was mildly pissed off about it."

So he did something about it.

"What are you *boys* doing?" a white police officer asked the two teenagers collecting signatures outside a grocery store. It was a normal afternoon in Washington, DC, except that fifteen-year-old Jo-Jo and his pal Leon were protesting a major food chain's hiring practices. They were a bit of a sight. Leon was short; Jo-Jo was tall. Leon was a little thick, and Jo-Jo was lean. Leon, voted the wittiest and the noisiest in the class, was popular; Jo-Jo was a bit more of a loner. But they had this in common: they liked to make waves.

"Safeway was a sizable supermarket chain in DC, and they didn't have—even in African American neighborhoods—they didn't have any black cashiers." The two teens were collecting signatures on a petition to allow Negroes to work where they lived. And someone had called the police.

"Sure enough," Joe said, shaking his head when he thought about the scene. The second day they were out there, they had some company. "We were very respectful and we had our pads and our petition sheets,

COMING OF AGE | 123

and the local cops showed up—the white cops." It is a moment in a black man's life that he is not surprised to experience, being stopped on a public sidewalk by the police—especially then in the nation's segregated capital. First, the officers rolled up in a shiny black Studebaker, a Metropolitan Police insignia gleaming from the metal grille on the front. For a while the officers watched as the boys asked locals to support their movement. When it became clear that Jo-Jo and Leon were not intimidated by their presence, the officers got out of their squad car and approached on foot.

"What are you *boys* doing?" demanded one officer.

Jo-Jo did the talking. He politely explained their mission and offered nothing more, knowing that the situation could end poorly. One of the stern-faced policemen took out a pad and gruffly asked for their names.

"Joseph Stewart."

The officer wrote it down and turned to Jo-Jo's friend.

"L-E-O-N-R-A-N-S-O-M. Leon Ransom."

The officer's demeanor changed quickly. "One of the cops recognized Leon's name."

Leon Ransom was the son of Leon A. Ransom, the NAACP attorney and civil rights crusader. After an awkward silence, the officer flipped his pad closed and said, "All right, you boys behave yourselves." They got back into their car and drove away.

"They figured if we do anything to these kids, it's going to be more trouble than it is worth," Joe Stewart said, chuckling at the memory.

At that time Leon A. Ransom, referred to as Andy by his friends, had been on the Howard faculty since 1931. He worked with fellow Harvard Law grad Charles Hamilton Houston, then dean of Howard Law School, and Thurgood Marshall, future US Supreme Court justice. They were all part of a generation of legal minds out of Howard who were on a mission to use the courts to unravel the tightly woven threads of segregation and rip apart legally sanctioned racism.

Ransom handled some egregious civil rights cases. He appeared in front of the Supreme Court and argued successfully for the freedom of several black men charged with murder in southern states. In DC, however, the problems were less flagrant than the police rounding up forty black males and forcing a confession out of one of them, as happened in Ransom's case *Chambers v. Florida*. In Washington, the discrimination, especially for the working class to upper-middle class Negroes, was felt in the schools, workplace, and housing. Litigation and legislation seemed to be the answer.

Activism was brewing in the city. The wide, stable, and educated middle class was all about achieving better jobs and gaining economic independence. The engine of the movement was an organization called the New Negro Alliance (NNA). The NNA's founders and legal team were made up of former Dunbar teachers and students, including John Davis (brother of Allison Davis), Kelly Miller, and William Hastie, who went on to become the first black federal court judge. Their first targets were stores that would not let Negroes clerk or serve in any administrative positions, even in Negro neighborhoods. Peoples Drug. High Ice Cream Company. A&P.

Despite threats from the Klan, the NNA was quite successful in integrating workplaces and empowering young Negro men like the team of Stewart and Ransom. Years later, when seventy-nine-year-old Joe Stewart was asked why, at just fifteen years old, he had participated in pickets like those started by the NNA, he replied, "I was pissed off."

Different families approached the segregation and the restriction of personal freedoms in different ways. Some didn't discuss it—it was just the way things were. Some tried to create a social force field around their children so they would not become infected by thoughts of inferiority or bitterness. James Grigsby, Dunbar '46, remembers his mother's sweet way of protecting her five kids from any sort of humiliation: she only took them to outside events.

My mother would always say she loved parades. And my parents took us sightseeing on Sunday afternoons. But my mother always told us when she was taking us out, "You are not going to go to the bathroom because those public toilets are too dirty." And so I guess we had to have strong systems. When I look at children that have to go to the bathroom when they go to the store, I realize that it was a way of keeping us from knowing that we were not allowed. That's why we love parades to this day. But they kind of shielded us. But the first time I really felt segregation was when I went into the service, and it was something about going down to Richmond. You had to eat in the colored sections, and that was just awful. That was awful. We never saw anything black and white in writing in Washington. But I guess our people were so sophisticated they wanted to protect us from that kind of thing. It was like an unwritten thing.

Living her whole life in segregation, one Dunbar student just had to satisfy her curiosity about her peers. One day she altered her route to Dunbar and chose to walk through a different neighborhood. "I wanted to see what they looked like," she explained. "I really wanted to see what these white children looked like."

When I met her, Yvonne Clayton (Dunbar 1935) was still as sassy as she had been on the day she decided to stroll past the white high school. All her life she had been a voracious reader, and was still getting through one or two books a week. "I read all the time. If you had come in yesterday, my books were piled here. I read my books several times. I just got through reading the *Twilight* series and Edward Cullen and the vampires. I fell in love with that man! The most romantic story I have ever read." She was a ninety-two-year-old Twi-hard.

Yvonne liked a good story, and could spin a good one too:

This particular day, I thought, "I'm going to walk down Eleventh Street to get to school." I was curious as to what it would look like to go past Central High School when students were there. So, I started down Eleventh Street. One block, I noticed it was like ten AM and all the students were—well, it was like the point of no return! I could have turned back a half a block and then walked down Sherman. . . . I said, "No, I'm going to see what they look like." I had never seen a lot of white children in my life. At any rate, I start down the street, and I suddenly realized that the children are on both sides of the street. OK. I was petrified. I was absolutely frightened to death. The talk about being afraid of us—I was absolutely frightened to death.

At that point the smile on her face and the gleam in Mrs. Clayton's eyes made her look fifteen years old again.

I was frightened that they might say something to me or hit me or, in some way, molest me, not sexually, cause that wasn't even in my thinking. I was just absolutely . . . but I said, "Oh, my God, I've got to walk." It was, like, between the boys, someone sitting on the curb and someone leaning up against the walls of the high school. So, I said, "OK, Yvonne. You're a stupid ——. Just make it to Florida Avenue." So I started walking. And, I didn't look left nor right. But, as I closed my eyes, I could see some of the boys are turning around, and I kept on walking. I tell you, I have never been so frightened in my life. When I got to Florida Avenue, I took off like a rocket. And I thank God that I had made it, and I ran all the way to school. And, I tell you one thing: I never did that again. But, that's the first time I had ever seen more than, maybe, one or two white children.

Of course, Yvonne couldn't keep her adventure to herself and had to tell all her friends at Dunbar how she had gotten to school that day and what she had seen.

"I got to school and told the other students about my experience and they said, 'You were crazy.'"

Hers is a funny story, but under other circumstances, her decision could have been a dangerous one. One graduate remembered his father telling him never to run, even if he was late. In some eyes, running while black justified the assumption of guilt. Another graduate remembered having to get a note to walk through a certain part of town. And no matter how hard Dunbar students studied or how much of *The Odyssey* they could recite, they still could not go into Garfinckel's Department Store.

And perhaps the most famous—and ultimately embarrassing—example of segregation in the nation's capital occurred in 1939, when world-famous opera singer Marian Anderson was banned from performing at Constitution Hall because the venue was for whites only. First Lady Eleanor Roosevelt arranged for Ms. Anderson to give a very public concert on the steps of the Lincoln Memorial instead.

The parents and teachers of Dunbar gave students a great gift: self-esteem. The students understood segregation was a tool of degradation and rejected any concept of inferiority. Dunbar students were taught to be the best—and in many cases were the best. They learned Negro history. They saw role models in their teachers and in Negro speakers, businessmen, and scholars. Dunbar drilled into them that they were as good, if not better, than any student in the city, if not the country. Dunbar graduates were armed with excellence.

"They didn't have that at my high school in New York, teachers who cared that way." And for that reason, Jo-Jo Stewart knew Dunbar was the place he needed to be, even if the social nature of the city wasn't his thing. His track coach, the always approachable Mr. Jacobs, was looking out for him. A common encounter went something like this:

> Jo-Jo: I've got a big test tomorrow, and I would like to skip practice so I can study for my test.
>
> Coach Jacobs: Boy, you go study for that test. That's the most important thing that you can do . . . But how come you've got to cram so late?

"He really cared what happened to all of us who were on his teams, and he talked to all of us, and he always enforced the idea that we should be gentlemen in terms of competition, that we should win the right way and that while sports were important to us, the reason we were in school was for education." When Joe reflected on the experience, he could see the good it did him. He had strong male role models, he ran track, was a class officer. He saw that people cared. But his sense of individuality was at odds with the advice given to young Negro men at the time.

> He [Jacobs] said, "Remember you have to be a credit to our race." I agreed with it, but it mildly pissed me off that it was a fact that had to be considered. And one of the things that interested me is that some people couldn't understand why I would be mildly pissed off. Why should that be a consideration? That I have to be a credit to my race? I need to be a credit to myself as an individual because people ought to not be looking at my race, they ought to be looking at me as an individual. I have very strong feelings about that.

Jo-Jo Stewart also developed strong feelings for a dear friend and girl he met at church, Carol Graham. At the time he was dating another girl in her class, but he and Carol became confidantes. "She was serious. A really good person. I mean, very genuine. I thought she was the prettiest girl I had ever seen . . . and the best part was that I could talk to her, and she was intelligent. She was so smart, and there was something about her." They were married for almost fifty-five years before Joe passed away.

Slated to graduate in 1947, Carol Graham cared about her studies and her two friends. "We were like the Three Musketeers," her dear friend Letitia "Tish" Young remembered. Under Tish's yearbook picture, the editors assigned her the description "charming." She was an elegant, lanky girl with big eyes. The third musketeer was a sparkling, voluptuous gal named Carolyn Cobb. Next to her yearbook picture was printed the word "entertaining." Next to Carol's, it read "vivacious." Tish and Carolyn lived near each other and walked to school together. There they would meet up

Joe Stewart and Carol Graham, the author's parents, 1951.

with Carol, whose family moved around quite a bit. They would remain friends for years, rotating as bridesmaids in each other's weddings.

Back then, Carolyn had the luxury and burden of being the daughter of a legend. Her father, Dr. W. Montague Cobb, was a notable presence in Washington. Although he would refer to himself as "just a printer's son," Dr. Cobb was a nationally recognized leader in medicine. His field of study was anthropology and the crossroads of anatomy and racial discrimination. In his lifetime, he was published more than a thousand times. He worked his whole life for integration in national medical organizations.

Dr. Cobb's intelligence and ability to weave words were both dizzying and terrifying. A Dunbar graduate himself (class of 1921), Dr. Cobb was the chair of the anatomy department at Howard University. He was a major obstacle for Howard medical students, but he was a good kind of obstacle. He wanted the doctors he trained to be twice as good, because he knew they needed to be twice as good to get half as far. Almost six thousand medical students—two generations' worth of black of doctors—endured Dr. Cobb's rigorous classes. Medical students could not graduate until they survived the "Cobb Cadaver Walk," a final clinical exam on gross anatomy. While the young students dealt with the dead bodies, Dr. Cobb would sit in the corner and play the violin as they struggled through the exam. Carol recalled, "He was a brilliant man, although he taught anatomy, so they all dreaded him because they said he was the toughest professor they had, but he was just showing them that they had to be better. They couldn't just go out and party on the weekend—they had to be ready to walk through what they call that cadaver walk. You ask my brother."

While Carol's younger brother dealt with Dr. Cobb as a teacher, she knew him as her best friend's dad. However, even if a young person wasn't a med student at Howard, Dr. Cobb would test him or her—say, at the dinner table. Like most girlfriends, Carolyn would often invite Carol over to hang out.

"I would go to dinner at the Cobbs', and they were very gracious, and her mother Hilda taught—she taught the fourth grade or something like that."

Dinner at the Cobbs' was a bit formal, with a white linen tablecloth laid on the long table in their lovely brownstone dining room. They had a maid, and sometimes Carolyn's grandmother was there also. Dinner could be going along well and then Dr. Cobb would start firing off questions to the teenage girls.

"He would sit at the table, and he would just start to ask questions: What do you know about? And I remember he scared me to death."

One evening the subject was anatomy. Dr. Cobb trained his eyes on his daughter's friend.

"Carol, what is *Australopithecus? Australopithecus!*"

The conversation at the table stopped.

"Oh, Daddy, you know, can't we have a peaceful dinner?" Carolyn was the only person who could talk to the great Dr. Cobb in such a way. "You are not lecturing—you are not in school!" Carolyn continued. She was like her father in that she had a quick mouth. Carol couldn't do that as a guest; she had good manners hammered into her.

"Dr. Cobb, I don't know . . ." was all Carol could manage to say.

This was an unpardonable sin. "But, oh you must know these things!" He would then give a little lecture to the girls. Carol went on to become a biology teacher and became well aware that *Australopithecus* is one of the oldest forms of extinct hominids closely related to humans. But in Dr. Cobb's world, it was something a fifteen-year-old girl should know. But even then, Carol knew there was a greater lesson Dr. Cobb was trying to teach his pretty daughter and her pretty friends: you must know things.

Carol continued to join the Cobbs for dinner because she understood that. "What he was saying is, 'You have to get beyond your little boxes. You have to think outside the box.' So I have always had a great deal of respect for him, because he would not be limited."

It was a lesson she took to heart. Despite a very conservative home life, she did her best to try new things. She would visit her relatives in Brooklyn when she could. She was able to ride the B&O Railroad for free because her uncle was a Pullman porter. She took part in local events in DC.

One day she was called to the Dunbar office and told she was going to meet Hazel Markel, "the First Lady of Radio" in Washington, DC. Markel spoke nine languages and during her career reported for NBC and was the White House correspondent for Radio One.[1] Carol knew this was a big deal. "She was a brilliant woman," she later explained, "really ahead of her time." And now Markel was the news director at WTOP in Washington. "Hazel Markel called the school—which is unheard of, because the school is segregated—and said, 'I'm going to start a program on

Saturday mornings for young people at the different schools, and I think Dunbar should be represented.' And it was called, 'Youth Takes a Stand.' Miss Brooks called me down to the office and said, 'There is an experiment going on, and we would like you to try it. We think you can handle it.' " It was a show on which black and white students got together and talked about current events, live on the radio.

Carol was a natural. "In the process, Hazel Markel said to me, 'Get out of the stereotype,' and I guess I was sufficiently verbal or articulate— I don't know what the adjective would be—but Hazel Markel was the one who really took a liking to me, and she said to me, 'We have to do something about you.' " Markel suggested that Carol think about going to one of the northern women's schools rather than staying in Washington and going to Howard or Miner Teachers College.

Carol Graham began to investigate the options as Markel guided her along. "Sarah Lawrence. Hazel Markel was the one who encouraged me, because she knew of the school, and she said, 'I think that would be great.' But, of course, the big problem was money."

Actually, there were two problems: money and convincing her conservative father to let his only daughter go to school in New York with the fanciest of girls. She was going to have to be a scholarship student. It was a simple calculation. "I had to keep my grades up."

Carol was always perfectly dressed in pencil skirts and peplum tops, her long jet-black hair pinned up and back perfectly, Andrews Sisters–style. She looked as if she came from means, but she did not; her mother made her clothes.

"She was an excellent seamstress, making beautiful clothes, so that I never felt that I was dressed down. I was dressed up because my mother made these beautiful clothes. And books and ballet lessons and all the things that a little girl in Washington, at that time, should have, I had. And my folks did not have a lot of money. They just both worked very hard. During the height of the Depression, my father had three jobs. Sometimes we didn't see him because he'd go from one, come home, take a shower, and then go." Though her father had a law degree, he had to moonlight as a maître d' at a country club.

Carol had been born in Washington, but her upbringing was fairly southern. She spent a lot of summers with her grandparents in LaGrange, Georgia. Her grandfather Charles Henry Kelley was a Morehouse man who became a teacher and professor. He met his future wife, Frances Goss, when she was a student. Frances was originally from Alabama but moved to Georgia as a child. She only had three months of school a year but her teachers told her she had a good mind and someday she would make a "useful" woman. She always remembered that and wanted to make it come true. By her teenage years she had heard of Spelman Seminary for Women, but her father, a farmer, passed away. Her mother was left to care for the six children and money was tight. In 1890 Professor Kelley came to her community to teach in their school. The brown-skinned, bright-eyed girl showed so much promise that Professor Kelley told Frances's mother that he would buy her daughter's books and pay for Frances's first semester at Spelman. Once she got to school, Frances paid for the rest of her schooling on her own by working as a laundress. When she returned to LaGrange, she and Charles Henry married in 1895 and had seven children. They both worked in LaGrange for forty-two years: he was the principal of the colored Union Street School and Frances taught. Upon their retirement, the city of LaGrange renamed the school the Kelley School in honor of Professor Kelley's dedication. The superintendent of the LaGrange school system said, "He has been actively identified with all agencies seeking to improve his race. He is considered to be of the best citizens in LaGrange." To Carol he was her loving yet serious grandfather while Grandma Frances was the sweetest woman Carol ever met. Although Carol was a goody two-shoes, her little brother was a rascal, and sometimes they would get into trouble for climbing a forbidden pecan tree in the backyard. When a whuppin' was punishment, she was ordered to pick her own switch from the forsythia bush. One of her uncles was to take her out back for a whipping with the branch. He'd just tell her to yell really loudly while he whacked the ground.

All the Kelley children were sent off to secondary schools in the early 1900s because the system in LaGrange would only take them so far. The boys went to Morehouse, and the girls to Spelman. Carol's mother, Juanita, had gone to Atlanta when she was just fifteen, accompanied by her big sister Kate. The children all went their separate ways. Kate married well-known theologian Howard Thurman. Uncle Forrest, the faux disciplinarian, was a football star in college whom they called Shipwreck Kelley. He went on to teach phys ed in Marshall, Texas. Carol's Uncle Charles became a doctor and set up the radiology department at Howard.

Juanita met and married one of Charles's Morehouse classmates, a staid, no-nonsense man named Mayhugh Arnold Graham.

Mayhugh and Juanita Graham became the proud parents of Carol Jocelyn only twenty-six days after the great stock market crash of 1929. The following years were not easy. He worked in the insurance business and took a beating. Planning for the future, Mayhugh worked while he also attended law school, and he was in the first graduating class of the Terrell Law School in Washington, DC, named after the former M Street teacher and judge. The Grahams had another daughter, Gloria, who died when she was a baby. Juanita's sister Kate died of tuberculosis, and there was a concern that Juanita had been exposed. She was put on bed rest for a year while Carol's baby brother was sent to live with his grandparents in Georgia. Carol stayed home and grew up fast.

With a law degree, her father finally found steady work after the Depression. He became a clerk for two powerful politicians who valued his legal training. Carol would not confirm or deny that he worked for Jesse Jones, chairman of the reconstruction finance corporation who was sometimes referred to as the "fourth branch of the government." Because of Mayhugh's hard work, serious manner, and contacts in the government, he was offered a big job, one that would make a lasting impression on his daughter. He would join the National Capital Housing Authority to help run the first public housing units in Washington, DC, the Langston Terrace Dwellings, and his family would live there.

"When he went into housing, he believed that you should live on the premises, that if [residents] could see that the manager lived on the premises, then they could use that as kind of a role model. But my mother was always very cautious." She did agree, however, because of the premise of the project.

Carol's father was drawn to the optimism of the project, which sought to provide clean community housing for people who had been, up to that point, marginalized. Carol recalled:

> The thesis was that poor people, if given an opportunity to have decent housing, that would be the critical issue which would help them turn their lives around. It sounds so idealistic to me now, but they really believed it. And because there was such a shortage of housing with people, not just poor black people, people coming to

Washington for government jobs. Many of them came from good southern families, they just had no place to rent houses. His theory was, if you could put a family with limited exposure [into] good housing between two families who knew more, they could imitate and learn. So the housing people deliberately tried to intersperse— and on some level it worked.

The city had cleared out all of the alley housing in the 1930s; and as part of the New Deal, public units were put up in the city. They were lovely, modern buildings, finely designed by Hilyard Robinson, a well-known black architect who was an M Street grad. There were small yards and beautiful public art. With only 274 units in Langston Terrace, the application process and tenant selection were important.

I know when [the tenants] came to live in the project, I remember Daddy used to have meetings. They had what they called the Tenants Council to try to get them to understand what the principle of the whole thing was and how everybody was going to be uplifted, rising tide. But in many cases, when they tried to put too many, and they didn't have enough of the ones with the middle-class values to intersperse, it went down instead of going up. And that's what I called, Daddy used to call, "the failed dream." Because their original dream was that this was going to be a turning point, but all over the country, I don't think they've solved that problem yet.

Originally the idea was to have a mix of people, and the process was a delicate balancing act. The balance was there for a time, but it ultimately tipped. It got to the point where half of the residents had come from crowded, single-family homes and areas of "disease and delinquency."[2] The Langston Terrace Dwellings became a slum.

Carol learned important life lessons during her time in public housing. She was friends with all kinds of people and learned to get beyond stereotypes. "I never regretted it, because it gave me a different approach, I think, to people. While many of my friends were what people would have called 'the elites,' because I had had that experience with the public housing, and I knew what my father was trying to do in his idealism, I could see both sides of it. And I never felt that I was a snob because of that. I never felt that I was totally in the bubble. My parents brought me up so I could walk on both sides of the street."

After years of living and moving from public-housing unit to public housing unit, Carol's mom, Juanita, wanted a house. She'd taken a job as a stenographer with John R. Pinkett, the big Negro real estate company in town founded by a Dunbar and Amherst alum of the same name. As she was working, a listing came across her desk for a lovely Tudor with a lawn. She fell in love with the house and knew it would be the perfect place to put down roots and plant a garden. And they could afford it. The problem was they couldn't buy it. "In order to buy that house, my father and mother had to get a white couple to do it," Carol explained.

So that is exactly what the real estate agent did. They got a friend to look at the place on Evarts Street, and the rest happened quickly, according to Carol.

"I remember Cliff and his fiancée went to the house, took pictures inside, took the property, and the little old man said: 'Oh, I'm so glad to see this lovely young couple. Everybody in the neighborhood will be so happy to have you.' Well—John Pinkett Jr. worked it out. . . . They sold the house to Cliff, and within an hour [he] sold the house to my parents."

The Grahams' story of breaking a neighborhood color barrier turned out well. They saw their children and grandchildren enjoy that lawn. But things were not so easy for one of Carol's teachers at Dunbar.

The young student answered a customary question in language class. "*Je m'appelle* Carol Graham."

The teacher did not miss a beat. "Mademoiselle, you speak French with a southern accent!" That was what it was like to be seated in room 92 and on the receiving end of Mary Gibson Hundley's sharp tongue. She was strict—very strict.

Another notable characteristic of Madame Hundley was her keen interest in the students she deemed worthy to be placed in the best schools. Carol's best pal, Tish, was clearly on her way to being class valedictorian, and Mrs. Hundley wanted to see to it that Miss Young had her choice of schools, including Hundley's alma mater, Radcliffe, Harvard's sister school.

"Mrs. Hundley was really responsible for bringing me to the attention of the Radcliffe Club of Washington. They gave me a book and all that stuff my junior year and all of this helped me get into the place," said Tish. More than sixty years later, she still had the book, a blue, leather-bound volume of the classic *A Treasury of Great Poems*. The inscription read, "Presented by the Radcliffe Club of Washington, D.C. To Letitia Young as the outstanding girl of the Junior Class, Dunbar High School 1946."

In retrospect, after a career as a teacher herself in Berkeley, Tish had a fondness for Hundley. "She was kind of amusing because she would do things like, my former husband was in the French class she taught, and she'd call on us to translate. Invariably, he would get up and he sounded like Reagan, 'Well . . .' And she'd say with this heavy voice, 'Don't fall in it.' "

Mrs. Hundley considered Dunbar High School hers, and her claim to it was natural. In fact, she was the granddaughter of William Syphax, founder of Dunbar's grandfather school. She had grown up steeped in the history of the colored high school, and her personal résumé was the height of "Dunbarness."

After graduating from M Street in 1914 at the top of her class, Hundley was accepted to Radcliffe. But she was not accepted into the dormitories, which were for white girls only. The opportunity was too great to bypass, so her mother accompanied her to Cambridge to look after her; the two shared a small apartment. And it was a good thing, too. Mary worked hard and made friends, but no amount of academic luster can protect a student from a racist professor. One day, young Mary came home and revealed, "A dean demanded that I work as a domestic if I ever had any hope of securing a scholarship."[3] That dean, Miss Bertha May Boody, was trumped by the president of Radcliffe college, LeBaron Russell Briggs, who arranged a loan for Mary.

Many M Street/Dunbar graduates felt the sting of bigotry when they left the protective cocoon of the Negro Washington school system. When Ed Gray (M Street 1915), went to play football at Amherst, he tackled a white opponent only to have the player get up and angrily call him an "African ape." The player later apologized and said he lost control because he had been outwitted and outplayed by a Negro. Dunbar teacher and graduate J. Leon Langhorne went to University of Michigan in the 1920s. A white student approached him and asked, "Don't you wish you were white?"

Langhorne responded, "Hell no. Why should I?" Later in his life Langhorne wrote of the episode, "My family, my schooling, and religion had given me a sense of security and accomplishment. Self-esteem would guide me in confronting obstacles. I was the first Negro to receive a sweater for playing tennis at Michigan. It was a hard struggle but I finally succeeded."

Langhorne, like many of the Negro men and women who went to college, found comfort and companionship in the Negro fraternity system. The Greek organizations began with small groups of men and women devoted to scholarship and support. Several of the most powerful of these groups have ties to M Street. Both Nathaniel Allen Murray (M Street 1905) and Robert Harold Ogle (M Street 1905) helped found Alpha Phi Alpha at Cornell in 1906. Two of the three founders of Omega Phi Psi were M Street graduates, Frank Coleman (M Street 1908) and Oscar J. Cooper (M Street 1908). On the sorority side, the Alpha Kappa Alphas count M Street graduates Margaret Flagg Holmes (M Street 1904), Sarah Meriweather Nutter (M Street 1906), Julia Brooks (M Street 1904), and Nellie Quander (M Street 1898) as pioneers of the AKA dynasty. And Vashti Turley Murphy was one of the original members of Delta Sigma Theta. They are all men and women whose names are committed to memory today by their modern-day brothers and sisters. Years ago these fraternities and sororities provided a real haven for Negro students in college and beyond.

Dunbar's college bureau was the domain of Mary Hundley. By the 1940s she'd spent her adult life at Dunbar guiding students to certain schools and making sure the colleges couldn't say no. In one piece of correspondence to an admissions officer she makes the case for reconsidering a girl of prominence whose application had been rejected. The Sarah Lawrence admissions officer wrote back politely declining and adding, "As perhaps you know, Carol Graham, another graduate of the Dunbar High School, also applied to us and the Committee has passed her application. . . . I hope we will have her at the College."[4]

Hundley kept copious notes about which faculty had gone to what colleges and how many students received Rosenwald grants. She even tracked student IQs. It was her mission, at all costs, to maintain Dunbar's reputation for placing students in highly selective schools. And often those students were the ones she selected herself. She had her pets and pushed those students she liked and admired toward greatness. Others felt left out. She was a woman to be both admired and feared. You couldn't argue that she wasn't accomplished and brilliant. You could argue about whether or not she played favorites.

By the time she was in her early forties, she was making about $3,200 a year, and her second husband, an art teacher, was making a little bit less. She wanted to buy a new home and found a great place at 2530 Thirteenth Street NW. It was modest, about 1,800 square feet, white brick with a nice front porch. The houses on the street were adjacent, built right up against one another. Sitting on the front porch, it would be easy to chat with passersby or the people next door. That is, unless those neighbors went to court to have you evicted from your new home.

The Hundleys took possession of the house on January 17, 1941. Immediately, the couple began to fix up the house and would ultimately spend a huge amount of money, nearly $2,000 on it—two-thirds of Mrs. Hundley's annual salary.

Three months later, the people who lived next door, Rebecca Gorewitz of 2528 Thirteenth Street NW, and the folks one house over, Mr. and Mrs. Paul Bogikes of 2534 Thirteenth Street NW, filed a lawsuit asking that the Hundleys be removed from No. 2530. The white neighbors said the Hundleys' ownership was breaking a restrictive racial covenant set in place in 1910. According to the neighbors' case, colored neighbors were undesirable and destroyed the value of their homes. The Gorewitzes in particular were upset. On one side of their home was a Negro family living in one of the few houses not covered by the covenant, and now on the other side were the Hundleys. They would not be surrounded.

The original developers of the street, Harry B. Wilson and Harry Wardman, placed a covenant on five of the six houses on the 2500 block of Thirteenth Street NW which provided that the property never be rented, leased, sold, transferred, or conveyed to colored persons.[5]

One Great Depression later, the white owners of 2530 Thirteenth Street NW lost the house. A New Deal program created the Home Owner Loan Corporation to take on underwater mortgages, and it absorbed the property. The house was snapped up by a white real estate developer on January 13, 1941, and four days later the deed was conveyed to the Hundleys.

The covenants were contracts intertwined with the deeds of properties, and the covenants' terms applied to all future buyers. No amount of education, no amount of money, no amount of prestige within Washington's Negro community could protect the Hundleys from the embedded racism in the District. The Hundleys needed a good lawyer, so they turned to Charles Hamilton Houston, former valedictorian of M Street, class of 1911.

Houston's passion for civil rights began after he graduated from Amherst and went into the army. The legend goes that the racism he suffered in the segregated army, including a near beating, informed the rest of his career. Houston's purpose in life became legally dismantling the racist underpinnings of America's legal system. As dean of Howard Law School, he made sure the students who passed through the classrooms at Howard understood the role of the lawyer.

> A lawyer is either a social engineer or . . . a parasite on society. . . . A social engineer [is] a highly skilled, perceptive, sensitive lawyer who [understands] the Constitution of the United States and [knows] how to explore its uses in the solving of problems of local communities and in bettering conditions of the underprivileged citizens.

Eleven months after they bought their home, the Hundleys were told to leave. A judge agreed that the covenant was enforceable. The Hundleys' deed was declared void. They found a renter—a white renter—while they pursued the case, but the situation was frustrating and embarrassing. One day when Mr. Hundley went to check on the house, the neighbors called the police on him. The Hundleys weren't even allowed to get the keys from the renter when he was leaving. In a letter addressed "Dear Mollie and Fred," Houston wrote:

> On moving out June 30, 1942, Mr. Gillian has arranged with the US Marshal to accept the keys from you and hold the premises. You should call Deputy Marshal Kearny, US District Court House and arrange for a convenient time for him to come to the premises June 30 and for you and your tenants to leave the same. As the property passes into and under control of the law, you cannot enter the premises after the Marshal takes possession, whatever you need to remove you should do so beforehand, and the same applies to your tenants.

The letter also requested $257 for printing so Houston could begin revisions on an appeal.[6]

It took a year and a half, but the Hundleys did return to their home. They technically won their case, but in terms of advancing civil rights, this one could go in the loss column. The judge did not rule on the basis of any of their lawyer's arguments about the Constitution or his clients' rights. The judge ruled that the covenant was a moot point because of the changing neighborhood, so they might as well be able to move in. The judge ruled that the neighborhood had "so changed in its character and environment" and that

> the present appellees are not now enjoying the advantages which the covenant sought to confer. The obvious purpose was to keep the neighborhood white. But the strict enforcement of all five covenants will not alter the fact that the purpose has been essentially defeated by the presence of a Negro family now living in an unrestricted house in the midst of the restricted group, and as well by the ownership by another Negro of a house almost directly across the street. And this is just the beginning.

————————— ✺ —————————

Joe Stewart and Carol Graham were married in Washington on August 7, 1954. The reception was held in the backyard of 1509 Evarts Street, the home their parents had acquired in the middle of the night. They were well on their way, both eager to leave Washington.

Carol went off to Sarah Lawrence on a scholarship, as Hazel Markel had predicted she would. Carol wanted to be a teacher, so she earned her master's at Columbia. One of her first teaching assignments was at New Rochelle High School in New York, where she was the first black academic teacher. "I remember one parent saying, 'Oh she must be from the Caribbean because she's probably been trained in British schools.' British schools? Oh brother. Do I have a British accent? No. I just spoke English." She made the local paper when a group described as "Southern students from Washington and Baltimore" made a field trip up north to see what an integrated school looked like. A photo appeared in a local paper of Carol talking to the teenagers. Three are smiling, one is frowning, and one has her arms crossed. The caption read,

Southerners see integrated schools. They were invited by the student body of New Rochelle High School to observe the various activities in which both Negro and White pupils articipate. Biology teacher Mrs. Carol Graham Stewart, the first Negro teacher at New Rochelle High School, greeting [*sic*] the student to her classroom. The students were surprised to learn from Mrs. Stewart that she was originally from Washington, DC, and attended Dunbar High School. Two of the boys expressed their special interest in the integrated activities of the football team. One of the girls said that she didn't come to New York to be photographed but to find out how the northern school handled the problems of their prom and other social events.

At this point in the story, her husband—my father—jumped in, clearly proud of his wife. "The best thing Mom did was that there are literally hundreds of bright kinds of people who spread out throughout the society who learned something of great importance to them from a person of color. And a whole lot of white folks have not had that experience."

"Many of them, the only people of color they knew were the maids in the kitchen," Carol finished the thought.

And then she suddenly recalled one confrontation with a young man who had not done his homework. She walked over to him and let him have it. "You are smart. And you are just being lazy. And you just want to go ride your motorcycle, and you should do your work. Now you sit down there and do that work, because I know you can do it and you know you can do it."

The boy stood up. "You don't talk to me like that!"

Carol was thrown for a moment, but just a moment. "What do you mean I don't talk to you 'like that'? *Sit* down!"

"My father says you never allow a woman to speak to you that way. No matter who it is."

"Well, you father isn't here, son. Now sit down and do your work." At seventy-nine she laughed remembering it all. "I'm sure they felt they had to test me."

Joe's tests came in a different form. He attended Kings Point Merchant Marine Academy. "In the plebe year, you got kids coming in from all over the country. And some of them came from places like Mississippi, and they had a bad attitude. And they had to undergo attitude correction, some of which I helped administer."

Joe spent his whole sophomore year at sea, sailing all around the world, which was transformative for all involved. "You come back juniors, changed. More mature, especially those with the bad attitudes. You'd seen the world." His worldview changed seeing the coast of Italy and North Africa. He learned discipline, naval etiquette, and "how to behave." His teenage edginess matured into a strong sense of right and wrong. He would send Carol long letters about their plans for the future along with gifts—small cameo earrings from Italy or a coral necklace from Spain.

While sailing abroad was liberating, Joe Stewart still faced racism in the States. By his last year he was an honors student and third officer on a military sea transport. Still, he found himself being detained at a New Orleans port trying to reboard his ship. The local official wanted to know where the "boy," the six-foot, two-inch twenty-four-year-old, had gotten the uniform. The captain came down with some stern words for the man who had detained one of his deck officers.

When Stewart returned home, he was accepted to the Harvard Business School, though he almost did not attend because he didn't have enough money. Carol searched and searched for scholarships for him. She'd done it a year earlier for herself. With his grades and experience, Joe was able to obtain a Whitney Fellowship and a Harvard scholarship. He graduated in 1952 and was one of three Negro students out of six hundred. Close to graduation, he was called to the dean's office. At HBS there was a tradition among graduates to only apply for four or five jobs because it was assumed that many offers would go out, and it was the gentlemanly thing to do.

The dean sat Joe down and was direct. "Look, we know you are going to have a bit of trouble finding a job. And while everybody is restricted to five applications, Joe, you can talk to as many people as you need to talk to."

Joe Stewart, future Harvard MBA, spoke to sixty companies. No from Raytheon. No from Union Carbide. Form letter after form letter appeared after his interviews, thanking him for his interest and regretting to inform him there were no openings at that time. Joe received two job offers. One was to run a family department store in Saint Croix, and the other was with a steamship company that he said "wouldn't pay me enough to starve on." Knowing of his troubles, his finance professor Charlie Williams asked Joe to come to his office.

Professor Williams said, "Look I think you'd probably be good at securities analysis, and I have a very, very good friend—old friend, good guy—down in Metropolitan Life Insurance Company. I want you to go. You are from New York, right?"

"Yes, sir," said Joe. He was excited. This could be the one break he needed.

"Good. I want you to go down to the Met. I've called him, and all you have to do is call and set a date." Encouraged at the possibility of returning home with a job and a lovely new wife, he called.

The interview went well, or so he thought.

"Now Mr. Stewart, I want you to go to one other gentlemen." Joe and his potential boss went down about four flights of stairs and shook hands. The man pointed him toward an office before leaving.

In the little office was a small, older Negro man in a gray Salvation Army uniform. Joe thought, "OK. Fine." Joe realized his professor had never mentioned to his contact that the student he was sending was a Negro.

"I understand you are here, son, for a job, but we are very sorry to tell you that we just don't have an opening for you in this company."

Joe asked him one question. "Look, is it your job to tell every Negro that comes in here that there aren't any jobs in MetLife at this professional level for Negroes?"

The man looked at him for a long time without saying anything.

"Never mind." Joe got up to leave.

Hearing the story again, his wife of over fifty years, Carol, smiled and said, "Best thing that never happened to you."

Carol went on to teach for thirty years, becoming the kind of teacher you admire—and fear just a bit. She was described by her superintendent as the definition of a master teacher. Occassionally she would get a letter from a university informing her that a student named her as as someone who had shaped her life. She believed in her students. Once she channeled Hazel Markel when she gently (and not so gently) suggested one of her students, a smart, quirky guy, go to Sarah Lawrence.

"Carol Stewart's influence on my life is immeasurable," said David Kessler (Sarah Lawrence 1975), who has been a biologist at the National

Zoo for thirty-four years and counting. "A week doesn't go by when I don't think of her and the lessons I learned from her. Aside from my parents, Carol Stewart was the most influential person in my life."

And Joseph Stewart? He spent his life climbing the corporate ladder and broke glass ceilings in a way that seemed effortless. And he never forgot to reach back. He was on the board of directors of large companies and civil rights groups. He would often speak to young students at inner-city schools. For example, he met one young man and made it his mission to help the bright teenager get into college. Stewart assisted him in filling out all his college applications, because both of the young man's parents were holding down two jobs. Joe Stewart helped pay for other people's children to go to college and would always find a way to help if he could. He was a naturally generous person on all levels. I received an e-mail shortly after my father died: "For what it's worth, Joseph Stewart was one of the most influential people in my life. He hired me in 1989. It was my second job out of school. At the time, he was a board member, and I was amazed when he came down to reception to collect me instead of sending an assistant for my first interview with him. He was a gem." The young woman who sent this note was fortunate to meet a man who never forgot what it feels like when someone believes in you.

He, like many black men of his generation, occasionally bumped into institutional racism and faced the silly displays of other people's prejudice that make a person either bitter or more determined. He was once mistaken for Senator Bob Dole's driver when he had personally invited the senator to lunch that day. Once a young junior executive came rushing into a hotel conference room looking for the very senior executive who was going to run a meeting, looked around, and then yelled to Joe, "Hey you, have you seen Mr. Stewart?" He replied, "Every day when I shave." Joseph Turner Stewart Jr., the young man who had been sent to the MetLife janitor only to be dismissed went on to become a senior vice president and member of the board of directors of a Fortune 500 company. The CEO of a competitor, number 231 on the Fortune 500, once wrote to Joe Stewart, "Let me say that in the world of class and accomplishment, whether it be relating to analysts, politicians, scientists, business people, corporate gameplayers, you name it—you have no peer."

9 | RIGHT TO SERVE

"I DIDN'T HAVE A roommate. I didn't want a roommate. And they didn't want to make somebody room with me, although a couple of guys offered." Even as a teenager Wesley Brown was wise enough to know that no good would come of the only Negro cadet at Annapolis living in close quarters with any other newly arrived white plebes.

"At the time, I said if I had a roommate, my roommates would be catching the same hell, or more, just for the fact that they live with me. And then I'd feel guilty, and it would be like the king's whipping boy," Brown said. "When the king was bad, he went over and beat the hell out of the whipping boy. And that was an incentive for the king to be good because he didn't want his friend, the whipping boy, to be whipped. So I said, I don't need that; I'm going to be busy enough as is."

In 1945, a year after he graduated from Dunbar High School, Wesley Brown was nominated for, appointed to, and enrolled in the US Naval Academy, a full three years before President Truman issued the order to desegregate the armed services. The navy, as a 1944 issue of *Time* magazine put it, "is not celebrated for liberalism in handling its race problem."[1] Originally, colored men could enlist but would be assigned to some sort of low-level duty. From 1919 to 1932, during a time of relative peace, Negro men couldn't enlist in the navy at all.

By the 1940s, despite being at war again, the navy continued to be particularly inhospitable to Negroes, from the top down. In the early 1940s, Secretary of the Navy Frank Knox continued to uphold the policy that firmly stated segregation was the best thing for all parties involved. The concept of Negroes and whites serving on the same ship and in close quarters was unthinkable to most sailors.

Knox saw nothing wrong with the fact that all Negroes in the navy thus far had been relegated to the role of stewards, cooks, or cleaners. He said it afforded them their best opportunity to serve, even though the positions were subservient, and grown men were often addressed as "boy" by other naval members.[2] That practice didn't become officially against the rules until the late 1940s.

FDR made a halfhearted move toward equality by allowing Negroes to enlist in 1942. They did, despite knowing that they would be assigned menial labor. In a few rare cases, a Negro enlisted man was given an assignment. Most notably, thirteen men, who became known as the Golden Thirteen, were chosen to train as officers but had to do so at a segregated facility. Secretary Knox barely went along with the plan, despite prodding from Adlai Stevenson, who was then special assistant to the navy. Stevenson suggested to his bosses, Knox and Roosevelt, that a navy with sixty thousand Negroes in the service but not one officer might be a problem.[3] Who knows what would have happened if Knox hadn't died in 1944? He was replaced with his philosophical opposite, James Forrestal, a true believer in pursuing equality in the services. The next year Wesley Brown arrived at Annapolis.

Five others like him had tried to penetrate the Naval Academy, and not one reached graduation, for various reasons including bad eyesight, flunking exams, and mental exhaustion from harassment.[4] The first colored cadets had been swept in and swept out during the short-lived hopefulness of Reconstruction. Sixty years passed before another Negro person attempted to enroll.

In the 1930s and '40s, as part of the emerging civil rights movement, Negro congressmen were intent on nominating a young Negro man for the academy. Congressman Arthur Mitchell of Chicago, the first Negro Democrat in Congress, vowed to search for appropriate candidates and to keep nominating them until one made it, even if the candidate did not live in his district.

Representative Mitchell was in close contact with the head of Dunbar's military training instructors. Because of the Naval Academy's intense academic entrance program, Dunbar High School was the natural choice to

be the go-to incubator for Annapolis. In the 1930s three Dunbar graduates had attempted to complete "fours years by the bay." James Lee Johnson (Dunbar 1933), flunked out, despite an excellent high school record.
"They mistreated him. Tearing up paper and pushing it through the
transom so when his room was inspected it was unkempt."

Dr. Adelaide Cromwell (Dunbar 1936) remembers it. "They dropped
him out of the academy because they said he couldn't read or speak English. James Johnson! He went to Dunbar High School, so you know full
well he knew how to speak and write!" James Minor (Dunbar 1933), the
son of a school principal, was said not to have passed the entrance exam.
However, George Trivers (Dunbar 1933), looked promising.

Trivers was mature, having already graduated from college. He
passed the entrance exam, and the day he walked into the academy and
registered, it made the Negro papers.[5] That was the last bit of good news
to come out of the experience. Trivers was spat upon. He was called a
nigger. Young men who had joined the academy and were expected to
develop "morally, mentally, and physically and to imbue with them the
highest ideas of duty, honor, and loyalty" pounded Trivers's walls at night
to keep him awake.[6] He left Annapolis when the physical abuse became
too much and because he realized the instructors let it all happen.[7]
When an inquiry was made about the treatment of Trivers, Congressman Mitchell was told by the navy, "There was no unpleasantness in the
resignation of George J. Trivers."[8] For the next nine years, not one Negro
applicant made it to the Naval Academy.

As a teenager, Wesley Brown thought he *might* attend West Point.
After Dunbar he enrolled in the Army Specialized Training Unit at Howard. The odds of succeeding at West Point seemed a little better than
Annapolis. While no Negroes had made it through the Naval Academy,
twelve black men had graduated from the United States Military Academy.[9] But Brown was on the radar of Congressman Adam Clayton Powell
Jr. of New York. Powell had nominated ten young Negro men to be considered for Annapolis, and Wesley Brown was one of them. He was the
only one who got into the program.[10]

Being a good student, Brown did his homework before getting to the
campus in Maryland. He spoke to Trivers and Johnson about the isolation and the lack of support they endured. He read the biography of the
first black West Point cadet for inspiration.[11] He tried to prepare mentally

and control what he could. He empowered himself by choosing to live alone at the academy, turning down one or two offers for a roommate.

Brown was not that concerned about the academics. He felt confident in his high school training, especially after witnessing some of his classmates.

"When I went to the academy, I noticed there were a lot of guys who had straight As in high school and so forth who weren't doing too well. And I concluded that a lot of them were not challenged because their schools were not competitive."

He observed that a lot of the cadets had poor time management skills and were unpleasantly surprised by the effect of curfew on their grades. The heavy workload and high expectations at Dunbar had taught him discipline when it came to schoolwork. "What Dunbar did for me, it taught me how to study. . . . I didn't have time. I learned to get to the meat of the assignment."

As a high school student, Brown had worked from after school until midnight as a mail clerk to help support the family. His mother was a laundress, his father a truck driver. "My family didn't have any money or any political drag," he later explained. "I had a very limited time to study. . . . I was working nights and drilling and participating in sports." In addition to working in a mailroom and running track, he was the cadet colonel of the Dunbar High School Cadet Corps.

Hundreds of Negro high school boys (as well as girls intermittently, and then full time beginning in the 1940s) learned discipline, integrity,

Lt. Cmdr. Wesley Brown during his first class (senior) year.

United States Naval Academy

and perseverance in the competitive Cadet Corps. More than an after-school military training activity or a club, the Corps was a life experience, one that fed the Dunbar ecosystem of excellence. The goal of the Corps can best be summed up by the US Infantry Drill regulations and the training manual from which lessons were modeled: "The object of all military training is to win battles. Everything that you do in military training is done with some immediate object in view, which, in turn, has in view the final object of winning battles."[12] The immediate objective at Dunbar was getting a good education. The final object was advancing the race. And what was success? Disciples of the drill knew the answer: "Success may be looked for only when the training is intelligent and thorough."[13]

At one point, military instruction was a mandatory subject for the Dunbar fellas. The Corps was made up of companies that consisted of platoons broken down into squads. The ranks of colonel, captain, and the like were based on academic standing and military aptitude.

The cadets were a part of everyday life at Dunbar. They could be seen marching in formation in the armory, the open center of the first floor of the Dunbar building. The space was about two hundred feet wide and quite deep. It was *the* gathering place for students. But, as the name suggests, it was where the cadets practiced formations and kept their Browning assault rifles. There was a firing range in the school. The cadets were expected to look sharp. The uniform was a cadet cap, cadet coat clean and pressed with the collar ornament of the company to which the cadet belonged, trousers clean and pressed, white shirt , policed black shoes, clean white gloves. A cadet's uniform was to be worn to at all drills and inspected. If not in the armory, the cadets practiced formations and the manual of arms behind the school. The precision of the rifle drills required focus and instant recall. Upon hearing the booming command "Port arms!" it was second nature for a cadet to snap his rifle to a diagonal position in one swift movement, using the right hand to carry the firearm across the front of the body, with the butt of the rifle in front of the right hip, the barrel of the weapon perfect aligned between the neck and left shoulder and the gun held four inches from the body. And this was one of the many sequences to remember. "Right shoulder arms! Left shoulder arms! Present arms!" They practiced over and over and over. Each combination had to be committed to memory and was put to the test at the annual drill competition.

The drill competition was the event of the year. Companies from the Negro high schools appeared before thousands of people. After 1914, the crowd could swell to twenty-five thousand people packing Griffith Stadium to see Dunbar, Armstrong, and ultimately two other Negro high schools which came later—Cardozo and Phelps Tech—compete. Girls wore armbands to signify which company their sweethearts were in. One year President Coolidge and the First Lady made a surprise appearance to watch the young men. One of the drills in the competition was the response to a simulated attack. The faux fight was recalled by a reporter much in the same way that color commentary is provided for today's sporting events.

One of the most pleasing spectacles of the drill was the extended order which came at the end of the competitive drill program. Each company advanced on the enemy composed of a detachment from the National Guard ambush. Starting from one end of the field the

24TH REGIMENT, 1ST BATTALION

Dunbar High School yearbook, 1946

companies moved toward the enemy in squads and platoons and as one volley was fired after each advance. The enemy was so weak and the attack so strong that the former was compelled to seek cover.[14]

The instructors were both mentors and tormentors. They insisted upon full attention to detail and expected a full effort. But the graduates say the instructors taught them more than formations and precision. They taught them how to become men.[15] One name comes up over and over again: Lieutenant Bill Rumsey, a military science instructor. Rumsey was encouraging and motivating. He was a teacher who was not concerned with a student's social class, only that the student develop class and character while under his command. He wanted the cadets to think about the bigger picture, about life and life as a Negro in mainstream America. But he could also be about the moment. He once took the cadets to a competition in a cattle car because it had no seats; he wanted the cadets to arrive at the drill with the stiff creases in their trousers intact.[16]

The colored high school corps started a few years after the white high schools began their military instruction in the early 1880s. After a couple of ragtag years, the colored cadets made their first public appearance at Metropolitan Baptist church in 1892. There was only one company. The instructor, Major Arthur Brooks, who stayed on for twenty years, began as an unpaid volunteer. And the young cadets wore uniforms that were borrowed, too big, and required padding because the pencil-thin boys could not fill them out. For a time they only had wooden "rifles." Any real arms they used were borrowed or decrepit. Although seventy boys made up the first organized company, the number was whittled to fifty-nine because that was the number of uniforms available after a fund-raising push. The first commander and founder of the cadets was a colored war hero named Christian Fleetwood, and his background made him the right man for the job.

Fleetwood stood five feet four inches tall, and three feet of it seemed to be comprised of his barrel chest. His obvious strength served him well when he was in the Union Army, especially on the September morning when he was part of a legendary two-pronged attack on the capital of the

Confederacy, the Battle of Chaffin's Farm. The whole operation was the brainchild of an officer whose effectiveness was questionable but whose dedication to integrating the armed services could not be equaled.

Major Benjamin Butler, a basset hound of a man, had repeatedly called for the inclusion of colored troops. "I deny the ignorance of the colored men of the South" was his operating principle and his answer to those who questioned colored men's ability to fight.[17] Major Butler handpicked the regiments of the United States Colored Troops, which included Christian Fleetwood's Fourth Regiment, for the Virginia attack. On Wednesday morning, September 28, 1864, twenty-three-year-old Fleetwood boarded a gunboat, arrived at Deep Bottom, marched on land, and bivouacked overnight near Richmond. The next morning, before dawn, six regiments of colored troops formed a line and attacked the Confederate camps. Fleetwood described the day succinctly in a diary entry: "Moved out and charged with the 6th [regiment] at daylight and got used up . . . saved colors . . . marching in line and flank all day . . . saw General Grant and staff. . . . retired at night."

The simple sentences do not describe the carnage or valor of that day. "Used up" refers to the hundreds of casualties—the battle, which spanned four days, would result in about five thousand soldiers being killed. "Saved the colors" refers to Fleetwood rescuing the American flag mid-battle after two others who had tried to do so were shot and killed. Fleetwood won the Medal of Honor that day for his heroism, one of the handful awarded to colored soldiers during the Civil War, many of them earned during this assault. A vindicated Benjamin Butler later wrote, "The capacity of the Negro race for soldiers had then and there been fully settled forever."[18]

Christian Fleetwood, the first commander of the colored cadets, had convinced Butler of colored soldiers' worthiness. The same was not true for Wesley Brown at the Naval Academy eighty-five years later. Despite all Brown's training in the Cadets and at the hands of the fine Dunbar faculty, there were some things he simply could not control or even foresee at Annapolis. Brown received an extraordinary number of demerits—so many that it was obvious he was being hazed. As a result, his grade point average and class rank slowly sank. In some of his course work, Midshipman Brown received low marks. He discovered in some cases there was not an objective form of grading.

They called aptitude for the service and leadership. So this is the most subjective thing you could do because it was not a subject review. You can't say, "Hey, this is unfair. . . ." Even if that person is saying, "Well, based upon my experience as a Naval Officer, I don't think this guy has it." So as a result I was barely passing.

Demerits and poor performance reviews did not destroy his record at the time, though. "But I'm still in the top half of my class," he remarked.

While Midshipman Brown knew that the other cadets talked about him, used racial epithets to refer to him, and wouldn't sit near him, he was unaware of a persistent lie being told about him.

A fellow cadet approached him in private and revealed, "There's a rumor that you are being paid by the NAACP. That you are getting money for every day you stay, and a bonus every year and a bonus if you graduate."

This was news to Brown, but he found out it was considered the truth by many classmates, one of them ominously saying within earshot, "Well, I am going to make sure he earns his money." However, after having a class with Brown in which he held his own, the fellow recanted. "You're a nice guy and a pretty capable student," he said to Brown. "But I decided the rumor is not true, because if the NAACP was going to pay someone, they would have gotten a much brighter, sharper student."

At the time of our interview, the then seventy-nine-year-old Brown was quick to say that some cadets were cordial or decent to him or at least had the decency to ignore him. In his home office—full of files, clippings, and history books—he didn't want to dwell on the negative parts of his experience and those who treated him poorly. He looks back at that time with the curiosity of a cognitive scientist investigating why some cadets were bigoted.

"Some were, some were. Now the question is why?" Brown posed the question to himself rather than rhetorically. "I don't know. I'd have to look in somebody's mind and say, 'Is this guy just a natural-born racist? Is he doing this because his parents taught him that way?' But logic says, this doesn't make any sense at all. Or is he afraid that the upperclassmen will punish him because he's friendly to me? The one person that helped me a lot was a guy named Jimmy Carter."

That Jimmy Carter?

"That Jimmy Carter." He smiled as he answered.

The former president recalled the time this way: "I had been at Annapolis for one year. I was in my second year when he came, and I was interested in getting to know what kind of person he was, and I was able to do this because both of us went out for the cross-country team. So, we were running together in training for the cross-country meets, and that's when I first met Wesley Brown." Sixty-seven years later, former president of the United States Jimmy Carter can easily recall those days. "I knew that some of the other midshipmen didn't like the idea, and they were concentrating on doing what they could to force Wesley out of the Naval Academy, which was a gross violation of proper conduct."

Carter was not trying to be a hero. He had spent his youth in the South playing with children of all hues. He didn't see Brown as a threat or a problem. He saw him as a fellow student. "I just treated Wesley Brown like I would any other midshipman." At the time it seemed like the natural thing for Midshipman Carter to do: lead by example, especially for his fellow southerners. But of course, President Carter knows Wesley Brown wasn't just any cadet.

"He was brave. And I think he was an outstanding person. I think had he been timid or had he lacked courage or had he been arrogant or so forth and he would not have been successful. This was before Jackie Robinson played baseball, and so forth. So this was a very early time. And he was brave, and he was very intelligent. He was well behaved; he responded to hazing and quiet persecution with equilibrium. . . . This was before the country moved toward equality in the armed services. It was not until two or three years later."

Carter remembers where he was when he heard about Executive Order 9981.

I was actually on a submarine after finishing at the Naval Academy. I was gratified when Harry Truman, our commander in chief and president, ordained that there should be no more racial discrimination anywhere in the military services. In the army, navy, coast guard, air force, and so forth. And the US Marine Corps. But this was the first glimmer anywhere in America of real equality between African Americans and whites as students. And it was an innovative time, and this was probably ten years before Rosa Parks sat in the front of a bus, before Martin Luther King Jr. ever got famous. So this was far in advance of trials where they measured education institutions for segregation and equality.

At the time Negroes, coloreds, blacks who answered the call to serve their country were treated as though they were there to serve the white soldiers whose decision to enlist was somehow more meaningful or important. Still, many Negroes wanted to and did fight for America, even if America didn't support their equal rights. The sanctioned bigotry of the army, navy, air force, and marine corps is well documented and was experienced by many Dunbar/M Street graduates who chose to volunteer.

Ollie Davis graduated from M Street and lied about his age to volunteer to fight in the Spanish-American War of 1898. After forty-two years of military service, Benjamin Oliver Davis Sr. attained the rank of general in the army, the first black to do so. The path to the four stars was frustrating for Davis Sr. and at times seemed futile. As a teenager he wanted to attend West Point and despite a strong family connection was told President McKinley would not nominate a Negro cadet for political reasons.[19] Instead, Davis enlisted and then excelled. After his stint in the colored national guard, at the turn of the century he managed to obtain a commission to the regular army as a second lieutenant, becoming one of two colored line officers.

Davis's rise was a problem for the army. He could not be superior to or command white troops, and his assignments reflected this reality. He was sent to teach military training at all-black colleges. He was stationed in Utah and Wyoming, became the attaché to Liberia, and was shipped to the Philippines for a while. No matter the assignment, he mastered it and was promoted for it—to a point. As a result, his two biggest contributions to the army were not made during firefights. One was the result of an assignment, after being made general, to advise President Roosevelt on race relations in the army at the start of World War II. General Davis traveled the United States and Europe to devise a strategy to handle the unsustainable state of things. His work figured greatly into the passage of Executive Order 9981. His other greatest achievement was his son, Benjamin O. Davis Jr. This son was able to accomplish many of his father's dreams because of what his father instilled in him and what his father had fought to achieve for him and those who came after.

Benjamin Davis Jr. was the fourth black graduate of West Point, an achievement his father was not even allowed the chance to try. A talented man with great leadership skills, Davis Jr. was given an assignment that on the surface seemed to reinforce all the negatives of segregation in the military. Yes, you can train Negroes to fly planes, but you have to do it separately, with bad equipment.

The year was 1941, and as Davis Jr. wrote in his autobiography, "In 1941 the Army still regarded all blacks as totally inferior to whites—somewhat less than human and certainly incapable of contributing positively to its combat mission."[20] His assignment to lead a flight squadron trained at Tuskegee seemed like a political escape hatch for an army under pressure to cure its own racism. The group became known as the legendary Tuskegee Airmen, made of the best and brightest Negro pilots, many of them Dunbar graduates.

Roscoe Brown (Dunbar 1939), was a Tuskegee Airman for two years. He joined up right after graduating from college. "During that period of time I flew sixty-eight combat missions and shot down a jet plane over Berlin and blew up a train." Brown was the first Negro pilot to shoot down an enemy plane in World War II. That was before the airmen got their most important mission: to escort white bombers behind enemy lines. Their record was flawless; they never lost a plane. When asked if he was treated better in Europe than in his hometown, Brown laughed and said, "That's like asking if the sun shines."

"Davis was a great leader." Brown remembers. "He was very demanding. Fair. He was very disciplined. Our job was to escort the bombers, and he indicated if we didn't stay with the bombers and try to shoot down planes on our own, he would court martial us. Being six three and ramrod straight when he said that, we knew he meant it."

The Davis family handled military racism by being great. Others, like Dr. Charles Drew, publicly pointed out the ridiculous nature of racism in the armed forces. Dr. Drew took aim at one of the military's most illogical policies: segregating Negro blood from white blood.

When Charlie Drew was a senior at Dunbar High School, he was known as a super jock, not necessarily someone who would become a super scientist. He played football and basketball, swam, and ran track. It was a good thing, too, because as the eldest of five and the son of a carpet layer, Charlie needed an athletic scholarship to go to college. His studies led him to a discovery that has saved millions of lives around the world.

Hematology—the study of blood—may not seem that dynamic or controversial, but it was both for Drew. The premise of his dissertation, "Banked Blood," proved to be true: plasma could be separated from cells and thereby stored long-term. He figured out how to make a blood bank at a time when war casualties were high and soldiers were often bleeding to death. Dr. Drew, who was also a surgeon, became the authority on blood preservation and was dispatched to the UK during WWII to help set up the Blood for Britain campaign. He also came up with the idea of refrigerated mobile blood banks, still in use today.

After his success in England, Dr. Drew returned home and was tapped to be the director of the American Red Cross Blood Bank, the first of its kind. His first assignment was huge: organize a massive blood donation campaign for the military at the height of WWII. At the time, the military had a strict policy: white blood for white soldiers. Black blood was to be separated out. There is type A blood, B blood, AB blood, and O blood—but not black or white blood. Yet the military directive stated, "It is not advisable to indiscriminately mix Caucasian and Negro blood for use in blood transfusions for US military."

Dr. Drew resigned his position in protest and returned to Washington, DC, to be the chair of the department of surgery as well as chief of surgery at Freedmen's Hospital, and to teach at Howard University. He spoke about the situation often, and once when accepting an award told the audience, "It is fundamentally wrong for any great nation to willfully discriminate against such a large group of its people. . . . One can say quite truthfully that on the battlefields nobody is very interested in where the plasma comes from when they are hurt. . . . It is unfortunate that such a worthwhile and scientific bit of work should have been hampered by such stupidity."[21]

The year after the military stopped segregating blood, Dr. Drew died as a result of a car accident. He was forty-five. A myth about his death developed and persists to this day because it rings of a truth of the time. The apocryphal story is that an injured Dr. Drew was turned away from a

North Carolina hospital because of his race and then bled to death. This didn't happen, but it is certainly believable that such a thing could have happened in 1950. Indeed, it had happened to Walter White's father.

------------- ✺ -------------

According to the Dunbar Alumni records, 200 M Street/Dunbar graduates served in World War I and 963 served in World War II. The school produced a brigadier general, nine colonels, a lieutenant colonel, twelve majors, and many captains and lieutenants. Of all the Dunbar-related military stories, the one that may have had the most lasting effect—not on the military, but on United States history—is that of Charles Hamilton Houston, second lieutenant in charge of field artillery. Houston graduated from M Street when he was fifteen and then was Phi Beta Kappa at Amherst. He taught for a bit before enlisting in the army at the age of twenty-four.

While stationed in Paris during World War I, the story goes, Houston happened one evening upon a group of white soldiers who were screaming at a Negro soldier about a girl. Within minutes, two trucks full of white soldiers arrived and surrounded Houston and the other soldier. He feared for his life as the white soldiers told the "uppity niggers" not to think too much of themselves because they were wearing uniforms.

This was one of many frustrating experiences for Houston, and his time in the army became the catalyst for his life's mission—to end segregation. Houston said of the time, "The hate and scorn showered on us Negro officers by our fellow Americans convinced me there was no sense in my dying for a world ruled by them. . . . I made up my mind . . . that if I got through this war, I would study law and use my time fighting for men who could not strike back."[22]

By the 1940s, pressure from legal minds like Houston, the Negro press, and the threat of marches by the NAACP made Presidents Roosevelt and Truman as well as the army brass uncomfortable. What made the situation morally impossible to ignore was the harm and harassment of Negro veterans. Truman, who had dropped the *N* word on occasion, was shaken by two acts of senseless violence. Isaac Woodward, a World War II veteran, was pulled off a bus in South Carolina and beaten to blindness by the town sheriff. George Dorsey had been home from the

Pacific for just ten months when he was shot to death by a white mob, sixty shots fired in all. Truman ordered a federal inquiry into his murder, but no one was ever charged.

By the end of the decade, President Truman signed the executive order that stated: "It is hereby declared to be the policy of the President that there shall be equality of treatment and opportunity for all persons in the armed services without regard to race, color, religion, or national origin. This policy shall be put into effect as rapidly as possible, having due regard to the time required to effectuate any necessary changes without impairing efficiency or morale." The order was issued July 26, 1948, one year before Wesley Brown graduated 370 out of a class of 800, demerits and all.

Lieutenant Commander Wesley Brown went on to a successful naval career. He was recognized in 2006 when the Naval Academy broke ground on the $52 million, 140,000-square-foot Wesley A. Brown Field House, a state-of-the-art athletic center at Annapolis.

Along the way, Brown married a groundbreaker in her own right. When he went off to the academy, his fellow Dunbar alum and not-yet sweetheart Crystal Malone headed north to the University of Vermont seeking fun and friends. And it wasn't hard for the gorgeous girl. "I'm a gadabout, so it was easy. I could make friends easily, and Dunbar prepared me to do anything in the world!" she remembers, showing me a *Life* magazine with a photograph of her with some friends. Crystal had accepted an invitation to join the Alpha Xi Delta sorority. "In the charter it said a girl of certain quality, certain academic achievement, certain recommendations, and I had all of those."

What she didn't have was white skin. When the sorority's national administrators realized a Negro had been pursued and accepted at the UVM chapter, the organization rebuked the local chapter. The national president in charge of sixty chapters and nineteen thousand students headed to Burlington to sort out the situation.[23]

Crystal was approached by the sorority's national representative, a Mrs. Beverly Robinson, who tried to explain to Crystal why she should gracefully bow out. Mrs. Robinson told the eighteen-year-old, "Life is selective, and maybe it's just as well to learn it while we are young." When the young women in the chapter refused to rescind the invitation, the chapter's charter was suspended.

Malone said later that she had talked to them about quitting. "I know for a lot of people that was the most important thing in their life, was the girls. And I would not want to take that from them. They said, no, no this is our choice; the national sorority was wrong."

When the story made the national press, Mrs. Robinson told a reporter, "I am sorry this happened both for [Crystal's] sake and for ours. But I expect the girls up there thought she was an exotic and interesting person—the way you would think of someone from a foreign country."[24] But Crystal was not a creature from a far-off land, she was a girl from the nation's capital.

Although the chapter was suspended, the school and the girls remained steadfast in their beliefs that they had done the right thing. Years later she recalled feeling that a new day was coming. "This was at the end of the war where we thought we were making the world a better place to live, everybody was . . . we were essentially dreamers. And it was supposed to be."

Looking back on their life together through newspaper clips and personal memories with her dear husband, Crystal Malone Brown had clearly retained some of the twinkle and moxie that had aided her throughout her life and helped her husband be a success. She cheekily suggested that her husband's life story should be called *Brown v. the US Naval Academy*.

10 | *BOLLING, NOT BROWN*

TECHNICALLY, *BROWN V. BOARD of Education* did not bring an end to legally segregated schools in Washington, DC. *Bolling v. Sharpe*, one of the five cases bundled under the *Brown* umbrella presented to the US Supreme Court, was the suit that made the difference. On May 17, 1954, at 1:20 PM, the Court delivered two striking opinions in favor of two different anti-school segregation arguments.

Four of the five individual cases involved South Carolina, Delaware, Kansas, and Virginia. The last was argued by Dunbar graduate Oliver Hill, who graduated number two from Howard Law School behind his buddy Thurgood Marshall. The Warren Court unanimously agreed that separating schoolchildren based on race was unconstitutional based on the Fourteenth Amendment's guarantee of equal protection under the law. The Fourteenth Amendment was the Reconstruction edict ratified ninety years earlier that had been so thoroughly battered by racist state laws and then neutered by *Plessy v. Ferguson*. It was revived by Thurgood Marshall and his team.

The long-term plan of the Howard Law School think tank established by Charles Hamilton Houston had reached its desired conclusion—for the states. However, the plan could not apply to the nation's capital because the District was a federal territory and the Fourteenth Amendment specifically addresses the states and *only* the states. The Howard scholars had learned this the hard way with a previous case. Defending the District's children took the Fifth Amendment. Attorneys James Nabrit and George E. C. Hayes (Dunbar/M Street 1911) didn't mess with the concept of school equality. Instead they went straight to the Bill of Rights and a founding principle of the United States of America: liberty.

C. Melvin Sharpe was the president of the DC Board of Education in 1950. Spottswood Thomas Bolling, a local preteen, was one of eleven students denied entry to the newly constructed, spare-no-expense facility that housed John Philip Sousa Junior High School. The school had plenty of spaces for students—but only white students. The principal turned the Negro kids away, and all the children were forced to return to severely overcrowded schools. *Bolling v. Sharpe* became the focal point of the District's movement toward educational equality. And it worked because two men did not let their differences get in the way.

Charles Hamilton Houston became involved with the case after he was approached by a local barber who told anyone who would listen that he was wary of a certain kind of DC Negro. Gardner Bishop, known as the "U Street barber," worked as a civil rights activist and leader of a group of local parents who felt he represented the "regular" working folks. He became well known locally when he led a "sit out" at his daughter's elementary school to protest the horrible conditions there. Her school was at double its capacity while a white school, closer to their home, was only about two-thirds full.

Bishop was a South Carolina transplant, not a native Washingtonian, and was not too trusting of Washington's well-heeled and highly educated Negro community. They didn't protest in ways that he believed would get much done. Bishop used the term "double Jim Crow" when he described being discriminated against by whites and looked down upon by "upper class" and "highfaulutin" Negroes who were the local civic leaders.[1] But Gardner Bishop knew he would need help navigating the legal system at some point.

He and Houston first met after a public event where Houston was speaking. Gardner stayed and listened and waited for his opportunity to approach the great legal mind. Gardner was hesitant initially, but soon his concerns wafted away. Houston knew of Bishop as well, and of the grassroots work Bishop had been doing around U Street. The lawyer greeted the barber warmly and invited Gardner to his home, and the two men became allies. The Bishop-Houston union was an important one. It was the antithesis of the "us and them" meme that had been festering in Negro DC. Unified, they led a consolidated effort for all children.

Houston (M Street 1911) was the architect of the fight to end segregation; he has been called the "man who killed Jim Crow." NAACP defense team: Walter White, Charles Houston, James G. Tyson, Leon A. Ransom, and Edward P. Lovett.

The author wishes to thank the National Association for the Advancement of Colored People for authorizing the use of this image.

There was one problem, however, and it was something that could only be left in God's hands. Though his mind was strong, Houston's heart was weak, and he knew it. One thing Mr. Houston did not leave up to the Lord, though, was the future of the *Bolling* case. Shortly before Charles Hamilton Houston died in 1950, he made sure Mr. Bishop and his followers were protected. Houston introduced Bishop to James Nabrit, a friend, fellow Howard law professor, and fierce attorney who understood the need for a hard strike at Jim Crow.

Nabrit was no stranger to the Supreme Court. He and Thurgood Marshall had successfully argued the case of a Negro man denied entrance to the University of Texas School of Law. In an bogus attempt to satisfy the separate-but-equal requirement before going to trial, the university hastily set up a "Negro law school" by leasing the basement of an oil company to serve as a classroom and having one white dean work part time as the "faculty."[2] In that case, Nabrit and Marshall were clearly able to challenge the notion that anything about that "law school" was equal to the one for white students. The US Supreme Court agreed.

When it came to facilities, by the late 1940s and early 1950s Dunbar was not equal to its companion white high schools. Neither were the other two Negro high schools—Armstrong, the trade school, and Cardozo, for business studies. In 1948, Dunbar was three hundred students past capacity. Armstrong was built for 875 students, but 1,114 were enrolled. Cardozo had it the worst: 1,721 students were attending a school meant to hold only 875. It was nearing double its capacity while a nearby white high school was 60 percent under capacity.[3] The Negro junior high schools and middle schools were bursting at the seams as well: five out of six were grossly overcrowded and one was at full capacity. This meant the students were arriving at the high schools with a compromised foundation in the basics.

The Dunbar Alumni Association approached the white superintendent of schools about the difficulties and how the overcrowding had an impact on the school's standards. At a board of education meeting it was revealed that there were only forty-five teachers on staff. The alumni felt that sixteen more were needed to save the school's academic standing. Superintendent Hobart Corning replied, "Dunbar is still doing a good job under very trying circumstances. I would like to say that Dunbar will tomorrow have sixty-one teachers but there is no way anyone can do that."[4] Forty years of underfunding was beginning to show. Dunbar's facility was becoming shabby. The parents had spent the better part of the late 1940s and the early 1950s trying to get the pool fixed and the filtration system updated. In its current state the pool had to be drained every two weeks.

Traveling to DC—or even moving from someplace outside Washington—to attend Dunbar had once been worth the trouble. But James Nabrit transferred his son out of Dunbar after one year so that he could attend a private prep school in the North and get a better education.[5] Yet there were perils involved in leaving the relative emotional safety of DC. Nabrit's son had been rejected by another private school because of his race. "Systematic racial segregation shaped our lives," the younger Nabrit recalled.

James Nabrit III followed in his father's footsteps and became a civil rights lawyer. "My father argued a voting rights case from Oklahoma called *Lane v. Wilson* in the US Supreme Court in 1939 when I was still in the first grade. Is there any reason to wonder why I became a civil rights lawyer and tried to do what he had done?"

The elder Nabrit was a maverick in many ways. At age fifteen, this son of a Baptist minister dropped out of school and delivered shoes for a year. His decision was the result of a dispute with his father about where he would go to school. He'd spent a lot of his childhood in Georgia being pelted with rocks because he'd had to pass a poor white neighborhood to get to school.[6] At sixteen he left home for Morehouse College, where he could finish his high school education.

As an adult, Nabrit was a striking man, about five feet seven with brown skin, auburn hair, and blue eyes. Although he went to Northwestern University Law School in Chicago, Nabrit set up his law practice in Texas. He was recruited to come to Washington to teach at Howard Law and be a part of Houston's civil rights dream team. A student in his first class at Howard in 1936 mistakenly remarked upon seeing the new teacher from Texas—who was wearing cowboy boots and a red tie—that "this dude will never last at Howard." Not only did he last, but Jim Nabrit Jr. would one day become Howard University's president.

Nabrit's cocounsel was an attorney who'd spent nearly his whole life in Washington, except the four years he had spent in Rhode Island while at Brown. George E. C. Hayes had graduated from M Street High School in 1911 and returned to Washington after college to attend Howard for law school. He also taught there and was a member of the District's board of education during the 1940s.

Hayes had personal insight into how to argue the case. He and Nabrit chose a different approach than the other lawyers arguing the other cases. Nabrit was tough minded and said they were going to attack segregation, period. Some feared this head-on collision; if it failed, would make *Plessy v. Ferguson* immutable. But the *Bolling* tack, while harder to prove, would be the bullet to the head of Jim Crow, if successful.

While the *Bolling* case was initially dismissed in the DC courts, it was heard with great interest by the Supreme Court in 1953. Nabrit and Hayes invoked the operating principle of America, the intangible bedrock of liberty. They argued that the children of the nation's capital were not receiving due process as provided by the Fifth Amendment, specifically the fifteen words that declared, "No person . . . shall be deprived of life, liberty, or property, without due process of law."

The two men took turns addressing the court for fifty minutes each. Mr. Hayes opened their case:

> The position we are taking with respect to these cases, that segregation, per se, is unconstitutional, and that without regard to physical facilities, without regard to the question of curriculum, and that if, as a matter of fact, there is a designation that one must

go to a particular school for no other reason than because of race or color, that that is a violation of the constitutional right; and as this Court has said, wherever the issue is raised with respect to color, then it is upon the Government to show that the reason for it, that there is a reason for it—that there is a reason that is a justifiable reason.

Hayes and Nabrit put the burden of proof on the city. Justice Frankfurter was full of questions and dominated the proceedings. He almost seemed to enjoy watching the defendants struggle.

Milton D. Korman represented C. Melvin Sharpe and the board of education. He presented a simple case that the dual system was legitimate because Congress said so. Congress repeatedly approved budgets for a dual system. Congress passed acts to establish separate administrations. His point was that Congress had always meant the education system to be like this, dating back to the first act to establish public schools for colored children in 1862.[7]

Korman and the team of Nabrit and Hayes used almost the exact information but came to very different conclusions. They cited Emancipation Day; the Acts of 1882, 1884, and 1886, which called for the school system; the 1900 consolidation of the school board administrations; and the 1906 reorganization of that school board. Korman even cited the ugly business of Anna Julia Cooper's battle with Schools Director Hughes as an example of how Negro and white educators couldn't get along and how each should be left to his or her own students. Korman contended that segregation was not discrimination.

I say to the court, and I say to my distinguished adversary Mr. Hayes, that these acts were not passed, this dual school system was not set up to stamp these people with a badge of inferiority. There was not this racial feeling that he speaks of with such fervor behind these acts. There was behind these acts a kindly feeling; there was behind these acts an intention to help these people who had been in bondage. And there was and there still is an intention by the Congress to see that these children shall be educated in a healthful atmosphere, in a wholesome atmosphere, in a place where they are wanted, in a place where they will not be looked up with hostility, in a place where there will be a receptive atmosphere for learning for both races without the hostility that undoubtedly Congress thought might creep into these situation. We cannot hide our faces and our minds from the fact that there is feeling between races in these United States. It is a deplorable situation. Would that it were not so. But we must face these facts.

Face the facts and then do nothing about them because there was no need—that was this argument's bottom line. There was no equal protection clause binding Congress.

The last thing the justices heard from James Nabrit before the case concluded at 1:27 PM on December 11, 1953, was this:

The basic question here is one of liberty, and under liberty, under the due process clause, you cannot deal with it as a quantum of treatment, substantially equal. You either have liberty or you do not. When liberty is interfered with by the state, it has to be justified, and you cannot justify it by saying that we only took a little liberty. You justify it by the reasonableness of the taking. We submit that in this case, in the heart of the nation's capital, in the capital democracy, in the capital of the free world there is no place for a segregated school system. This country cannot afford it, and the Constitution does not permit it, and the statutes of Congress do not authorize it.

The *Bolling* decision was announced after the four others, which is important for one reason. The justices said that if the states could desegregate, then surely the capital must. As for Nabrit's argument about liberty, the court agreed with caution.

Although the court has not assumed to define "Liberty" with any great precision, that term is not confined to mere freedom from bodily restraint. Liberty under law extends to the full range of conduct which the individual is free to pursue, and it cannot be restricted except for a proper governmental objective, and thus it imposes on Negro children of the District of Columbia a burden that constitutes an arbitrary deprivation of their liberty in violation of the Due Process Clause.

Left to right: George E. C. Hayes (M Street 1911),
Thurgood Marshall, and James Nabrit celebrate the
1954 desegregation victory.

Library of Congress, Courtesy of AP/Wide World Photos

President Eisenhower wanted Washington to set a good example for the rest of the country when it came to integration. "A model for the nation" had been his public proclamation. Ike had laid the groundwork for the transition. In anticipation of what was to come, he'd stacked the DC Board of Commissioners, the District's governing body, with integration-friendly men. He'd ordered the Justice Department to support the *Bolling* case during the Supreme Court arguments. He'd appointed Earl Warren to chief justice with full knowledge that Warren would shape the *Brown* decision. Eisenhower once said he believed every vestige of segregation should be erased from DC and "not a penny of federal money spent to discriminate." However, that didn't mean he could control racist members on the appropriations committees from ignoring pleas for more money to help the schools. The president also couldn't directly control Washington's board of education.

"A model not a mockery!" was the rallying cry of Dr. Margaret Butcher, one of the three Negro members of the board at the time. The District teacher with a PhD was reacting as many Negroes did to the integration plan announced by the superintendent. On May 18, 1954, Superintendent Hobart Corning told the press he didn't know how and when the schools would integrate, and he'd wait until the Supreme Court explained it all.[8] Within a week it became clear this was not a position he could hold. Instead, he and Board President Sharpe announced a slow rollout of desegregation. A chosen block of elementary schools would integrate first, in September 1954. High schools would not begin the process until January 1955. However, there was an optional clause that angered people like Margaret Butcher. A student could stay in his or her school until graduation, even if the student was zoned out. Or if students preferred, they could transfer to schools serving the zones in which they lived.

According to the integration guidelines as they were laid out on paper, the superintendent's full plan would be in effect by September 1955; but with the stay-put grandfather clause, technically, the schools might not be fully desegregated until 1959. The president of the local NAACP sent a letter to the board saying that the phase-in plan would so "violate the spirit of the clear decision of the Supreme Court that its acceptance by you seems inconceivable." Dr. Butcher and the NAACP wanted the Supreme Court's ruling to go into effect immediately. The final vote on Corning's step-by-step plan was 5–1, with Dr. Butcher the only member voting against it. She confronted Corning publicly in the spring of 1954.

"I want this board to instruct Corning, regardless of cost, to sit here this summer and order his staff to rezone these schools and the students and the buildings involved this September. Mr. Corning, are you vacationing this summer?"

"Yes."

"Well perhaps you could appoint someone to do it for you."

"Mrs. Butcher, I don't think someone could stay continuously on this job integrating and live," Corning snapped back. But he did eventually cancel his plans. The new boundaries were decided by July, just six weeks after the decision.[9]

Some called Dr. Butcher a militant—a militant with perfectly manicured, painted nails, who favored shirtwaist dresses with block-pleated skirts and three-string beaded necklaces.[10] Dr. Butcher was a Dunbar graduate, and her father was one of the Ivy League–educated teachers there, the famous scientist Ernest Everett Just. She had two children in the school system and was a professor of English at Howard.

At the beginning of the 1953–54 school year, before the Supreme Court decision was made, Dr. Butcher wanted to ensure that the board of education record reflected the disparities between what white students received and what Negro students received. Perhaps in anticipation of an unsuccessful Supreme Court outcome, she wanted everyone to tell the truth about what was happening in the schools. She wanted the word out there that the southern congressmen who were on the appropriations committees had little concern for the colored schools and that those institutions were withering. The board of education would not allow Dr. Butcher to go on the record with her concerns.[11] She hounded the other board members, especially the other Negro members, to back her up. Her efforts to do so and to demonize or oust the board members who didn't agree with her caused some to see her as a "danger."[12] But she'd seen what not exactly benign neglect had done to the Negro schools.

And it wasn't a secret. The Senate and House District Appropriations Subcommittees had commissioned a report to survey the District's schools. The extremely detailed Strayer Report found the Negro children in Washington were getting the educational crumbs. According to George Strayer and the report's other authors, in September 1948 the average white high school teacher taught 548.1 pupil-hours per week, while black high school teachers taught 711.3 pupil-hours per week. In the 1947–48 school year, 25 percent of the white school buildings were fifty years or older as compared to 40 percent of the black school buildings. In the white grade schools, 67.9 percent of the classes had more than thirty pupils. Black schools had classes of that size or more 88.1 percent of the time. In the white grade schools, 18 percent of the classes had more than forty pupils. The corresponding figure for black schools was 40.3 percent.[13]

The Negro population in Washington grew 113 percent from 1930 to 1950. The schools were either overcrowded or Negro students were shuttled into hand-me-down schools when white children vacated the old building for nicer or newer facilities. Division II (Negro schools) got Division I's (that is, white schools') old books. Negro students in the system at that time were not nearly as prepared as those thirty years earlier. How could they be? The average number of minutes spent in the classroom was diminishing. Some Negro children were only attending classes for three hours a day because most of the black elementary schools were on shifts to accommodate so many children. The disparity would have long-term consequences for Washington and its potential for integration.

Even in the final weeks before the decision was due, Dr. Butcher was out looking for support. She had a big public appearance lined up for which the poster read, HEAR DYNAMIC FREEDOM'S CHAMPION, DR. MARGARET BUTCHER. She was the headliner at the Trinity Baptist Church program to honor the late Charles Hamilton Houston, whom she considered a personal friend, which remembered him and his fight as the world awaited the Supreme Court's decision. The poster invited Washingtonians to "come in honor of the memory the man who gave his life that you might enjoy greater freedom."

Legally desegregating Washington was a complex undertaking because the Negro and white DC school systems were like a set of fraternal twins whose parents liked one better. The favored twin got the nicer things, the better room. Even in the most subtle ways, the hierarchy was displayed: Division I was the category for the white schools; Negroes were in Division II. Now the systems would have to merge and share. Up until then, there had been two sports systems, two cadet systems, two sets of teachers, and two student bodies. In the entire system there were only six jobs that bridged both systems, and they were support positions like food service and grounds maintenance.[14] There were 3,588 teachers—1,895 Negro and 1,693 white. There were 108,816 students—57,716 Negro and 43,100 white. In total, 165 schools had to be realigned.[15]

It would all come down to those new boundaries drawn up by all the principals using spot maps and tabulations of the pupils, block by block and grade by grade. In the summer of 1954, Washington, DC, was carved up on paper. Dr. Butcher pressed Superintendent Corning on every detail during those school board meetings during the summer of '54.

"Will new boundaries be fixed every year?" Dr. Butcher asked.

"If boundaries cannot be absolutely fixed then they must be flexible for the reason that there are many changes in the population and the best use must be made of the schools," Corning replied.

Did the superintendent assume white flight? "I thought the board was trying to make an integrated system," Butcher responded.

"This is all integration," Corning shot back.

"I am talking about a decisive school plan whereby children will go to the schools nearest their homes and to accomplish it seems that the city should be decisively zoned," said Dr. Butcher.

"That is what I discussed in my report," replied Corning.[16]

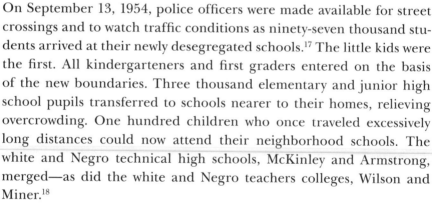

On September 13, 1954, police officers were made available for street crossings and to watch traffic conditions as ninety-seven thousand students arrived at their newly desegregated schools.[17] The little kids were the first. All kindergarteners and first graders entered on the basis of the new boundaries. Three thousand elementary and junior high school pupils transferred to schools nearer to their homes, relieving overcrowding. One hundred children who once traveled excessively long distances could now attend their neighborhood schools. The white and Negro technical high schools, McKinley and Armstrong, merged—as did the white and Negro teachers colleges, Wilson and Miner.[18]

Washington's transition was calm as compared to that of other cities. Yet as smoothly as the first day went for the students, the next few months were rocky. In October white high school students staged a walkout from their classes, protesting pending integration. The board of education was inundated with letters from white parents concerned about the proximity of Negro children to their own. The Capitol Hill South East Association expressed concern about "the spread of communicable diseases such as tuberculosis, venereal disease, pediculosis, scabies, and scalp ringworm."[19] Seventeen parents signed a petition that read, "We strongly protest the policy of the BOE, which results in the assignment of Negro Teachers to teach in schools which are predominately white in enrollment. It is not in our children's best interest because of the 'close relationship' between teacher and pupil."[20]

Some questioned the Supreme Court's authority. Mrs. Kate Steele wrote, "The court makes decisions, but Congress makes the laws and changes in laws such as the abolishment of segregation should be by the people or by a constitutional amendment, as the constitution does not say that the court can rule the country by force."[21] In September a Mr. Ellicot Dudding suggested that two night watchmen be placed in every school building—one white and one Negro—because he believed there was a "very bitter feeling among a vast part of the White population on the matter of integration, although I have no ill feeling toward the Negro but I heard rumors that not a school building will be left standing in Washington by Christmas."

By 1957, Superintendent Hobart Corning declared, "Desegregation is complete." But he then added this: "Desegregation is the moving about of people and things. Integration is a much longer process depending on the creation of a community."

Those who had gone to Dunbar up until that point were selected in the sense that they were highly motivated academic students almost sequestered in an environment dedicated to their advancement. They had earned the right to be there by virtue of passing the appropriate tests and maintaining their records. For eighty-seven years, Dunbar High School had operated like a combination of a closely monitored charter school and a private college prep school. By 1954, more than sixteen thousand young men and women had graduated from the institution. The year the Supreme Court decisions came down, Dunbar sent 80 percent of its graduates to college, the highest percentage of any Washington school, white or Negro. That same year it had the highest percentage attending college on scholarship: one in four.[22]

In the little picture, Dunbar was a mighty force in the District. In the bigger national picture, it was a rarity. But now that there would no longer officially be Negro or white schools, what would happen to Dunbar? What would happen to the teachers? The facility? The student body? In his parting note to the Dunbar class of 1955, the first to graduate post-segregation, the principal signaled that he knew Dunbar as a concept was ending. He wrote:

> As graduates of Dunbar High School, you inherit the mantle of thousands of sons and daughters who have preceded you. They have carried the banner high and made the name of Dunbar a noble one by their fine accomplishments all over the world. With this our proud heritage, I have no fear that you will nurture it and that it will blossom and become more fruitful as the years pass by. The opportunities are manifold for you to add increased laurels to your Alma Mater. I have every faith that this will be done.[23]

In retrospect Margaret Butcher said, "Integration—integration was the rallying cry. No one really thought about Dunbar."[24]

Dunbar, like every other school, became a neighborhood school, and attendance was based solely on the boundaries in which a child resided. From 1955 onward there would still be academically gifted students who attended Dunbar, as long as they were zoned in. But now there would also be students who had been cheated out of adequate elementary schooling. And the neighborhood around Dunbar was not great.

"First and O Street is infamous as a gathering point for young men who are either out of school or out of employment or both out of school and employment," reported one educator about Dunbar's location. "They gather there and are indecent in their public conduct. I say that without reservation."[25]

Four years after DC schools were legally desegregated, Dunbar was still all Negro. In fact, that has never changed. The student body just became a more diverse academic population. The faculty changed, too. Many of the teachers moved on to other jobs once opportunities became available across the system.

The 1959 Dunbar handbook offered a different greeting than in previous books. It reflected not only some of the changes in the new population, but also the attitude about the population entering the legendary halls of Dunbar High School. The greeting—"Dear Newcomer"—was a sign of tensions to come.

Dear Newcomer,

We are very happy to welcome you to Dunbar High School. The fine traditions of Dunbar and the achievement of her alumni are a challenge for you to emulate. Through the years, Dunbar has sent forward a host of young men and women who have become worthy citizens of this great nation. We feel that you are fortunate in being assigned to this school, and we hope that your days here will be happy and fruitful. This little booklet is given to you as a guide during your first days at Dunbar High School. Keep it and consult it frequently for you will find it a valuable aid in orienting you to this new experience.

11 | ELITE VERSUS ELITISM

"YOU DON'T WANT TO go to that place. That's a horrible place. They don't allow Negroes in that place."

"Well, I've been accepted, so I am going to do it and take a chance."

Dr. James Bowman's friends were warning him about the perils of accepting a medical residency at St. Luke's Hospital in Chicago. But Bowman, Dunbar 1939, was keen on taking advantage of the opportunity. He had interviewed with and wowed a highly respected pathologist, who then personally offered Bowman the position. At the time, Bowman couldn't have known that he would one day become an internationally recognized pathologist in his own right and an expert on inherited diseases. Back in the early '50s he was a rare breed: a young Negro doctor entering a specialized field.

His friends remained unconvinced. "But you know you have to go in through the back door of the hospital. You cannot walk into the front door of the hospital."

"Well," Bowman responded, "that's absolute nonsense. If I'm a resident there, I'm going to walk through the front door."[1]

And he did. On his first day, Bowman walked down Indiana Avenue and into the main entrance of the hospital. He looked around, and people were looking right back at him, mostly Negro cleaning staff, janitors, and maids who stared at the bold young man calmly walking down the hall. And just like that, James Bowman integrated a hospital. He was the first and, for a long while, the only Negro resident at the institution.

While making just $100 a month, he had to commute to the hospital because Negroes were not allowed to live in resident housing.

After completing his residency, Dr. Bowman made a bold decision: he left the United States. He had been offered positions in Chicago, but was dismayed that they paid lower salaries than for his white counterparts.[2] "I was only going to make ten thousand dollars and my colleagues were going to make twenty-five thousand? You're going to take advantage of me? Good luck. So we decided to leave the country." It was the principle, not the pennies. "My wife and I decided that we were not going to go back to anything that smacked of segregation."[3]

Dr. Bowman accepted an offer to become the head of pathology at a newly opened hospital in Iran. The Nemazee Hospital was named after a rich and powerful Iranian, scion of a family comparable to the Rockefellers or Carnegies.[4] It was in Iran that Dr. Bowman began to study the link between genetics and blood. He went all over the country taking samples and doing research to help find the root cause of specific blood diseases. Much of the time he worked in-country and was followed by the shah's security operation. This came in handy when he and his assistants were returning from a research trip in a remote community and got lost in the desert in the middle of the night. The government watcher who had been surreptitiously tailing them was kind enough to approach them and lead them back to the city.[5]

The Bowmans had been keeping up with the civil rights activities in the States by listening to the radio. The movement was of interest across the world. Dr. Bowman remembers hearing "Little Rock, Little Rock, Little Rock . . ." being discussed in Russian and Farsi. Apparently his young daughter also heard these conversations over the years. One day his little girl, who had been born in Shiraz, looked up at him and asked, "Daddy, what's a Negro?"[6] Dr. Bowman knew at that moment it was time to return to Chicago with his wife and young daughter.

"That is what he says, yes." Valerie Jarrett, senior advisor to President Obama, has heard this story before. She has that look of amusement and mild irritation common to those whose parents repeatedly tell stories that are embarrassing, yet funny and true. "I don't remember, but I'm not surprised at all by that. My parents have said that that was the reason why they came home, because they didn't feel like I had any black identity. Because they [Iranians] didn't distinguish between white Americans and black Americans. We're all Americans." It was something the Iranians were able to do that many in the United States could not.

Jarrett's office in the White House looked like almost any other office of a prominent executive, with wooden chairs around the conference table and the all-knowing assistant about ten feet away, just outside the door. Her days were scheduled in increments, and she was all business. Yet her voice was warm when she spoke of her father.

While Jarrett didn't remember asking the "Negro" question, she did remember the first time her father told her about Dunbar.

"I was a very young child. Dunbar was critical in my father's past, to his life's path. He gives it full credit for having been educated—he, together with his colleagues—at a world-class level. Anytime I would ever say anything that was grammatically incorrect, he would say, 'As Dunbar High School taught me . . .' and then he would correct me. And he's a big believer in, 'Do not be lazy with grammar'; 'Do not be lazy, period.' Certainly don't be lazy in how you speak. And, I think that, as a young child, I remember him telling stories about Dunbar High School. And, really, to this day, just gives it an enormous amount of credit for the shaping of his life." That life led him to be a pioneer in hematology and a professor at the University of Chicago as well as the director of the Comprehensive Sickle Cell Center at the University of Chicago. He was keen on education and spent years as the medical school's dean of minority affairs.

Bowman's yearbook superlative was "enthusiastic," and he was voted "Most Energetic."[7] His energy and love of his school were apparent when, at age eighty-eight, he traveled to Martha's Vineyard to join four other 1930s Dunbar graduates for a Chautauqua about the school's history. Martha's Vineyard had for years been a haven for black Americans, a place for friends and family to reunite.[8] Most important, it was a place of relaxation for people who lived their days working hard to stay upright in the mainstream. As one historian put it, the Vineyard was a place for black Americans to "carve out niches . . . a place to celebrate with friends and not have to explain a damn thing."[9]

Regularly on the island there are lectures and happenings highlighting African American culture, including Harvard's Charles Hamilton Houston Institute's annual event. On an August day in 2010, the audience at the high school on the small island was filled with curious history buffs,

Dunbar graduates, and their families, who had come to listen and honor the octogenarian and nonagenarians on stage, including Dr. Bowman. Jarrett's father, sporting his usual bow tie and suit, told the audience, "We were always told, almost brainwashed, that you can do it and when you leave here you can compete. That's the most important thing. And we believed it. When you get out, you can compete with anybody." Bowman was making the point that Dunbar's children were never, ever made to feel inferior to or less than anyone else. It was a perverse benefit of the times. He explained it this way. "One of the advantages of segregation: we were there in a closed world. We couldn't communicate with the other side. We couldn't go to theater downtown. We couldn't go to a restaurant but we *believed* we shall overcome."

John King Rector III (Dunbar 1939) and Harold Nelson (Dunbar 1939) spoke of their families' involvement in the school. "Then there was the school unity," Rector recalled. "All the people I knew went to Dunbar. That is what it was. It was a community." Harold Nelson got a big and knowing laugh from the audience when he added, "My mother kept saying, 'You are going to be somebody.' The other part of being somebody is 'You will never embarrass me.'"

The two women on the panel both went to Smith after graduating from Dunbar. Laura Cole (Dunbar 1930) sweetly recalled her days at Dunbar as "time and treasure," while Professor Adelaide Cromwell (Dunbar 1936) displayed her well-known frank and funny side. She let loose memorable one-liners about the boys' dean of discipline, remembering that "he was not underemployed," and about local politics, which she called "chicanery in secondary education." She once returned an interview request letter sent for this book corrected in red ink. Wearing her white hair in her signature two braided buns on either side of her head, Princess Leia–style, she was unfiltered in her thoughts about Dunbar: "They took care of the student. . . . Some felt there was predjudice on the basis of color . . . there probably was a little of that. But when you get down to the truth it—it was the brains of the child that counted. The teachers put their faith and hope on the intelligent students, students who came from simple homes. A lot of the parents had modest jobs. Regular jobs. Government jobs. It created a stability. It allowed people to plan."

Such a simple idea, the ability to plan and have dreams for one's own life was one of the many gifts from Dunbar that, Mr. Nelson reminded the audience, needed to be paid forward. "Walter Smith was the principal for twenty-three years. During that time he tried, he emphasized service, redefining what service was. It was all determined because you were receiving this phenomenal black education, you were supposed to take it and use it and promote something else for someone. It was not just enough for you to receive it. You had to take it, build on it, and pass it on." Dr. Bowman summed it up this way: "One thing about Dunbar students was determination, stick-to-it-iveness. Keep pluggin' away." The same was true of Dr. Bowman into his late eighties.[10] Ms. Jarrett was amazed her father made the trip, because he had not been well.

"He took pride in the fact that he could go to this school and receive this world-class education. And his father was a dentist, and so they lived reasonably well. Obviously, DC wasn't as bad as if he went further south. But their neighborhoods were segregated. But, he also grew up with a sense of right and wrong and so, for example, [when] he went to his residency in Chicago, he walked in the front door of the school as a resident. 'I am deserving.'"

By the 1960s and on the national stage, Dunbar's alumni were breaking ground that had yet to be broken, propelling the civil rights movement and climbing political ladders. Dunbar graduates were creating the school's legacy. Dr. Bowman used his expertise to influence and change a governmental policy of random and indiscriminate use of genetic blood-sample testing in black communities. Other noted scientists include Dr. Herman Branson (Dunbar 1932) who codiscovered the alpha helix, the basic structure of protein, while working with Linus Pauling. Pauling won the Nobel Prize for his work, but there are those in the scientific community, including one University of California professor, who went on the record as saying Dr. Branson was as pivotal as Pauling in the groundbreaking work and should have shared in the glory. Dr. Linc Hawkins (Dunbar 1928) was the first African American on the technical staff at Bell Labs, where he coinvented the polymer cable sheath, the plastic tubing that insulates all underground phone wires to this day. Dr. James Henderson (Dunbar 1935) was a noted plant physiologist, and Dr. Evelyn Boyd Granville (Dunbar 1941), who earned a PhD in mathematics, helped write the orbit computations for NASA's Vanguard and Mercury projects.

The Chambers brothers, Andrew (Dunbar 1950) and Lawrence (Dunbar 1948) were on their way to becoming great leaders in the army

(Andrew) and the navy (Lawrence). Lawrence was the second black graduate of the naval academy, right after Wesley Brown. He would gain international fame as Admiral Chambers, who commanded a ship that saved three thousand Vietnamese during Operation Frequent Wind, the largest helicopter evacuation in American history. He made a gutsy choice to push millions of dollars of equipment off the aircraft carrier in his command so that a plane carrying refugees could land.

In the business world, Naylor Fitzhugh (Dunbar 1926) was on his way to becoming a legend. He went to Harvard at age sixteen and then on to the Harvard Business School, becoming one its earliest black graduates. Yet even with two Ivy League degrees, he could not get a job with a company, so he returned to Washington to teach business at Howard. He finally had an opportunity in 1965 to join Pepsi, and he changed business forever. He developed campaigns for specific consumers and became the man who invented target marketing. Large corporations sought his counsel for the rest of his career.[11] He was called the "father of black business."

In the arts, Olga James graduated from Julliard, appeared on Broadway, and was a lead in the film *Carmen*. Ellis Haizlip (Dunbar 1947) became a concert and TV producer, known for his Emmy Award–winning variety show *Soul!* He had originally been asked to create "the black *Tonight Show*" but chose instead to present something not yet seen on television. He described it as a "meeting place for black ideas and black talent with undertones of New York's Apollo Theater."[12] Dunbar graduates in the arts had a unique opportunity in the 1960s to use their talents and their education to advance civil rights. Two became famous worldwide: Elizabeth Catlett and Billy Taylor.

Given her mind and memory, which both remained sharp well into her nineties, it is no surprise Elizabeth Catlett remembers liking Dunbar because it was an "intellectual place."[13] Her genius was expressed through finely sculpted metal, stone, and wood, or through her intricately detailed linocuts and prints, in which each line adds something to the story the pictures want to tell. The young woman born in DC's Freedman's Hospital in 1915, Elizabeth Catlett (Dunbar 1931), became one of the most acclaimed, if not the most acclaimed, female African American sculptor of the twentieth century. She was the chair of the art department at Dillard and taught at Hampton. She was a celebrated artist whose work in the 1960s demonstrated her strong sense of social justice. "I was politically engaged before I was an artist," she replied when asked how politics affect her work.[14] Her piece *Black Unity* is made of mahogany wood. On one side are lovely serene faces; on the other side a strong fist punches toward the sky. Her bronze statue *Target* is a bronze bust of an African American man surrounded by a metallic crosshairs. She created posters for Angela Davis's Freedom Movement. By the '60s, she had moved to Mexico. After being arrested for protesting with railroad workers and her continued political activity, Catlett was deemed an undesirable alien by the State Department. Catlett adopted her husband's home country of Mexico and became a citizen, working on her own and socializing with "Diego and Frida." She stayed in Mexico for the rest of her life "because I was just a person. I wasn't a black person. They accepted me as a person."

In the United States she both observed and experienced struggle as an outspoken black woman. "I was ignored as a woman and experienced prejudice as a black person." Once, as a professor of art in New Orleans, she was not allowed to take her class through the front door on a field trip to the museum. When she graduated from high school, she applied and was accepted to attend the Carnegie Institute of Technology, but the school rescinded its scholarship offer once it learned she was black.[15]

Instead she stayed home in DC and went to Howard, where she was influenced by James Porter, the father of African American art history. Later, when studying art at the University of Iowa, Catlett was mentored by Grant Wood, painter of the iconic *American Gothic*. He advised her to create from what she knew, her real experience. As a child she would spend the summers with her maternal grandparents in North Carolina, where she was struck by the poverty of sharecroppers who worked so hard. "The nasty thing about it: the owners. The owners took part of what they grew. When they had all the plants, corn, and cotton, then the owner would come and run their hounds on the land, let rabbits close, trampling the crops. No respect for anything. That was my impression."[16]

It was far from the world of books and art in DC, but in Catlett's mind the sharecroppers were the dignified people. She always felt the grace of the women she saw working in the fields should be celebrated. She was able to catch their beauty and strength in a series of linocut prints called *I Am the Negro Woman*, which depict women working in fields, in homes, and with their children. Perhaps her most famous image is *The Sharecropper*, a three-quarter linocut print portrait of a strong-jawed black woman wearing a large straw hat. She gazes out with a serene but determined look on her face. It was recently described as "a graphic masterpiece" and was acquired by the Los Angeles County Museum of Art.[17] Her work is in the permanent collections of major US art museums including the Museum of Modern Art in New York, the Art Institute of Chicago, the Philadelphia Museum of Art, the High Museum in Atlanta, and the Smithsonian in her hometown of Washington, DC.

"I Wish I Knew How It Would Feel to Be Free," which became an anthem of the civil rights movement, was written by the brilliant jazz musician Billy Taylor (Dunbar 1939). "It really is one of the best things I ever wrote," Taylor recalled in his expansive apartment in the Bronx. The white paint on the walls was barely visible because every inch was covered with striking art of and for African Americans. And of course there is a piano. "And it was most useful," said Taylor of his composition, "one of the most used. Because it's [also] been used by the women's movement. Dr. King used to ask me—he couldn't remember the title of it." Taylor smiled as he remembered back fifty years. "He'd say, 'Billy, play that piece, that Baptist piece that you always play for me.'" Tay-

Elizabeth Catlett's *The Sharecropper*, 1952.
© Catlett Mora Family Trust/Licensed by VAGA, New York, NY

lor's life as celebrated musician, director of the jazz series at the Kennedy Center, and television personality was not on his mind at that moment.

He was reliving in detail working with Dr. King to raise money for the 1963 March on Washington.

"I went to several places for Dr. King. I was in Alabama with Dr. King."[18] A fund-raising concert had been planned, and the roster for the event was stellar: Joe Louis, Ray Charles, and Frank Sinatra. "We had had a problem, and because it was a mixed concert, they would not allow us in Alabama to do a mixed—so they said they refused to let us have the town hall, or wherever we were going to play. So we had to makeshift; we had to get another [location]—we had a school athletic field, and quickly built a makeshift bandstand." When it came time to get to the concert venue, the local police had another idea. "Now, we are in a rented bus that can't go any faster, I mean, if you are pushing it, it wouldn't go any faster than twenty-five miles an hour. And the guy gave us a ticket for speeding. And I mean, just little things. And so that was the kind of atmosphere we were in."

"I had this radio, the microphone, and I'm standing out there, and the people are coming. And the people are coming. They are really coming. I'm saying, 'My goodness, this is a big crowd. A lot of folks are going to come.' And as I'm standing there, this guy is coming toward me, and he looked just like any of the white guys that we have problems with—he looked like a redneck. And so he's coming right toward me. And so, I say, 'Sir, I beg your pardon, sir, how did you happen to come to this particular concert?' He said, 'I want to hear Ray Charles.' That blew my story."

Back in Washington, a young woman named Norma Holloway (Dunbar 1950) was in law school and on her way to becoming the first black woman justice on the federal bench in Washington and the only woman to serve as chief judge of the court. She presided over the grand jury in the Starr/Lewinsky/Clinton case. Robert Weaver (Dunbar 1925) became the first black presidential cabinet member when LBJ named him the secretary of housing and urban development in 1966. And the following year, an impressionist painting of a handsome black man graced the cover of *Time* magazine. The only text on the cover, aside from "February 17, 1967," was U.S. SENATOR EDWARD BROOKE (Dunbar 1936). He was the first black senator ever elected by popular vote and someone considered to have "moved the arc of history."[19]

"I think everything that happened to me after Dunbar—Dunbar had an impact upon it," Brooke said. Even at ninety-three-years-old,

Billy Taylor, New York City, 1947.
William P. Gottlieb/Ira and Leonore S. Gershwin Fund Collection, Music Division, Library of Congress

breast-cancer survivor Senator Brooke can clearly recall the Dunbar teacher who sent him on his way toward politics, which hadn't been his plan at all. Indeed next to his yearbook picture is the caption, "To be a surgeon." "I always thought I was going to be a brain surgeon. I wanted to be a brain surgeon. Don't ask me why, but when I was a kid I used to take dead animals up in my attic and sneak them up there and do biopsies and just crazy things like that. And I really had no real affinity for it. No one in my family—my immediate family, of course, was in medicine, but I somehow—maybe because the doctors were the community leaders. They had the biggest cars, and they had all the girls, and medicine was quite something at that time. And the doctor was very well respected in the community. So, maybe some of that had some influence upon my young mind at the time. So, when I went to Dunbar I was taking courses sort of leading to that. But when I went to Dunbar there was a teacher there by the name of Shippen."

Cyrus Shippen taught history and civics. The Yale-educated teacher took a shine to young Mr. Brooke. "Mr. Shippen said to me, 'You know, you ought not be following with the sciences. You have a mind for civics.'" Up until that point, despite his surgical aspirations, Brooke had been more focused on playing tennis than on academics; he was captain of Dunbar's team. He had just assumed he would go to Howard's medical school.

But Mr. Shippen was insistent. "He said, 'You know, you are a people person.' And I said, 'A people person?' He said, 'Yes, I've noticed you with the kids around here. You're a people person. You get along; you know how to get along with all people. And I just think that'd be a better career goal for you.' So that, in its way, had a great impression on me and [was] a great inspiration. Now, he was not a counselor or anything like that. He was just teaching civics. And I had taken it as an elective, I think, just because I couldn't find anything else to take. And I was not a great student—a scholar. You know, I did what I had to do, and I graduated from Dunbar, but I met a lot of people there because we had such a wonderful student body." And the most important thing—even now in his last years, his voice deep and slow, the senator remembers this: "And he said, 'I believe in you,' and that was quite an inspiration to me."

Brooke referred to his experience at Dunbar as a bit of a cocoon. He lived in an area so segregated that if you wanted to walk through the next neighborhood you needed a note from a white person. He served in the military and, like those who came before him, was marked by the way the US Army treated its black members.

Once Brooke was in the real world, he made sure he would find a way to make things better for those who were not privileged. Before he was elected senator, he became the first black state attorney general ever in the United States. He called himself a "creative Republican" who worked on fair housing issues. He said he was a senator for all people, not just blacks. He was out front on women's issues: Brooke fought hard to change the Hyde Amendment, which bans the use of Medicaid money for abortions. Some legislators did not want to include the language that made abortion available "in the case of rape, incest, and when the life of the mother is endangered." He held firm until that clause was included, and to his surprise the portion about the life of the mother was the sticking point.[20]

Black activists who were angry that he wasn't more supportive of the Black Panthers suggested he was an Uncle Tom. Still, Dunbar's class of 1967 dedicated its yearbook to him. In his later years he was one of the first people to call for a national holiday for Dr. King, and in the 1970s he was the first person to call for President Nixon to resign. And while he was not an activist legislator, he did champion a law against housing discrimination in 1969 that aimed to help the poor find homes. The war on poverty was something the senator chose to address in a commencement speech that year.

On a May morning in 1969, four hundred graduating Wellesley College students sat eager to get their diplomas. The Seven Sisters school in Massachusetts was full of smart young women, most of whom came from Republican families.[21] Brooke, the current Republican senator, seemed

Edward William Brooke III, US Senator (R-MA) from 1967 to 1979.

US Senate Historical Office

like a perfect fit for the occasion. There was a bit of extra excitement at this commencement as well. For the first time in its ninety-four-year history, Wellesley was going to have a student speaker at commencement. The students had requested the opportunity; it had been happening all over campuses in the late '60s. The chosen speaker would address her classmates after the senator.

By this time, the senator was fifty years old, the same generation as many of their parents. He made a nod toward the age gap and then continued to offer some thoughts about the roots of protest and the point of political protest given the tumult of the decade.

He began:

> I hope you will permit me to offer some reflections on one of the safer and less inflammatory topics of the day: the protest movement in general, and the character and function of student protests in particular. Standing as I do somewhere between fading youth and advancing obsolescence, I hope it will be possible for me to speak both to your generation and to my own.

And he offered this thought about protesting:

> Potential allies are more often alienated than enlisted by such activities, and their empathy for the professed goals of the protesters is destroyed by their outrage at the procedures employed.
>
> In short, it behooves the disciples of protest as politics to reconsider the alleged merits of coercive tactics. By now they should be able to see that, apart from being morally insupportable, such methods are politically ineffective.

And then he concluded:

> This country has profound and pressing problems on its agenda. It needs the best energies of all its citizens, especially its gifted young people, to remedy these ills.
>
> Let us not dissipate these energies on phony issues or misguided missions.
>
> Let us not mistake the vigor of protest for the value of accomplishment.

Let us direct the zeal of every concerned American to the real problems.

Let us forsake false drama for true endeavor.

Let us, in short, recognize that ours is a precious community that demands and deserves the best that *is in*.

The president of the college took to the microphone and made the long-awaited introduction of the student speaker.

In addition to inviting Senator Brooke to speak to them this morning, the Class of '69 has expressed a desire to speak to them and for them at this morning's commencement. There was no debate so far as I could ascertain as to whom their spokesman was to be: Miss Hillary Rodham.

Twenty-one-year-old Hillary Rodham walked to the microphone. She was exactly twenty-eight years younger than Senator Brooke, with whom she shared a birthday—October 26; she was born in 1947 and he in 1919. She had a prepared speech, but first she decided to deliver an off-the-cuff, unscripted rebuttal of the senator's speech. Miss Rodham began with these words:

I find myself in a familiar position, that of reacting, something that our generation has been doing for quite a while now. We're not in the positions yet of leadership and power, but we do have that indispensable task of criticizing and constructive protest and I find myself reacting just briefly to some of the things that Senator Brooke said. This has to be brief because I do have a little speech to give. Part of the problem with empathy with professed goals is that empathy doesn't do us anything. We've had lots of empathy; we've had lots of sympathy, but we feel that for too long our leaders have used politics as the art of making what appears to be impossible, possible. What does it mean to hear that 13.3 percent of the people in this country are below the poverty line? That's a percentage. We're not interested in social reconstruction; it's human reconstruction. How can we talk about percentages and trends? The complexities are not lost in our analyses, but perhaps they're just put into what we consider a more human and eventually a more progressive perspective.

The young woman's nervy rebuttal of the sitting Senator was written up in *Life* magazine's feature on future leaders.

What happened that day was a pure example of the strange position middle-class, middle-aged blacks found themselves in during the 1960s. The "don't trust anyone over thirty" mantra meant they got the brush-off from very liberal young whites and very conservative old whites, while experiencing insolence from some young blacks.

In Washington, DC, the rise of Marion Barry exemplified the moment. He harnessed the grassroots energy of young blacks who felt underrepresented or plain old forgotten by the black middle class. Barry swept into town and made an immediate impression with Pride Inc., a successful campaign to put young, out-of-work, unrepresented black men to work cleaning the streets of their own neighborhoods. Many young men got their first job opportunities through Pride Inc.

It was a landmark event when LBJ appointed Walter Washington mayor of Washington, DC—he was the first black person to run a major city. Washington was a product of Howard Law School, a longtime government leader, and married to a Dunbar graduate from a prominent Washington family. Yet he was seen as the establishment by some young blacks. He fought off challenges to his power from J. Edgar Hoover. And he had to appeal to racist congressmen still holding the purse strings. When Mayor Washington sent his first budget to Congress in 1967, the head of the appropriations committee in charge of financing DC's government, John McMillan, a Democrat from South Carolina and an infamous bigot, gave Mayor Washington some watermelon.

At Howard University, students protested and occupied buildings. They wanted certain concessions from the president of the university, and some called for him to step down for being what they considered to be unresponsive to their current needs. At the time the president was James Nabrit. When Nabrit had first come to Howard as a teacher, he came on two conditions: that he be permitted to do pro bono civil rights work while working at Howard and that he be permitted to start and teach a class in civil rights law.[22] Of course, he also successfully argued the Supreme Court case to integrate DC schools. Nabrit was prescient about the social upheaval to come in the late 1960s. He gave an interview to the *Washington Post* when he became president of "the nation's largest Negro college." In 1963 he told the reporter that "the Negro looks at this year of Emancipation centennial and sees how far he is from obtaining rights of first class citizens. He is alarmed, disturbed and angry when he realized that 100 years after the Emancipation Proclamation he is still struggling for elemental justice, the right to register and to vote, the right to educate his children along with other citizens, the right to avail himself of public accommodations and the right to live where his income enables him to live. . . .[He is] tired of excuses, tokenism, and discussion about how far he has come. This mood is not the result of the mood of the leadership but is the usurping mood of the masses of Negroes."[23] He did not suspect, however, that he would be on receiving end of the anger five years later.

Nabrit's achievements on the students' behalf did not seem to earn him any points. The Howard students of that time were just four and five years old when the *Brown/Bolling* decision was made. Students boycotted classes and occupied the administration building. Jay Greene, a law student who had led demonstrations said, "Students who walk into the administration building are treated worse than a beggar off the street. We seek dignity, respect, and real student autonomy."[24] It sounded a lot like what President Nabrit had said years earlier. Nabrit retired not long after the protests. Protests were bubbling up in the lower schools as students began demanding changes in the curriculum to include Afrocentric courses.

One Dunbar teacher found himself consumed by it all. Madison Tignor had begun teaching at Dunbar in the 1930s. He adored the written word. Milton was his favorite writer. His son described him as loving the English language and trying very hard to pass that love along to others, sometimes doing it by force.[25] He was an avid collector of photographs and carefully arranged pictures in his albums. He wrote small narrations, descriptions, or poems next the snapshots of his beloved family. Under a picture of his wife and two of his sons, he wrote:

Both Hands Full
Both hands Happy
With two young lives
Facing the Morning of Life

Madison Tignor was born in 1902 in the house where his mother and grandmother had been born. The home had been built by his great-grandfather, a master carpenter, who also helped construct parts of Howard University. While proud of this fact, his elders were reluctant to talk about slavery or the past. Their motto was: "The world started with us, and that's all that matters."

Tignor's mother was a strict adherent of Booker T. Washington's philosophies, and despite the insistence of other relatives, she enrolled Tignor at Armstrong instead of Dunbar. She did yield to his taking Latin at Dunbar when it became obvious he was going to be valedictorian at Armstrong. Young Tignor was headed to college, and he'd have to help pay for it. Money was not plentiful in his household, and he learned the value and necessity of hard work early on. As a child he took his wagon to Eastern Market, where he would haul groceries for change. As a young adult, he worked in a Library of Congress reading room eight hours a day all through his years at Howard University. He was not of Washington's affluent black class and had little time for social climbing or clubs.

As hard as his childhood was, Tignor knew he had it better than those who lived in the alleys near his home. His mother always took him along on church outreach meetings. The ministers would go into the alleys and pray with the folks who lived there. Food and clothing would be distributed to those in need. Tignor's mother would play on a portable organ while he handed out hymnals.

Tignor found the segregation of his hometown both absurd and frustrating. At times he made light of it. The family joke, upon seeing signs for "colored" water fountains, was that they knew the water was not colored. He was infuriated that blacks couldn't use the public toilets in the Capitol Building. And when he worked at the Library of Congress he discovered a separate shelf labeled "colored authors." He felt the labeling of authors and their works by race was "the ultimate inhumanity" and resolved to do something to change the system.

That something was to become a teacher. He believed his purpose at Dunbar and the goal of the school was "to create leaders of color in every field of American life." His students described him as a gentleman, elegant and composed. He restarted Dunbar's student newspaper and dubbed it the *Dunbar Newsreel*. He was the advisor to the Correspondence

Club, which started out all female except for one round little boy. Tignor was a father of three boys who in the 1950s also went to Dunbar.

Mr. Tignor was known to do whatever it took to help a child master the English language. One young man of privilege spent a year or two away from Dunbar when his father relocated to Haiti to teach. Mercer Cook remembered, "When I returned to Dunbar, my grammar was jumbled. I had difficulty. He took extra time with me, really helped me."

Tignor always came to school impeccably dressed, wearing a well-fitting suit with a pocket square and sometimes a bow tie. He usually had a serious expression on his long face, which was bisected by a small thick mustache. That's not to say he wasn't warm. "He had personality and a sense of humor, and he was a good teacher. He was dedicated, yeah. He was very good to me," Alfred Derricot recalled at his fifty-fifth reunion.

In the 1960s, after thirty years of teaching at Dunbar, Madison Tignor was offered a new opportunity. He accepted an invitation to become assistant principal of Eastern, the largest high school in Washington. The job meant more money and more responsibility. His sons had graduated from Dunbar and gone off to Yale, Columbia Medical School, and Howard. The time was right.

Before 1954, Eastern had been all white. Initially its principal reported that desegregation had not caused any problems. He told the curious press, "In our school, integration is doing well."[26] However, some of the students did not like the new arrangement and took part in a four-day boycott during which white students refused to go to school.

By the time Tignor moved from assistant principal to principal of Eastern in 1963, the school had flipped from 100 percent white to almost 100 percent black. Principal Tignor, who'd been there through the transition, had taken control when Eastern was in a bit of a crisis. There were some fights at sporting events. The white flight from the neighborhood and the sharp shift in the student body had left the faculty feeling unsettled. Principal Tignor led by example with his old-fashioned belief in discipline and focus. One of his teachers said she felt that his presence really helped calm the school and that he was dignified and conscientious.[27]

Tignor told the teachers and the student body of nearly twenty-four hundred that he wanted to reestablish Eastern's good name. He expected every student to be involved in at least one extracurricular activity. He helped establish new nursing and business clubs, a stamp-collecting club, and even a baton-twirling club. He promised assemblies with noted figures, including Ralph Bunche, the first black person to win the Nobel Peace Prize, and Secretary of State Dean Rusk. He informed his students he expected an improvement in school citizenship.

Until 1964, his tenure as the first black principal of the largest school in the District had gone well. The seniors in the class of 1964 respected Principal Tignor and would remain close to him throughout their years, nominating him for leadership awards. The freshmen that year were another story. Some of these new students would grow to resent his Old Dunbar ways in just four years' time.

In the late '60s, a group of students calling themselves the Modern Strivers began making demands of Tignor's administration. The first

Madison Tignor.
Courtesy of the Tignor family

demands were small—for example, music in the cafeteria. They became bigger: the inclusion of a black history course. By 1967, the list of demands had grown to include freedom to dress as they liked, wear political buttons and publish papers without censorship, organize groups, protest grievances, and listen to classroom speakers free of any prior censorship. The Modern Strivers also sought for students to choose all of their nonrequired courses. They called this their bill of rights.

The students also wanted to establish what they called a Freedom School. It would be a school within a school, focused on Afrocentric studies including black history, and offering Swahili as a language course. All through this process, a young teacher at the school named John Lord guided the teenagers; he became their advisor. Lord, a recent graduate of Amherst College, taught English and was white.

"Black is Beautiful and it is Beautiful to be Black" was the Strivers' credo.[28] They took their handle from the name given to a neighborhood of Washington, the Strivers section, settled in the early 1920s. The formerly white neighborhood had become home to black doctors, lawyers, government workers, and professors who moved in as they made it. Their homes were beautiful row houses with lovely gardens. Originally, the term "strivers" was meant to be negative, as if the people moving into the mixed-race area were striving to get away from less affluent people of color. A respected cultural writer and historian successfully countered this concept and promoted the idea that the blacks living there at the time—citing former residents Frederick Douglass and Charles Hamilton Houston as examples—were pioneers, striving for better things for all blacks.

The Modern Strivers saw themselves as pioneers on the forefront of a social and educational revolution. Their platform clearly stated, "We the Modern Strivers of Eastern High School, ask not for favors, we ask only for the return of our stolen education. We do not ask for a mountain, not for luxuries, but for a necessity. That necessity is an education, a meaningful education."[29]

The students were referring to two issues. The first was the post-desegregation practice of tracking. The superintendent of schools had introduced ability grouping, and students were funneled into one of four tracks: honors, college preparatory, general, and basic. Basic students were considered "mentally retarded but educable." In 1962, 99.99 percent of the children in the basic track were black.[30] Black children, who had received half—or sometimes just a third—of the time or quality of elementary education available to their white peers, were being shuttled into the lowest two categories. They never got a chance to strive for advanced education because the playing field wasn't just uneven, it had giant, gaping holes in it. Black activists called the tracking de facto segregation. They argued that segregation had perpetuated the black educational lag and that it wasn't possible to tell whether a black student's record was poor because he was a poor student or because he had attended such inferior schools.[31] Board of education member Julius Hobson sued the superintendent of schools to abolish the practice, and in 1967 he won. But for students like those juniors and seniors at Eastern High School, it was too late. They'd be stuck in the lower tracks for their whole lives.

The second issue of "stolen education" was the lack of black history taught in schools. The subject had been a part of both Dunbar and Armstrong's curricula. The Modern Strivers didn't just want black history taught here and there; they wanted a whole school within a school based on Afrocentric culture.

When the students did not get the results they desired, their response made it seem as though they had made a New Year's resolution for 1968. Every month from January 1968 on, they appeared before the board of education. On February 7, four Modern Strivers told the board that students should have the right to be involved in the recruitment and hiring of teachers and administrators for Eastern High School. They demanded an immediate reevaluation of Eastern's curriculum, and they submitted a proposal to establish the Freedom School. The leader of the group, a charismatic young man named Greg Taylor, singled out Principal Tignor in his remarks.

> I am a student at Eastern High School. I'd like to read a caption from the *Washington Post*. This story appeared on January 13th and was about the Eastern students' protest. Eastern's principal, Madison W. Tignor, said in this article and I quote: "The students have no right to be disappointed in the school as a whole just because the reading scores are low. They don't take into account the odds we're working against. . . . We have every kind of student at this school. Some come from fine professional homes, but we have many from other kinds of homes, you know."

I, myself, come from one of the other homes, my parents are not professional so what do you do with me? Am I inferior because I am not from a professional background? I, myself, believe that it is because you do not want me to be a professional person. Last year I wrote a letter of protest to a faculty member. The faculty member responded to my letter by saying, "You need to go back to the first grade because of the misspelled words. A first grader could have presented it better than you presented it to me."

My feeling about what she said was if I'm down and I want to get up, she is going to make it as difficult as possible for me to get up. I am a 19-year-old junior and too old to go back to elementary school, so what do you do? You give the so-called basic student, me, anything just enough to get me out of the way. I have been officially labeled basic since the first grade and I'm still unofficially now. As an example of this, I have been trying to go to college. But this is the program they gave me at the beginning of the year: 1st period, gym; 2nd period, applied math; 3rd period, lunch; 4th period, English; 5th period, U.S. history; 6th period, cooking; and 7th period, wood shop. I have had courses like cooking and woodwork all my life. In place of these courses, I could have taken a foreign language and a meaningful science course to help prepare me for college. But I know the answer now. I must depend on myself and not on the school system.

The Strivers-Tignor clash was a painful example of how the traditional approach and progressive approach to black self-determination were at odds in the 1960s. Up until then, education, education, education had been the bedrock of advancement. Academic achievement was the way that men and women like Houston and Hayes, Cooper and Terrell, Dykes and Davis had clawed their way up the social and economic ladder and forced the mainstream to accept them.

But the experiences of the current generation still living in the District were different. The decades of chronic underfunding of black schools by racist congressmen had produced two generations of angry and/or undereducated blacks in DC. But undereducated does not mean stupid or ignorant by a long shot. Students like the Modern Strivers knew and understood what had happened to them in the tracking system.

The generation that had had their opportunities scuttled and could not afford to leave DC wanted DC to bend to them. And they were the majority, so why not? They viewed the Dunbar generations as part of the problem. The description of Dunbar and its principles went from the "elite" to "elitist."

One school board member, a Dunbar graduate, supported the tracking system, calling it part of the "art of teaching."[32] The men and women who had graduated from Dunbar were recast as the lucky few who were not in touch with what being black in DC in the late '60s meant. However, it was an odd suggestion that people who had lived through legal segregation that could rob you of your house or your job, and could tell you where to eat and sit, didn't understand being black. The generations had different fights to fight.

Principal Tignor was a believer in a classical education. He had his standards, and he wanted the students to reach for those standards. He had done just that. He had come from humble beginnings without a father. He knew hard work was the way to succeed. Some of the suggestions, such as students swapping Swahili for French, seemed counterproductive. The idea of a separate school within a school was untenable. But there was one element of the whole Modern Strivers issue that really angered a normally even-tempered man: Madison Tignor was particularly irked with the student's advisor, Mr. Lord.

Gregory Tignor, Madison's son, is today a retired Yale professor. He can recall his father's anguish at the time. "I contend it was an era in which whites and blacks sponsored pseudo-freedom among black youth that was only going to be destructive in the long run. These white kids who had fun—I saw them at Yale—they could protest, they could lead. . . . They were great at it, and then when the stuff hit the fan, they could put on a suit and could go work for daddy. And black people had nothing like that. Now that is the frame of mind my father came from. You have to remember when he was born and what influences he came under. I have pictures of him with Du Bois, who was a hero. That was called radical stuff then. He expected discipline. In that era there was discipline. I mean a teacher at Dunbar got respect. It wasn't that they demanded it, they got respect."

The lack of respect from the students and Mr. Lord was foreign to Principal Tignor. He had gone out of his way to help the young teacher.

The Vietnam War was swallowing up young men who were drawn into the fight, and after Mr. Lord arrived at Eastern he asked Principal Tignor to write a letter to the draft board to get him out of service by saying he was a necessary part of the staff at Eastern. Gregory Tignor remembers it well: "I know this for sure. A white teacher came to him and said he was going to be drafted and he would do anything to avoid Vietnam. My father never helped us avoid military service; all three of us were in the military. But he wrote a letter to the draft board saying he was an essential part of teaching. Now draft boards in that era exempted people. The reason I know that is . . . it happened to me. I was at Yale, and I had a student come to me crying, he wanted me to write a letter saying how important he was as a teaching assistant."

But then Principal Tignor wrote a second letter to the Lansdowne, Pennsylvania, draft board on January 31, 1968.

As a patriotic gesture I am advising that I am withdrawing my request that Mr. John G. Lord Jr. be deferred from the draft. He has been a teacher of English in the Eastern High School on temporary status since September 1965.

Within two weeks John Lord learned from the draft board that he had been reclassified and why, and he took the issue to the board of education, the teacher's union, and the press. On March 12, 1968, the students of Eastern High School were asked to report to the auditorium. The students were informed that Principal Tignor was on an "extended" medical leave and the assistant principal would take over.

The audience responded with a mix of cheers and jeers. The Modern Strivers were in the first row of the auditorium when the announcement was made that Mr. Tignor was not returning. They stood and clapped.

Just a few days before, four hundred students had walked out of class during last period in support of Mr. Lord. Everyone knew from the accounts in the *Washington Post* that the teacher's union had called for Tignor's removal and the board was lukewarm in supporting him. John Lord had announced in a press conference that he was seeking a reversal of his draft status given what had taken place. When asked if he'd had any previous run-ins with Principal Tignor, he responded, "He once chided me for using the word 'stuff' to describe something in class."[33]

After the announcement of Principal Tignor's leave, students approached the stage with questions. A young woman took to the mic and looked at the Strivers' leader, Greg. She asked, "Do you think that it was because of you that Mr. Tignor did what he did?"

"I don't think it was because of the Modern Strivers," Greg responded to the girl. "The letter wasn't a very nice way to handle the situation."

A young boy named Dennis took to the microphone. "I'm speaking on behalf of the minority which feels that a school can be run by teachers and administrators alone. It's hard to get up and speak against a strong group like the Modern Strivers, but as far as I am concerned, you are striving in the wrong way."

Another Striver named Roger spoke up, saying, "We never claimed to be the majority. But if you look at the American Revolution or any other revolution, you will see that it is not the majority that compromise it but a hard-fighting minority."

"Mr. Tignor brought Eastern through many a crisis," another student added. "We should stand behind Eastern and we should stand behind Mr. Tignor because that's what he represents." The assembly ended, and it was clear Mr. Tignor would not return. He retired early.

Professor Gregory Tignor said of his father's last days at Eastern, "He couldn't cope. I think he just couldn't cope with what transpired."

Two weeks after the assembly, Dr. Martin Luther King Jr. was murdered and Washington, DC, imploded.

12 | NEW SCHOOL

BORN IN 1897, MRS. Mary Hundley lived long enough to bear witness to many transformational moments in history. She was twenty-three years old when women got the right to vote. She had lived through two world wars and saw a man land on the moon. In her own life she taught Latin and French at Dunbar for more than thirty years, wrote a book about the school, and was even involved in a breakthrough racial covenant case.

It is unlikely that Mrs. Hundley ever thought she'd live to see a wrecking ball hit Dunbar High School. But there she was, long retired and nearly eighty years old, watching the city leaders plan the demolition of a school she had witnessed being built, with a school culture she had helped to develop.

Mary Hundley was not having it. "There is no justification for destroying this famous school that is nationally known for training colored black youth for high education," Mrs. Hundley said to anyone who would listen—politicians, news reporters, former students. "For years it was the only opportunity for the development of these underprivileged boys and girls to their utmost potential."[1] Hundley's use of the word "colored," and her definition of underprivileged were signs of a divide within black Washington that was growing bigger with each decade.

The District was remaking itself in the 1970s after the explosion of rage, anger, and pain that manifested itself in three days of turbulence following Dr. King's murder. For four days starting on Thursday, April 4, 1968, Washington, DC, was heading full tilt toward self-destruction.

When the embodiment of hope was gunned down, a wave of despair flooded U Street. For generations, U Street had been the main artery of black-owned and black-run businesses, surrounded by lovely family neighborhoods full of Victorian row houses. Duke Ellington lived in the area. Langston Hughes did for a time. The Howard Theatre was where black Washington was able to see the best entertainers of the times. U Street was where you could find the barbershop of Gardner Bishop, the man who had joined forces with Charles Hamilton Houston to bring the landmark *Bolling v. Sharpe* case to its powerful conclusion.

Within seventy-two hours of Dr. King's death, U Street was burned out and the stores that were still standing had been looted. Ultimately 6,100 people were arrested, 900 stores were lost, 1,097 people were injured, and 12 were dead.[2] The armory at Dunbar was used as a staging area for the national guard. A fifteen-year-old Dunbar student went missing on the first night. He was last heard from when he called his mother to tell her that in the chaos he had gotten her some pantyhose, the kind she liked. His father was later called to identify his body.[3]

Lives were lost. Property was lost. And a reason to stay in DC was lost for black Americans who wanted to make a living, send their children to decent schools, and know their kids would come home safe.

In February 1968, just prior to the riots, the board of education had been following up on a two-year-old request for funds to modernize Dunbar High School. After fifty years of use, including some years of neglect, Dunbar High School was showing its age. The pool was in such bad shape it had to be closed; it was finally repaired only because private donors provided the money. New lighting had been installed in the labs. But these projects were just patchwork measures. The school needed a significant rehab.

The original request in 1966 was for $1.3 million to build a 65,994-square-foot, air-conditioned addition that would include thirty extra classrooms, double the gym space, and install fifteen hundred new lockers to accommodate another twelve hundred students.[4] Dunbar was going to be a huge school, as big as Eastern, capable of accommodating twenty-five hundred students. The plan was to spread the financing over two years, 1967 and 1968. There was some concern about building the new addition, as some houses in the neighborhood would have to be sacrificed, but the point became moot. Six months after the riots, the board of education requested funds to replace the 1916 building entirely.

A movement emerged to make the Shaw area around Dunbar a phoenix that would rise from literal ashes. The Shaw Urban Renewal program was launched to rework the neighborhoods that had suffered from the demise of the U Street commercial corridor and all the good things it attracted. The city planning commission created a whole proposal for a post-1968 version of the neighborhoods near Dunbar. The plan tackled parking spaces, affordable housing, and even the width of the sidewalks. The plan also stated that "obsolete schools should be eliminated and sites meeting established standards should be provided. New schools and associated play space and recreational facilities should be grouped as unified campuses to provide richer academic offerings and to provide economies in the use of scarce land."[5]

The 1916 building was a remaining piece of connective tissue to Old Dunbar. Many changes had come to the school in the years since legal segregation had been knocked down. The school now served one neighborhood, not the entire city. In the course of fifteen years, Dunbar had become an average public school in the sense that there were smart kids who did well and there were students who didn't care about their grades. There were students who were dedicated athletes and students who barely showed up. There were the well behaved and the disruptive. There were students from families who valued education and students whose parents did not. It was a general-population school, and all segments of the population were represented.

The change became evident almost immediately. In the fall of 1956 Principal Charles Lofton realized he now had students who had been robbed of a good early childhood education. In 1956, out of 110 new students, 108 came from other school systems, primarily the Deep South.[6] Lofton said the students were "ill prepared" as compared to students from Washington's "old order" homes. But he was hopeful, "Our new students are soon to pick up the ways of old students. . . . These students need love and affection because nine times out of ten, they aren't getting it at home. Once our faculty realizes these students aren't going on to college or professional careers and recognize the fact that they must work after graduation the biggest hurdle is over and we all pull together."[7] Lofton and his team did not lower standards for behavior. An anti-vandalism campaign was started. Attorney General Robert Kennedy was invited to the school to address the students. Dunbar still maintained a dress code: no jeans, and the young men were required to wear ties. Lofton reminded the students of the "thousands who have preceded you." Lofton did not find discipline to be a problem with some of the new transplants but Lofton did note that there was a problem "of economics." As the student body changed, so did the teaching staff. One 1962 Dunbar graduate told me she felt that some of the Dunbar teachers were snobby and just didn't want to teach neighborhood kids so they left for other jobs. Many of the greatest teachers who had taught at Dunbar for decades died in the 1960s. Anita LeMon, who went to Dunbar herself and taught Latin there since 1930, passed away in 1961. Clyde McDuffie, who taught French at M Street and Dunbar, departed this life. Other teachers, like Mr. Tignor, took advantage of new opportunities. Charles Lofton, a Dunbar graduate himself, had been the school's principal since 1948. He saw the school through the transition but then accepted a promotion in 1964 and left his post. Suddenly, there was a new group of educators on the scene.

The first officially elected school board flexed its muscle and decided that Dunbar was the definition of obsolete. The building in its current form didn't and couldn't address the needs of the modern student, and its history seemed as if it belonged to another school. This point—that Dunbar's days in the superlative category were over—was punctuated during the last week of 1969. At the end of a decade that brought change in how students were grouped, where they went to school, and what their neighborhoods looked like, the *Washington Post* ran a shocking and enormous headline that offended more than a few people: YEARS BRING CHANGE TO DUNBAR HIGH SCHOOL—"BLACK ELITE" INSTITUTION NOW TYPICAL SLUM FACILITY popped off the front page of the City Life section on Sunday, December 28, 1969. What a way to end the 1960s.

"It wasn't scary or anything. It was just seriously deteriorated. The trophy case just stopped at 1954," recalls Lawrence Feinberg, who wrote the article just over forty years ago.[8] "The school itself stopped functioning as a selective school. Blacks could go anywhere in the city, but it was no longer a selective academic high school." He called the change "ironic." After the reporter had observed Dunbar's high absenteeism and noisy halls, but generally orderly classrooms, for some reason Principal Howard F. Bolden was extremely candid with him.

Bolden had been the assistant principal at Dunbar for ten years, from 1953 to 1963. When Bolden took the the top post he found the school a different place. He had to deal with crime, specifically drug dealers in the area around the school. One Dunbar student left school at 10:20 AM, walked a few blocks, bought six capsules of heroin, and was back in class and high by 11:00 AM.[9] Five years after his return, Bolden felt compelled to tell the reporter, "The old Dunbar was no more like this school than it was like the man in the moon."[10]

Bolden was not a favorite of many of the students, including Blanche Heard (Dunbar 1969). She was a cute-as-a-button cheerleader, a class officer, and a budding activist. She organized a sit-in at Principal Bolden's door to protest the demolition of the school. She and her friends felt he did not fight for their school, "the castle" as she calls it, and that he didn't take the student's concerns about Dunbar seriously.

It was Principal Charles Lofton who had made the announcement to Dunbar students the day the big Supreme Court decision came down. Representative Eleanor Holmes Norton (Dunbar 1955) was there. "I remember that day because Charles Lofton made me remember," she said. "There was a gong, and Mr. Lofton said he wanted the attention of every student. He said the Supreme Court of the United States just declared school segregation to be unconstitutional. It was a moment that nobody who was there would ever forget. There were teachers who nearly cried. It was the kind of announcement you'd make at Dunbar and know everyone at Dunbar would understand what it meant to us. The point was, it was one of the great teaching moments of all time, and he understood it."[11]

Later in life Lofton reflected on what that day in May meant for Dunbar in the long term. "I wouldn't want it to go out that I'm not for integration—I am. I'm not for what it did to Dunbar and to students."[12] It is bitterly ironic that three of the key players in dismantling legal segregation—Charles Hamilton Houston, George E. C. Hayes, and Oliver Hill—learned their lessons at a school that became an unintended casualty of necessary civil rights action. The legal arguments that led to the 1954 rulings were compelling and correct—on paper. Fifteen years after *Bolling v. Sharpe*, the Washington schools were not integrated; they were simply legally desegregated. The "covert" segregation, as some called it, perpetuated the same problems in education.

By this point the tracking system had been abolished for two years and all levels of students were in classes together. It exasperated at least one teacher who would go on the record: "I don't care what Judge Wright says. How can you teach a class unless you group students?"[13] Some teachers were dedicated, and on the flip side were teachers who showed up just for the paycheck. This all played out at a school board meeting when a bright Dunbar senior named Deborah Powell got up to educate the board about what was and wasn't happening in the classrooms at Dunbar.

"Many of the teachers at Dunbar are inadequate. The Dunbar curriculum seems very limited, since they offer only three years of French." Powell had become upset when she discovered something as she was applying to colleges: one of her top choices required four years of a foreign language. She was out of luck because a fourth year wasn't even offered. "The number of counselors needs to increase. And board members should have a closer relationship with students by visiting the schools and talking with the students on our own ground."[14]

"Miss Powell, do you think that a student representative on the Board of Education would help to begin to communicate some of the problems you have mentioned?" asked a board member.

"Yes, but you, the board members, should come into the school, and meet the students on their own level. It would be a greater benefit."

"Do you think students should serve on the board?"

"It is a good idea but students who are failing would not likely be placed on the board and that type of student would probably have more to relate but would never have the chance because that student would not have an opportunity to serve on the board." Several teachers at the meeting agreed with the brave senior, except for one who told the board, "I do not think the children in Dunbar are as dissatisfied as they are in some of the other schools I have visited."

"The reason so many of the students aren't dissatisfied," Powell countered, "is because they did not know why they should be. They do not know how deprived or how remedial their preparation is until they go away to school to find out that they can just get by."

"Miss Powell," the teacher responded, "students have to do some things on their own and cannot sit by and wait for teachers to make assignments. They have to learn to read."

"Yes," Powell agreed, but she would not back down. "But that requires motivation, and unless a student was motivated, it wouldn't work. I have been lucky because I have been motivated."

At this point another board member jumped in with a provocative question. "Miss Powell, do you think students should be involved in the evaluation of teachers and principals?"

"Yes, the students really know a teacher after he or she has been taught for a semester. I would like to evaluate my teachers at Dunbar after four years, if I had the opportunity."

Dunbar High School was like any other community school—the highs, the lows, and the average. However, average was a concept that was anathema to pre-1954 graduates of the school. The columnist William Raspberry wrote about the change in Dunbar in the 1960s and '70s: "The idea of academic excellence that Dunbar symbolized has fallen victim to the sort of democratization that achieves equality by reducing everything to mediocrity."[15] Principal Bolden put it in much plainer terms. "Between the Old Dunbar and the New Dunbar, there's day and night."

Bolden was reassigned shortly after this article appeared, but he had identified the formation two groups of Dunbarites—Old and New—who would clash over the old and new building.

1971-73

The cover of the sleekly designed submission portfolio was blanketed with pixelated dots that spelled DUNBAR DUNBAR DUNBAR DUNBAR DUNBAR DUNBAR. There was one line of copy: DUNBAR SENIOR HIGH SCHOOL REPLACEMENT, WASHINGTON, D.C. The presentation's introductory page was an eye-popping orange sheet explaining the need for and scope of the new building. This was followed by forty-three pages of intricate detail about the facility that could be Dunbar Senior High School—no one could ever say they didn't know what they were getting. And no one really mentioned why Dunbar High School was now Dunbar *Senior* High School, but there it was in Neutra font on the front of the school.

The well-regarded firm Bryant and Bryant prepared the proposal, knowing that there were two audiences for this project. The introduction began, "Dunbar Senior High School is a historical institution in

Washington, D.C." for audience one. And then for audience two, the introduction continued, "The new demand on education and technological evolution have rendered the facility increasingly obsolete and the quality of program responsibility has been greatly restricted."

The school board had chosen the firm with input from the community. It seemed like a good fit. Brothers Charles and Edward Bryant had started their own firm in the 1960s and grown it into the largest black-owned architecture firm in the country. Their ultramodern work was on display around the District, and they seemed more than capable of handling the job.

The design presented took into account research by a Dunbar school planning committee, the administrators in charge of building and grounds for the city, and the "architectural convictions" of the firm Bryant and Bryant.[16] The sell's big finish included an explanation of the intermingling of progressive education pedagogy and a progressive building.

"The concept here is a school within a school. It is articulated in a vertical expression, and is urban oriented towards a more intensive use of a restricted site. We firmly believe that this approach to planning will yield a facility which will do justice to its history and in turn be one which the community, the School Board, Washington, D.C., and the architects will be proud to be associated with." No doubt if an old-school Dunbar graduate had proofread the plan, he or she would have informed the copy writer not to end a sentence with a preposition.

If you looked at the new Dunbar layout from above, the L-shaped complex comprised of hexagonal units looked a bit like a Buck Rogers–style ray gun. From the street level it resembled a bar graph: the length of the school was the x-axis, and the first wing to the left was about halfway up the y-axis. The academic tower in the middle spiked up ten stories high, the tallest bar on the imaginary graph, and then the next section of the school returned again to midlevel on the y-axis. The tall tower was the centerpiece of the school and it consisted of multiple levels and mezzanines connected by ramps. It was a single building complex made up of three components: The southern part of the complex housed the auditorium and art and music facilities. The central portion housed the adminstrative suite, career education area, and what were described as "learning centers" in the high-rise tower. The rest of the building was where you would find the physical education component. Starting at the top was the Penthouse West, then down to the Level Five Mezzanine West, Fifth Floor East, Fifth Floor West, Fourth Mezzanine East, Fourth Floor East, Third Mezzanine West, Third Floor East, Third Floor West, Second Floor East, Second Floor West, First Floor, Ground Floor, Second Basement, First Basement Ground, Basement One, and Basement. The designers claimed it would "present a more pleasant net psychological effect than a conventional space." The levels were stacked one on top of the other like a big concrete layer cake. In fact, almost everything about the school was concrete. The foundation would be made of reinforced concrete. The interior walls would be precast concrete slabs poured and formed off-site and installed later. The exterior walls called for brownish aggregate concrete, which had an industrial chic look because the smooth outside layer of the concrete had been removed to show a coarse, rough-hewn texture. The entryway floors were going to be a shiny composite material and the rooms carpeted. The doors were to be painted metal, and the roof was terne metal. These were all long-lasting materials if properly maintained. The school looked impenetrable. Given the violence in the area, that was a good thing; however, it did have a lot of exterior doors—ninety-seven of them.

The school would be so modern, so groovy, so contemporary, so thoroughly 1970s, from its architectural design all the way to its educational philosophy. The New Dunbar was designed around the educational concept of the moment: open classrooms. The reform movement had fallen head over heels with the British concept of open learning environments. Rather than the strict, formal model of a classroom, an open concept space didn't have any official delineated areas so that so-called learning communities could develop.

In theory, without strict walls, teachers and students could work back and forth between these learning communities. Good ideas could flow easily. Students could be put into flexible groupings, which could grow or shrink organically. To accommodate this plan for Dunbar's academic curriculum, the new school was designed with demountable partitions rather than walls. These were prefabricated walls that could be disassembled and relocated based on the needs of the classroom.

The design made an interesting statement about the times. While the interior was open, the exterior was a fortress, keeping the real world

Dunbar Senior High School opened in April 1977.

Courtesy of Charles Sumner School Museum and Archives

out there in the real world. The architecture critic for the *Washington Post*, who had seen the plans for Dunbar II, was all for the change it represented. "Its brick and mortar arrangement does away with the confining authoritarian rigidity of the old egg crate classrooms and recognizes the constant in our time is change and that education is a fluid process." In his review, the German-born critic also expressed fascination with the form of the new building. "New Dunbar is a container that will surely give most promising shape not only to the stagnant fluid of education in our ghettos but also to the life of the neighborhood."[17]

Dunbar II would be 354,896 square feet and take up 1.5 acres of the new 12.89-acre site. It would be fully air-conditioned, housing close to eighty rooms in different sections including labs, an auditorium, a pool, underground parking, and in a sign of the times, a day-care center. And a really big sports field.

One of the architects' stated objectives was to achieve "a dignified building located on the main thoroughfare to the Capitol."[18] For this to happen, the school would have to be built in a slightly different location. Bryant and Bryant proposed sliding the site of the building west and a little north, almost diagonal from where the current building stood. It was a radical move that would require completely shutting off O Street and putting the back end of the proposed football field right where the 1916 building had been. It had been a sore point for years that Dunbar did not have a regulation-size football field or stadium, even though the school was growing into a sports powerhouse. A little stadium and field had been constructed forty years before, when alumni raised the money themselves, but by the '70s the grounds weren't anything anyone would want to play on or sit in.

The challenge for the firm, aside from DC politics, was that the new facility needed to be ready before the old school could be razed, which was something the architects fully expected would happen. According to the Bryant and Bryant plans, Old Dunbar would have to go. The board of education and the National Capital Planning Commission signed off on the final site and building plans on January 4, 1973.

It seemed like a fait accompli until a former Dunbar French teacher said, *Arrêt!* Mary Hundley and her supporters, who opposed Dunbar's demolition, had two things on their side: bad accounting and a fierce command of the English language.

1974

The accounting issue became clear almost immediately. In mid January 1974, Board of Education President Marion Barry received a letter from the director of the general services office with bad news—about $1.9 million worth. The amount of money approved by Congress for the project was simply not enough. The budget for the new Dunbar school project was $17,353,000. The lowest of the bids submitted by six different construction firms was $19,493,000. That bid covered everything on the wish list: the building of the new school, the interior amenities, the tennis courts, basketball courts, track, football field, stadium and electronic scoreboard, plus a contingency amount of $600,000.

Given the approved budget, there was only enough funding to cover the basics, the building and basketball and tennis courts. The director stated clearly, "The demolition of the original building, the building of the stadium, and the track cannot now be awarded." The catch was that the $19.4 million bid was only guaranteed for the next sixty days. And it could easily climb. The city council needed to find the money fast, and the best way to do that would be to shave money off existing, approved finances rather than risk the time and effort to get congressional approval of a whole new budget. The director of general services wrote to Barry, "We will initiate reprogramming action to obtain the necessary funds."

A few weeks later at a board of education meeting, the chair of the Dunbar Community Committee for the new school knew something was up. He said the committee wanted answers to the following questions:

1. When could the groundbreaking be expected?
2. Had the contracts for construction been negotiated?
3. Had all support facilities such as gas, water, electricity, and sewage been completed?
4. What channels are available to the New Dunbar Committee for seeking up-to-date information?
5. In the event that they run into a money problem, were there other funds available?
6. Had the architects, Bryant and Bryant, completed all contractual obligations so far as plans were concerned for the new building?

The stenographer taking down notes said the questions would be transcribed and presented to the administration in the morning.

This glitch in the financing gave the "save our school" faction time to show the world the fine work of the English teachers at Dunbar. A legion of excellent and extremely opinionated writers unleashed a letter-writing campaign. Over two hundred letters were sent to civic leaders, the mayor's office, and the planning commission. Mary Hundley personally wrote to all of the District's television and radio stations and newspapers, and she activated Dunbar alumni groups. The letters poured in from alumni.

Former Tuskegee Airman Dr. Roscoe Brown, now the director of the Institute for Afro-American Affairs at New York University, wrote that he was shocked and dismayed at the thought of Dunbar's demise.

> As one of the literally thousands of Dunbar graduates who gained their personal competence and sense of Black pride and awareness from their years at Dunbar, I sincerely hope that this decision will be reconsidered. I am certain that the city planner in the District of Columbia can find alternate plans to avoid the destruction of this landmark of Black education.

From Henry Robinson, PhD, professor at Morgan State College:

> If it is at all possible to save the building, please let's do so. If it is only possible to save the main entrance, incorporate it into the new building, then I believe we should work for that goal. To completely destroy an historical landmark like the Dunbar High School runs counter to all the values and tradition, which we alumni have been taught. Would you please reconsider the decision, which I understand has already been taken by the District of Columbia Establishment to demolish our alma mater?

Dr. Montague Cobb, who was about to assume the role of NAACP president, called it an unbelievable paradox and a terrible contradiction that Dunbar would be torn down.

> The government of the District of Columbia, whose officials are now mostly black, should be moving to destroy the only symbol of black excellence in the City, one unique in the country and in the world.

And he offered a comparison, without irony but with a dose of hyperbole.

> Would the Greeks allow the destruction of the Parthenon? . . . In the People's Republic of China all the ancient buildings of the Forbidden City of Peking are intact and well maintained and every Chinese child is made familiar with the whole range of achievements of the oldest continuous civilization in the world, along with the accomplishment since the Revolution of 1949. Also, St. Basil's off Red Square in Moscow has not been torn down just because it represents a Christian Institution.

The historical significance of the school was impossible to dismiss. Even those who wanted the new football field and stadium acknowledged it. But there was something else to this fight, something more emotional that would cause each side to dig in. It was the twisted assumptions of superiority and inferiority that pushed people apart and was causing strife for black Washingtonians. The nasty, gooey issue of intraracial class politics was revealed in a letter from a representative of the class of 1934.

> People new to the Washington scene cannot appreciate the tradition and sentiment associated with Dunbar High School. . . . At a time when Blacks are searching for their roots in Africa, we seem to be hell bent on obliterating a portion of our American Black heritage. The architectural beauty of Dunbar High School alone is enough to have it declared a landmark. Unlike the European tradition, reverence for the past does not seem to be a part of the American value system.

The old guard had grown up in segregation when the black community, on some level, was one. They still thought of Dunbar as a beacon of possibility for all black people. They were proud of the fact that despite the law and despite all notions that black children couldn't learn, not only had they learned, they had excelled. The letter referred to "*our* American Black heritage" (emphasis mine).

But those identified in the letter as "new" might just as well have considered Dunbar's past as part of someone else's heritage, not their own.

They had not been included in the pre-1954 bubble around Dunbar. Their educations had suffered from their parents only being allowed to attend school for two or three hours a day, if they could attend school at all. For a large swath of DC circa the mid-1970s—when its 71 percent black population earned it the nickname Chocolate City—Dunbar seemed to represent parts of black American history that should be forgotten: segregation and even elitism. "A reservoir of nostalgia for a segment of the D.C. populace" is what the new superintendent of the DC schools, Barbara Sizemore, wrote about Dunbar in a letter to the board of education.[19]

Mary Hundley's response: "Don't listen to that Barbara Sizemore, she's only been here four months."[20]

The *Washington Star News* sided with the preservationists. It called upon the city council to be imaginative and show a little effort toward investigating possibilities other than demolition. But it was the cartoon accompanying the editorial that captured the moment. It was of a conservatively dressed black teacher, a lady of a certain age, wearing sensible shoes and a demure dress with the words "Dunbar Alumni" hidden in the dress's pattern. She holds a ruler in one hand, and with the other hand grabs the ear of a large man, dragging him along. The man has a small Afro and wears a leisure suit with platform shoes. He holds a folder that reads, TEAR DOWN DUNBAR HIGH SCHOOL, and the words SCHOOL BOARD are on his jacket. The caption underneath is assigned to the older teacher. It reads "You'll thank me for this one day!"

A week before the DC council would vote on whether or not to "reprogram" funds, Mrs. Hundley pulled out her big gun, a former student of hers who was by then a US senator. After a series of very lovely and carefully worded letters between the former teacher and pupil, Senator Brooke said he would be glad to weigh in on the issue. Showing his considerable deftness and walking a fine line, Ed Brooke, the alum, typed a personal note on the letterhead of Edward W. Brooke, the senator, and sent it off to the mayor of Washington, DC.

Dear Walter,

I am sure Mary Hundley has already contacted you in her efforts to save Dunbar High School from demolition.

As a Dunbar graduate, I would like to lend my voice to Mary's in the hope that a consideration be given to designating the old building as an historic site and incorporate the structure in plans for the new school. While I would not like to deprive future Dunbar students of a football field, I would hope that an alternative site for the field could at least be explored. Dunbar is so rich in the history of the District of Columbia and Black Americans that it should not be demolished without a full hearing.

I would most appreciate your thoughts on the fate of Dunbar and ways we might be able to spare its apparent fate.

With warm regards,

Sincerely,

Ed Brooke

And just to make sure the point stuck, Senator Brooke's colleague, Senator Ted Kennedy, took up the cause for a moment. On March 27, 1974, Senator Kennedy entered into the official congressional record a newspaper article about the Dunbar demolition issue.

"Mr. President, I would like to enter in the record an account," said Senator Kennedy addressing Senate President Gerald Ford. "A proposal to replace one of the oldest high schools in Washington, D.C., Dunbar High School, [which] has become a historical landmark in the eyes of many Washingtonians because it serves as the training ground for so many men and women who are today prominent Americans." Not once during his short speech did the senator mention race.

On April 1, 1974, the DC City Council rejected the "reprogramming" of $1.4 million to demolish Dunbar. Three of the nine federally appointed council members were Dunbar alumni. They, along with a deluge of correspondence, persuaded the other six members that Dunbar I was worth saving in some capacity. However, at least one of the council members wasn't sure they had done the right thing. Sterling Tucker told the press, "The building has seen its day."[21] The council did approve the additional money to complete the building of the new school, just not the money to demolish Dunbar and build the stadium. But it was a statement made by one of the council members that nailed why there was such a harsh reaction to those who wanted to save the building. Dr. Marjorie Parker (Dunbar 1932), a council member and a lifelong Republican who had been appointed by President Nixon, said that day, "Black history, black culture, black heritage did not begin with Cornelius Green and the Green Bay Packers."[22]

But this wasn't over. Shortly after the denial of the funds, the board of education renewed its call for the new school. Reverend Ray Kemp was chairman of the Capital Outlay Committee. A known civil rights advocate, Reverend Kemp told the board that any compromise on the design of the building at this point would be "very severe and costly."[23] Reverend Kemp had at one time gone by Dunbar every day on his way to school. "It was classic," he said. "I would see the cheerleaders out there. Go big D. Go Red." He was one of the progressive young idealists on the school board who wanted to do what they believed to be good things. "I thought the children needed a better facility," he explained. "That's it."

This had been a close call for the Dunbar preservationists. They couldn't rest now. The mayor could still ask the city council to reconsider the reprogramming for the next fiscal year. Plan A was for the alumni to start researching viable alternatives for the location of the sports field. Along the way, comments like Dr. Parker's cast them in the role of out-of-touch old people who wanted to deprive young students of their athletic field. Plan B was to formally pursue registering Dunbar I as a DC landmark. Hundley and her supporters hoped it could become a library, museum, or exam school. "I could never see any route to what they wanted that was even remotely feasible. And, by the way, no developer wanted to do anything over on First Street Northwest in those days," remarks Bill Treanor.

Treanor was on the board of education from 1973 to 1977, and he remembers Dunbar I being in bad shape, a rambling old structure past its prime as a facility. When he joined the board he was surprised this hadn't all been figured out long before, given that they were on the verge of breaking ground on Dunbar II. "The only thing that was left was what to do with the old one, which should have actually been dealt with years before. It was just a testament to the paralysis of the system. They should have been tearing down the old one at the same time they were putting up the new one so they could put the fields in right away."

A funny thing happened during all of the commotion over this little piece of land: democracy. A month after the council's decision to deny the funds for demolition, Washington DC's home rule went into effect. For the first time, the current population of DC could vote and elect a city council and mayor. In various configurations and ways, up until 1973 Congress and/or the president selected the leaders of DC. Now, for the first time in DC, everyone had a voice. The majority in DC had spoken. When the new city council was elected, there was not one Dunbar graduate on it.

There were three ways the decision about Dunbar could go. Would the DC council get its reprogrammed money, would Dunbar I gain landmark status, or would Dunbar II be completed before the problem was resolved? The answer: yes.

Within weeks of Dunbar being designated a DC landmark, the newly elected city council approved the reprogrammed funds for fiscal year 1976. It was expected that the money would become available about the time the stadium bleachers were being installed. The elected officials believed they had won, and it was all over.

1976

The mayor's office made a big mistake: it did not respond to a letter from DC's landmark commission. Now that the building was a Category II local landmark, the commission required there to be substantive discussion about alternatives. When the government of the District of Columbia, the owner of Dunbar I, sent in its application to raze the building officially located at 1320 First Street NW, Lot 857, Square 544, the application was denied. The city was informed that officials at the DC Landmarks Commission and the State Historic Preservation Office deemed that demolition of the building would be contrary to public interest and should be delayed for 180 days so that alternatives could be discussed further.

The State Historic Preservation Office acknowledged all the reasons the District of Columbia presented for demolishing the building: unavailability of an alternative site, cost and hardship of relocating families to provide an adequate site, cost of rehabilitation and maintenance should Old Dunbar stand, and desire to provide new academic and athletic facilities for the next generation. The official preservationist said the purpose of the six-month delay period was to afford enough time to resolve all issues. On March 23, 1976, the following was ordered:

The State Historic Preservation Officer is of the opinion that the demolition of the building should be delayed for 180 days to permit [the official preservationist] and the professional review committee to negotiate with the owner or owners of the building and civic groups, public agencies, and interested citizens to find a means of preserving this building. Ordered: The issuance of a permit to raze is DELAYED for 180 days from the date of this order.

At this point, the pro-demolition forces had been outwitted and outlobbied by a group of septuagenarians who knew how to use language and litigation to sway opinion.

As the public fight lingered on, proponents of the new school became more visible. In the papers, for every pro-preservation letter to the editor that appeared there now seemed to be a case made for the demolition—and a case made against the legend of Old Dunbar. In one day on the *Washington Star*'s letters to the editor page, these three letters were printed:[24]

On the last day of school I sheepishly appeared in the office of the dour Walter Smith, principal of Dunbar High School, to inform him that, out of economic necessity, I must quit school and go to work. He listened at first incredulously, then realized I was indeed serious. He began to lecture me in a fatherly way on the course I had in mind. I told him that I had had no choice; I had to help support our large family. He just shook his big black head and wished me well.

A man who identified himself as having a wife and children who had gone to the school felt this way about good Old Dunbar.

I am not so sure we want to preserve those traditions of segregated education and black elitism for which Dunbar stood. Many of us remember well when Dunbar was a school for the children of the black bourgeoisie when light skin and good hair and family were paramount prerequisites for admission and success. Many black kids went to other schools and "made it" also.

And this letter came from a Granville Woodson (Dunbar 1926), who happened to be the assistant superintendent in charge of buildings and grounds for the city:

We must remember the new Dunbar is for young people beginning their education and for the thousand more not yet born. It is not for those of us with only a few years to live. The young need and should have the best high school we can provide and not an unnecessary compromise based on dubious emotional rhetoric.

Sixty current Dunbar students protested the 180-day delay by showing up unannounced at the mayor's office and demanding to talk to him. His response was, "I'm with you."[25] Nothing happened in the 180 days; spring turned to fall, and the city seemed to be running out the clock. The new school was set to open in the new year, about six months away, yet the old school loomed in the background. The council hoped to get Dunbar I down by April 1, 1977, during spring break.

1977

After the 180-day delay came and went, the alumni association filed suit in the DC Superior Court for an injunction to stop the April 1 demolition. The alumni claimed city officials had not adhered to the Landmark Commission's conditions. There was no evidence of open, good-faith meetings or discussions of alternatives to knocking down Dunbar. A judge gave the city a week to produce proof of any such meetings or provide any transcripts of public hearings held for concerned citizens to discuss options for a DC landmark. City officials failed to provide any such evidence. The judge issued an order to stop the demolition of Dunbar High School until three public hearings were held and the city fulfilled its obligation to make a good-faith effort to hear plans to save the landmark. Old Dunbar was still standing on the day New Dunbar opened.

"We have been second-class citizens too long. Now we have a building that's first class, and we must have pride in it!" announced Principal Phyllis Beckwith to her students—or at least she said it to the ones who showed up for the opening day of Dunbar II. Attendance was off by 20 percent that first day, Tuesday, April 12, 1977. At that point, the auditorium wasn't quite done, and the budget had climbed to $20.6 million.[26] Still, it was an exciting and slightly confusing time. The new building was big—big enough for 1,500 students, and the current population was 1,350.

Students were given a handbook with eleven floor plans so they could find their way around the huge campus. For lunch in the cafeteria, head to Third Floor West. For the library, take a ramp to Second Floor East. The main office was on the first floor in Building B. It was ramps up and ramps down, past all the classrooms in the big tower. By midafternoon, a few kids had turned off the escalators. Apparently the easy proximity of an emergency button was too big a temptation for some teenagers. The problem continued throughout the year, so much so that the student newspaper took a stand on the issue. "The students should be more mature and learn that responsibility plays an important role in their lives," wrote the assistant editor of the *Dunbar Newsreel*. "If the immature students play with the escalators for kicks, imagine how the school will look before the end of the year!"[27]

The building was an experiment with a new way to use space as part of the teaching plan, and the students and faculty were excited. The noise level might be an issue, but everyone assumed they would get used to it. The teachers didn't have a choice because the walls didn't reach the ceiling and a maintenance worker was needed to adjust the partitions. One outstanding issue loomed larger than the rest. "We need our athletic field." Beckwith wanted her school complete. "Who ever heard of a school in this day and age without an athletic field?"[28]

This time the city followed all the rules. Three meetings. Well advertised. Very public. The requirements were specifically these:

> The owner of the building, the Government of the District of Columbia, has proposed the demolition of the building. D.C. regulation 73-25, as interpreted by the court in *Dunbar High School Alumni Association et al v. Government of the District of Columbia* as requires the State Historic Preservation Officer and the Joint Committee on Landmarks of the National Capital to negotiate with the owner, civic groups, public agencies, and interested citizens to find a means of preserving the building. Participants are requested to direct their comments to the question of realistic alternatives to demolition."

What happened next would come down to semantics. Long before there was any debate about what the definition of "is" is, the two sides in

Alumni v. City had very different understandings of the words "negotiate" and "realistic."

By the end of the three mandated meetings, all fifteen alternatives presented to the city by concerned citizens were rejected. Among the suggestions were to place the stadium/field on an angle in a northeast/ southwest direction and only remove 15 to 20 percent of Old Dunbar; to have Dunbar use RFK Stadium; and to convert Old Dunbar into a community center or an administration building for the board of education, which was currently renting space there. The city had tables, charts, facts, and figures to explain why every suggestion was not a cost-effective, *realistic* alternative.

When the city returned to the court with proof it had adhered to all the requirements put forth by the judge and the various preservationist organizations, the Dunbar alumni tried one last maneuver. The group filed a motion objecting to the city's position that it had *negotiated* in good faith. The alumni's motion even included *Merriam-Webster*'s definition of "negotiate": "conferring with another so as to arrive at the settlement of some matter."[29] The alumni plaintiffs believed the city had never given any serious thought to any of the suggested alternatives or presented a single new option, and that the person presiding at the meetings worked for the city, which meant he was inherently biased. It was a last-ditch attempt to keep the demolition ban in place. The motion read:

> The plaintiffs request that this motion be therefore not granted but that instead this court should require all parties to return to the bargaining table, with a truly neutral person designated by this court to preside at the negotiation sessions.

Judge Harold Greene's mandate was to rule on the law, not on the actual issue of whether or not Dunbar High School was worthy of saving. Judge Greene ruled the city had met its obligation and engaged in "meaningful negotiations."

On Thursday, June 2, 1977, Judge Greene lifted the ban on the demolition of Dunbar. The first wrecking ball hit the building that weekend.[30]

13 | CHILDREN LEFT BEHIND

2008

Michelle Rhee, the lightning-rod chancellor of the DC schools, told me she respected the history of Dunbar High School. "I had definitely heard about the school and knew its kind of longstanding reputation before. And then I also knew that in the 2000s the school had really gained a reputation as being one of the lowest-performing high schools in the city."

Almost exactly thirty years to the day that the wrecking ball toppled Old Dunbar, Rhee was appointed the DC schools chancellor, arriving on the scene in June 2007 like an ER crash unit. Many of the city's public schools had been left for dead, too sick to cure, or too far gone to bring back to life. Dunbar was one of the particularly ill patients.

"When I took over it was a school that had not met an adequate yearly progress in more than five years, which means that according to the No Child Left Behind Act, it was categorized as a failing school that they were mandating restructuring in. And if you looked at the achievement levels of the kids in that school, they were dismally low."

The achievement data coming out of Dunbar revealed that the basics were just not there. In English, only 21.79 percent of students were proficient, with 1.07 percent considered advanced. In math, 18.57 percent tested proficient and just 0.36 percent advanced.[1] That meant only three or maybe four Dunbar students could solve an advanced math problem. The brightest kids at Dunbar were the minority. And those who did well at the school weren't up to national standards. One student, a girl who worked hard, participated in clubs, earned good grades, and was in the top ten of her class, scored in the mid-400s on both her math and English SATs. The handful who were recruited to very competitive colleges were outliers. By 2007–08, in fifteen categories rating school quality, Dunbar scored unsatisfactory and unsound in eight, and only partially up to standard in the other seven.[2] It was found that:

> Dunbar did not meet one standard for a successful school.
> . . . The administration does not always use a systematic, school wide approach for supporting teachers and meeting student needs.
> . . . Efforts to implement consistent professional development program are fragmented, ineffective, and void of any staff input.
> . . . Although valiant efforts are being made to successfully manage the open space environment all stakeholders have voiced concern regarding the extreme challenges and dangers that student and teacher face each day in this unique learning community.[3]

It is extremely unfair to single out Dunbar High School's recent record, however. The school is like so many other urban schools in economically distressed areas, absorbing the blows of drugs, violence, and dysfunction. A list of statistics showing the problems with the DC school system could fill its own book. In the year Rhee took over, DC seniors scored the second-lowest SAT verbal scores in the country and the lowest math scores. The national average of high school graduates who currently enroll in college is 48 percent. In Washington, that number is 29 percent, and only 9 percent of those enrollees make it to college graduation.[4]

A concrete example of Dunbar's place in the DC academic landscape was revealed by a *Washington Post* reporter. Jay Matthews, who covers education for the newspaper described Dunbar this way: "Dunbar is your classic inner-city school with well-meaning teachers who have—who've been given no mandate to raise standards, and so they've limped along with their little engineering program." To give an indication of the school's academic health, Matthews pointed to a practical example: how few students took advanced placement tests. "AP is a good measure of their efforts to prepare kids for college, and they were doing next to zip.

You know, twenty kids were taking an AP test, and none of them were passing, and that didn't seem to bother anybody. They were happy to have a few of them taking AP, but [there was] no real determined effort to raise the school up to a new level."

The principal was bothered but appeared resigned.[5] Principal Harriet Kargbo's daily professional life was tough. A reporter covering DC schools pointed to Dunbar to get the flavor of a DC high school poised for transition. She told him, "The mentality of excellence? . . . We wish we could have that. . . . But this is the reality."[6] She was referring to the metal detectors. Earlier in the year, nineteen Dunbar girls had been arrested for fighting. When he asked about the smell of pot in the hallways, she didn't acknowledge the telltale odor.[7]

Kargbo was dealing with other safety issues. Armstrong, Dunbar's former counterpart, was abandoned and had become a way station for the homeless and drug addicts. The schools are adjoined, and some of the vagrants were migrating onto Dunbar's campus, setting up mattresses near the back doors of the school. And given the inadequate maintenance of the building, not all of the ninety-seven doors closed.[8] It was a wonder Kargbo could do her job—or maybe she didn't do it. The very afternoon on which she gave the reporter the tour of Dunbar, Kargbo was fired.[9] She was one of twenty-four principals ousted by the end of May 2008.[10]

The twenty-first century Dunbar High School wasn't a particularly special case, and that is what made its condition sad, because it had once been a very, very special place. The only thing the school had in common with its former incarnation was that the population was still all black.

Rhee was not afraid to introduce race into the conversation and was clear about the disparity in DC. "We have, in some circumstances, 70 percentage points' difference between our white kids and our black kids, and that makes me so angry. This is the result of the adults in this system not doing their jobs."[11]

However, one thing was obvious about Dunbar's situation: the physical plant itself. "I don't know if you've been to the school recently," Rhee added, "But we often say that whoever designed and built this building did not like children. It's this concrete structure that looks like an institution of some kind. It is not conducive to learning. It's not the kind of place that you would look at and say, 'Oh, I want my kid to go to school in that facility.'"

That might be the one thing Michelle Rhee said during her explosive tenure that almost everyone would agree upon. People said Dunbar looked like a parking garage and worse. "It looks like a prison," one alumnus said, echoing many others who observed the same thing. "What kind of message does that send to our children?"

The Dunbar building serves as a bit of a warning about the pitfalls of considering the now and not the future. In the 1970s, the energy crisis was at the top of most people's minds, so the school was built with very few windows in an effort to conserve energy. It was also built with the 1968 riots in the not-so-distant past. So much had been broken in the black community, and this was a concrete fortress, a muscular monument that could not be penetrated. In the 1970s, brutalist architecture like this (from the French *béton brut*, meaning raw concrete) was cutting edge, but its aesthetic appeal aged about as well as the avocado-colored refrigerator and the orange shag rug. And no building can function, or at the very least look good, if it is not maintained. From 2002 to 2007 there were ninety-three open repair requests for the school. Some were routine—a broken intercom or faucet. But many were urgent—siding hanging off the exterior of the building; no working shower in the locker room; dangling, broken windows.[12]

The outside was not pretty, but what was happening inside was uglier in some ways. On any given day students could and would wander the halls, wings, and mezzanines, cursing their way up and down the five ramps that traversed the building. Who knew when the escalators had last worked? The grooves on the steps were jammed with wrappers and paper. An evaluation of the school revealed, "The condition of the building demonstrates at least a lack of respect for a learning environment, and at most a physical hazard to the students and the staff."[13]

And then there were the walls. Or lack of walls. Another holdover from the 1970s was the momentary fascination in education circles with the open classroom methodology. Forty years later, the lack of barriers in the urban school opened up the building, grounds, and students to constant disruption. Dunbar's teachers complained of noise and students wandering in and out of each other's classes. Some teachers went as far as to create makeshift walls just to define their own space.

One thing Dunbar did have was a really nice football field. One of the main reasons the 1916 building had been torn down was to accommodate the athletic teams. The field got a lot of use, and it was important. For a lot of students, sports was a way to a scholarship or of staying out of trouble or of creating some kind of family if the structure at home wasn't there. Dunbar was a powerhouse when it came to sports. Between 2005 and 2011, the girls track team had racked up twenty-eight cross-country and track titles.[14] Today, Dunbar has one of the best high school football teams in the country. The Dunbar Crimson Tide made it to the citywide championships in eleven consecutive years, winning over half the games to be the district champs. The NFL is home to Dunbar alumni Vontae Davis, Vernon Davis, Arrelious Benn, Joshua Cribbs, and Nate Bussey. The sports teams have come a long way from the days when they were called the Poets. But when it came to academics, back in the day, the Poets were champions.

"I think it was a school that many people who have lived in this city for a long time—people kind of used to sort of orient me to kind of what had happened to the school district overall in the city. And they just sort of used Dunbar as a sort of prime example of that," Rhee recalled as more and more e-mail pings rang from her computer. She was a master multitasker.

> They said years ago Dunbar was a place where African American students could get an excellent education, and though the city's school system was largely segregated at that time, it was not only a place where learning was going on, but [one] that produced a significant number of some of the most premier African American scholars today. And then they sort of described from that as the kind of pinnacle high point to where it had gotten when I took over was this sort of nosedive over time, and that there was this huge desire to sort of see a rebirth or a regrowth of that institution in particular to go back to sort of glory that it once had.

The economic and social woes of DC were Dunbar's woes. As Dunbar became a neighborhood school, the neighborhood's problems became Dunbar's problems. On a Wednesday morning, January 26, 1994, gunshots were heard on the third floor of Dunbar High School. The shooter ran down the stairs and out of the building where the shooting continued— fourteen more shots. The seventeen-year-old shooter was charged with assault with a deadly weapon. The incident had allegedly begun as words over a girl.[15] A few days later, Vice President Al Gore traveled the two miles to Dunbar to visit the school and talk to the students about what had happened and about their safety in school. A handpicked group of students was invited to give Gore their perspective about gun violence and how they felt as teenagers. One senior asked a very direct question to the sitting vice president. Alenia Fowlkes looked at him and asked, "What are you going to do? . . . And when are you going to do it?"[16]

Years later, thirty-six and a clothing designer, Lena remembered that day. "Of course I was nervous—it was the vice president of the United States. I almost chickened out. But there were so many young people, we were losing each other. Every week there was a report of who got shot. I remember my first year in college I returned home for at least three or four funerals. Most of them were drug related. Three young men. It was sad. It was really sad."

Although only a teenager, Lena was wise enough to not let the opportunity go by as just an I-feel-your-pain photo-op. She found the backpack checks, metal detectors, and lockdown drills disconcerting. She had the chance to perhaps, in some small way, make a difference. "I hope he was listening, and I think that was one of the reasons why the question was so provocative. I wasn't the only person to ask a question of that nature, but I was the only one who said it with such simplicity. He is a politician, and they are infamous for roundabout answers, pacifying answers. It was such a simple question. As kids, you just want a straight answer." The students' doubt did not go unnoticed. A day after the visit a memo was sent from Keith Boykin, a young African American aide, to then–White House advisors Ricki Seidman, George Stephanopoulos, Mark Gearan, and Alexis Herman.[17]

When Vice President Gore on Thursday visited Dunbar High School, the scene of a schoolyard shooting the day before, students reacted skeptically. "What happens tomorrow?" one student asked. "What happens after the press is gone?"

In response to the students, Gore said crime bills being considered by Congress would put more police on the streets and could pay for more metal detectors for schools. However, "he made no proposals that would specifically help Dunbar," the *Washington Post* reported.

Before the Vice President left the event, several students virtually cried and pleaded to him. "Don't forget us. Don't forget our faces. Don't forget the fear," one girl said as network TV cameras recorded the exchange.

The fear, distrust, and cynicism felt by our youth is alarming and must be addressed. These kids are no doubt impressed by the stature of the White House, but they also know that their real life concerns will not be eliminated by photo ops and compassionate rhetoric.

The issue mattered to her because Lena really loved her school. The violence in the school and neighborhood was incongruous with her experience. From her perspective, Dunbar was "awesome." She wasn't from the area and had tested into Dunbar's rigorous pre-engineering program. The magnet program focused heavily on the sciences and was partially financed by corporate sponsors—General Motors, IBM, Potomac Electric, and METCOM. It had been set up in 1982 by the superintendent, Floretta McKenzie, and Dunbar's principal, Thomas Harper.

The first pre-engineering class had fifty students. "We had physics. We had Calc II. Statistics. Differential equations. It was tough, but it was a lot of fun," said Lena. "We kind of felt like we were all in it together. I liked math from the creative part. I was interested in the hands-on part." She couldn't believe the troubles Dunbar was facing. "It was awesome, everything you could want or needed. It was so good at the time, I thought it would go on forever—youthful naïveté." Lena had been encouraged by how much DC had improved in the early 1990s. The drug epidemic of the 1980s was waning in school in her opinion. She loved the fact that Dunbar's athletic teams were so great. She just wanted to be a teenager.

Many kids did live their lives that way, not wearing Kevlar to school. A '90s yearbook offers a snapshot of what was on young Dunbar students' minds at the time. Normal teenage stuff.

In: Tommy Hilfiger	Out: Calvin Klein
In: HBCU	Out: Ivy League
In: Your hair	Out: Store hair

"It was the best of times and worst of times. There was a day care for all the young mothers. There was a strict lockdown rule. You couldn't go out at lunchtime because we had drive-by shootings. There was a student who was paralyzed from the waist down. If you pop a balloon, everyone would hit the deck. We were trained to clear out."

In looking back, Lena really believed that despite the societal issues in the 1980s, kids at New Dunbar could get a good education. She earned a great scholarship and maintained nothing but love for her alma mater. "It was probably more rosy than one might think. Dunbar was a beautiful, state-of-the-art facility when I was there." No longer full of youthful naïveté but with the wisdom of an adult, she added, "Yes, there were dark spots—some scars last forever."

"For me it was all about getting out of the ghetto. I can't play basketball, and I can't sing, so I got to figure some way out." Ron Worthy laughed, but he was very serious about how pivotal the Dunbar pre-engineering program had been in shaping his life. Unlike the general population at the school, like Lena he had access to advanced math, more science, dedicated computer classes, engineering drawing, physics, and advanced-placement courses and options.

"Math and science was the thing. Engineering was how I was going to get out of the 'hood." Like Lena, Worthy had lived in another neighborhood and tested into the program in the 1980s. He was the valedictorian for the pre-engineering program as well as the general population. But before he went to college, he had one debt to settle. "I was forced to work in General Motors in Michigan because they were private partners for pre-engineering. After I graduated, within two days I was in Detroit. The idea was 'We [GM] are giving you guys computers. . . . Your top guys need to come here.' " It was just a couple of months, and soon after he would be a freshman at Stanford.

Worthy recognized that he had been fortunate to make it into the magnet program at Dunbar given that he had gone to school during the time of DC's drug epidemic. "You got a lot drugs—this was in the middle of crack. There was a lot going on externally, so that kids are either guys . . . selling the drugs and the girls [who] are trying to be with drug dealers because they got money. So if you are poor . . . you want to be around money. Socially, for me, it was difficult because I was a hard-core nerd, aggressive nerdy."

The nerd thing worked out well for him. After business school he got involved with an up-and-coming thing called the Internet. Long story short, Ron helped facilitate the $80 million acquisition of Blackpeople meet.com by Match.com and now runs his own consulting firm.

Worthy's high school success came down to his own motivation and what he described as "solid" teachers. Ron felt that many of the teachers tried to live up to Dunbar's history, "especially Ms. Rousseau—the way she carried herself. She was a power presence. She put in mind, like, a female pastor. Every time she walked into her room. For us, it was 'Don't embarrass us. We have a history here. Do not act foolish. We do not need people in the broader community to look at us Dunbar students in a negative light.' There was a sense of that."

Dr. Eva Rousseau has something in common with Ron; she was Dunbar's valedictorian, in 1962. "When I came back some of my teachers were there. It was a tremendous source of pride to have a student return as a educator." Dr. Rousseau still has the manner and the tone of someone to be respected. The sound of her voice immediately makes one sit up straight. She won't comment on Dunbar's decline but she will tell you what worked when she was there: locking down the school. She was fierce about keeping bad elements out. Expanding the pre-engineering program to twenty partnerships, including a program with NASA. And the school being the first comprehensive public high school in Washington, DC, to be awarded the Blue Ribbon School of Excellence by the US Department of Education in 1993. Into the 1990s, there always seemed to be some custodian of the spirit of Old Dunbar. Dr. Rousseau still held her school and herself to high standards. "And most importantly our children went to college and stayed in college." Her message to her students: "Believe you can succeed and you will."

If a student at Dunbar had the will and was lucky enough to encounter teachers like Rousseau or Arman Mazique, a former marine who challenged his students every day, there was a good chance he or she could graduate and do well. Mazique was the kind of teacher whose students, now as adults, find him and friend him on Facebook. He is still a wall of a man, broad and strong, which came in handy in the 1980s when he had to help escort gang members from the property. Mazique, an engineering teacher, considered the economic and academic diversity a strength in some ways because it taught students to get along with all types. He felt Dunbar's biggest problems came from the bureaucracy at the central office downtown, which he called "the puzzle palace." "I have a saying

I like from the Japanese: 'Fix the problem, not the blame.' " He didn't want to waste his energy on politics outside of the classroom. While the pre-engineering program attracted math and science whizzes, Dunbar of the late twentieth century also produced a few successful writers. The poet Thomas Sayers Ellis graduated in 1982. Yaba Baker, class of 2000, started a cottage industry with his "Just Like Me " books and Princess Briana books, featuring a self-sufficient princess of color who needs no prince to get it done.

Jewel Haskins (Dunbar 1997) is now the head park ranger at the Paul Laurence Dunbar house in Dayton, Ohio. "Mr. Mazique was my favorite all-time teacher. He made learning fun. The work was daunting and he would sit down and work with you. Sometimes all you need is the confidence to know you can do it."

For a huge part of the population, the concept of believing that a public DC education would enhance their chance at mainstream success was a cruel joke. The DC underclass was either entirely absent from the school system or being passed along, competency just an afterthought. Leon Dash, a journalist at the *Washington Post*, covered the student uprisings at Howard University in the 1960s and won a Pulitzer Prize for his long-term reporting about DC's forgotten poor, most of whom are black. What he found helps explain how the problems of the DC school system are deeper than building structure and the lack of AP classes.

For years, Dash investigated and wrote about a woman who spent her life spinning in the poverty cycle. The woman's parents were part of the second migration of hardworking farm laborers, descendants of slaves, who couldn't find work or housing in the big cities. They wound up first in alley housing and then in housing projects, where they were largely ignored. The woman he followed for years, Rosa Lee, went to Washington, DC, public schools in the 1940s, dropped out of seventh grade, and was illiterate.

Most of Rosa Lee's children cycled through the public school system until they too dropped out. The public schools had failed her, and she failed to fight to educate her children. As an adult, Rosa Lee was too intimidated to even approach a school on behalf of her many children when they were in trouble or didn't show up. She did not have the knowledge or skill set to protect her children's futures, unlike middle-class white parents and middle-class black parents. "They [the middle class] were not intimidated by anyone in the school system—teachers, administrators, vice principals, anyone in the school—because they were as highly educated as these people, and that is not the case with poor parents. They are easily intimidated, and sometimes treated with disdain." The Rosa Lees of this world were succumbing to the societal quicksand of poverty and a lack of education. And the public schools reflected this every day.

Dash felt the issues of race, poverty, and class, all of which were showing up in the public schools, needed to be out in the open, and he worked for four years on the *Post* series. He received nearly one thousand voice mails from middle-class and upper middle-class blacks admonishing him for this reporting. The common thread was that what he wrote confirmed stereotypes, not just about poor blacks, but all blacks. Dash, who is African American and now a journalism professor in Illinois, observed something that had plagued Washington for years: "The psychological burden of the black middle class [is] proving yourself worthy of inclusion. Dunbar grads and middle-class Washington had worked so hard for inclusion, or at least access to the best things. The larger society has all these myths about your humanity, and they had to work hard to overturn them."

But Dash felt that they, too, had been harsh on those left behind, and that was where the classism in DC came in. "The majority of the black poor haven't even made it [to] working-class society. They don't speak the King's English, and that is a social marker—a distinct class marker. They also distinguish themselves by generations going back in Washington. The social markers are very clear."

For the last forty years, various reports and studies have been released, all citing the same problems with DCPS: the 1989 COPE Report (DC Committee on Public Education) called "Our Children, Our Future," the 1995 "Our Children Are Still Waiting" report, and the 2005 "Restoring Excellence to DCPS" report from the Council of the Great City Schools. The problems remained: Failure is tolerated. The buildings need repair. And bureaucracy and poor academic performance plague schools.

So why does the District of Columbia, a place with some of the greatest minds, the most educated white and black people, the capital of the United States of America, have such a problem fixing its schools? Journalist Bill Turque theorized, "I think, because it's in Washington, because it's the backyard of Congress, it's been a laboratory for a lot of reform. The charter school movement started here. I think it all feeds—it makes it very passionate, it makes an interesting cover, but it also makes it hard to get by in a community that simply wants to get things done because everything is created with huge suspicion."

Turque has covered education for years. We met at a middle school cafeteria where a meeting about the structure for a new middle school was being discussed. The conversation between parents, mostly African American, and the DCPS representatives descended quickly to a stand-off. The African American parents knew the importance of protecting middle schools. They knew what had happened in the 1940s and 1950s, when the middle schools were in bad shape.

"That was pretty much a typical DCPS meeting. They always follow a very familiar arc." Turque said the tension and raised voices were par for the course. "You know, the DCPS people will come [with] a lot of energy, the best of intentions, but they end up serving in a posture of instead of soliciting ideas and input, they're basically there, it feels like a fait accompli. You know, it feels like, 'This is what will happen, but we're asking your opinion.' But it's a pro forma exercise so the anger is more than the anger of that situation. It is also residual resentment. Decades of bad decisions about schools, about neighborhoods, about being disenfranchised. You cannot separate all that resentment of being disenfranchised. It colors literally every decision in every meeting like that, so they're all like that."

Today, with the chancellor's position tied to whoever is mayor, another layer of politics is added to an already saturated situation. Turque makes an excellent point about the bigger issues at stake: "Education has become so politicized and mechanized. It's really a civil rights issue. . . . It packs in all the stuff in one small space. Race. Class. Income inequality. Every flammable issue is packed in to this very small school district."

Pre-1954 Dunbar had protected itself and protected its students' educational civil rights. The principals had a lot of power. The community helped raise the kids. The teachers were highly educated and fairly compensated. The parents and caregivers made a living, and the students had basic life needs fulfilled. Yes, the rooms were overcrowded, the books old, and the commute long for some students, but basically when the playing field was close to level, Dunbar proved that black children of all classes and shades could learn and excel. In the modern Dunbar, the average student appears to have been left behind.

In 2008, Dunbar was set for restructuring with nine other district high schools. To get on this academic hit list, a school had to fail to make adequate yearly progress for five years. The federal No Child Left Behind Act mandated that Dunbar accept one of these five options:

1. Reopen as a charter school
2. Replace all or most school staff relevant to AYP [Academic Yearly Progress] failure
3. Contract with an external partner
4. State takeover
5. Other major restructuring, which could include being shut down.[18]

Closing down the first public high school in the country for African Americans was politically impossible. One-third of Washington's schools were already charter schools, and charters weren't necessarily the panacea they originally seemed to be. A state takeover didn't apply. It was decided that the second and third options were the best courses of action for a school described as having "significant obstacles." The restructuring recommendation concluded:

> The school has a rich history and promising future, but the organization needs a massive cultural shift in the present to bring about the changes necessary to cultivate a climate conducive to student achievement. The right outside partner will bring to the table extensive capacity to manage change in Dunbar's challenged environment.[19]

A massive cultural shift requires either revolution or the patience for evolution. The plan was broken down into phases. The first phase would take place during the 2008–09 school year. The outside partner would observe, learn the current culture, craft a plan to be implemented in the following year, and then take over.

The subtext of the Rhee administration was that the revolution was going to come from non-Washingtonians. So far, the locals had not made changes for the good, so they should let someone from outside the Beltway try. For Dunbar, the idea was to bring in a private educational management company with a proven track record. New blood. Independent. No ties.

But was that even possible in the most political town in the country?

———————✺———————

The gravelly voice of an elderly, yet feisty, man on the other end the phone was insistent. "You *don't* need to write that old story. Everybody knows the old story. There's a new story going on at Dunbar. An exciting story! Forget all that old stuff. It's a new day." For twenty minutes Dr. Lawrence Graves, Dunbar class of 1940, told me what he thought I needed to write about Dunbar. And he was determined that I look forward not back. "You are witnessing something new. It is a great story to write down. The past is the past."

All roads of Dunbar history, legacy, and truth led to Lawrence Graves. A career educator in Washington, he was active in spreading the word about all things Dunbar. Passings of graduates. Accomplishments of current students. Once you were on his mailing list, he would send you obituaries, updates on scholarships, and photos of students' accomplishments. He could tell you exactly who had and had not contributed to the scholarship funds and why or why not. He was a firm believer that the graduates of Old Dunbar needed to embrace and support those at the school now, to once again build a community around the kids—and fill in the gaps DCPS or a difficult home life had left empty. When a student named Ronald Rivers asked to interview Dr. Graves for a project about Dunbar's history, Dr. Graves summed up the reasons why Dunbar was something special in its day and why it had changed.

> Dunbar placed me in a very powerful environment of associated people who had great vision and who were going places. You felt it. I don't feel that this exists on a wide scale in the regular public schools. At Dunbar, this air of excellence permeated the whole building. Even though no one spoke to you particularly about any event, you knew you were a part of something very powerful. It did have its effect on my life. . . . I have observed the transition of our

children since integration. It appears to me that in my neighborhood we had all levels of people, professionals, laborers, or whatever—middle class, upper class, lower class—we were all together. And so you always had element of people, who you gave a lot of respect. We went into one another's homes. Played Monopoly. We enjoyed one another, yet there was an overall sense of discipline and purposefulness for whatever you were doing. The way it is today, it appears to me that many of the professional, upper middle class or whatever, have moved out of these neighborhoods. Kids are being impacted by other children who do no aspire to really high levels of living. I see that and I have seen it not only at Dunbar but in many schools.

Graves articulated what many Dunbar graduates believe: that charter schools and vouchers have depleted DC's public schools of human capital. The parents, no matter their economic status, who were in the school system fighting for their children's education are now putting all their focus on getting their kids into charter school lotteries. Their children who, despite their home life or amount of money in their pockets, had the aspirations Dr. Graves described were no longer part of the public school community. Washington, DC, introduced charter schools in 1996, with 160 students attending. Currently 34,673 students—43 percent of DC public school students—attend charter schools.[20]

Dr. Graves came and went as he pleased at Dunbar. For over twenty-five years he volunteered in the Dunbar guidance counseling department. He was a bit stooped over by his late eighties, but he could make good time up and down the ramps of Dunbar. He would arrive in the library, folders under his arm, warmly greeted by teachers and the staff. No one said no to Mr. Graves. He'd ask someone to type this letter for him or copy that newspaper article. Yes, Dr. Graves.

He also served as a walking museum of knowledge about Dunbar. A young special-education teacher approached him in the library. She was very pretty and her hair was wrapped in a colorful scarf. With a light Jamaican accent, she asked about the new school where she would be working. "I read, and I was just trying to learn more. I'm just mesmerized. I'm overwhelmed really."

Graves addressed her the way he would any of his students. "You have a right to be," he said. "All that I've been through, all the fifty or sixty years, are the years that helped me emerge, to be the kind of person I am, but they are years also that are gone. They've gone by. We are in a different period now. What you are doing and what the people down the stairs are doing is the new day!"

The new teacher still wanted to know more about the history of Dunbar. "What I want to get these kids to do is to appreciate the history of Dunbar. So many of them—"

"Don't waste your time doing that. What you want to do is get them revitalized, energized to be something. The histories are right to talk—that's what I've been doing for all these years."

"OK."

"It has no powerful effect on the kids today. The kids are trying to make it out of their dire environment."

"Sure."

"I can't get that over to you enough. No. These are principals who've gone from Dunbar who could beautifully state what old Dunbar was like, how beautiful it is. We try to set the tone, and they could articulate magnificently. That is not where you are."

"Mm-hmm. Mm-hmm. OK."

"You're in special ed, aren't you?"

"Yes."

"Well, there you go. You've got to get those kids feeling good about themselves."

"Sure, sure, it's a different time and—"

"It's a different time. So, don't waste your time. Yeah, touch upon it lightly."

"Mm-hmm. Yeah, I did that."

"I'm speaking as an eighty-seven-year-old man who's been through all of that now, see."

Originally I had contacted Dr. Graves seeking his permission to cover the Dunbar triennial reunion, a gathering of all the classes dating back to 1928. I wanted to approach it as a fly-on-the-wall journalist. Instead I got a date with an eighty-seven-year-old man who wanted to make sure I did not just celebrate the past. He wanted me to met the new team in charge of Dunbar.

No one said no to Dr. Graves, which is how I found myself returning from a Dunbar reunion in his rusted-out Toyota as he peered over his thick glasses while making some liberal interpretations of the traffic laws.

On a bright October day, Dunbar graduates of all ages, shapes, and ambulatory capacities arrived at Martin's Crosswinds banquet hall in Greenbelt, Maryland for the Dunbar All Class Triennial Gala. Some walked in, some walker-ed in, and some wheeled in, too. It was a Sunday afternoon event, but some of Dunbar's ladies turned out with brightly colored silks and sequins. The gentlemen were in suits and ties. James Grigsby (Dunbar 1946) sported a bright red sport coat among a sea of crimson, black, and white, the school's colors. Upon entering the reception area, alumni exchanged hugs and kisses with old friends and shared fond remembrances of those who had passed. The grand ballroom was filled with circular tables, each with a class year displayed on a stand, dating all the way back to 1928. There were white linen tablecloths and silver, carefully arranged flowers.

There was a lot on the agenda. Several Dunbar graduates were honored for their achievements. Among the honorees was Dr. Harold Freeman (Dunbar 1959), the son of a truck driver, who went on to found the Ralph Lauren Center for Cancer Care and Prevention in Harlem. He was the director of surgery at Harlem Hospital for twenty-five years. His greatest contribution to the medical field may have been his implementation of the first patient navigator system. Dr. Freeman believes it is a moral obligation to raise health standards for the poor. The navigation system, which has been adopted across the country, helps guide poor and struggling cancer patients too intimated by the system to continue their care. It has doubled life expectancy in the areas where it is used.

Also honored were Dunbar alumni who had graciously funded scholarships. And of course there were star sightings too. The master of ceremonies pointed out, "In the room, we have a very special guest, a young man with the Dunbar High School. He played football [and other sports; he was a] three-sport all high. He graduated in '72. He was a quarterback on the football team. He went from playing before two or three hundred friends, family, and classmates to 102,000 people at the Ohio State University, and he was the most valuable player in the Rose Bowl in 1974, and he taught his roommate, Archie Griffin, all he knows about football. Ladies and gentlemen, please greet Cornelius Green. Let him be known by his nickname, Flam!" The same Cornelius Green an old Dunbarite, forty years earlier, had brushed off as a role model.

Dr. Graves and his date (me) found their place close to the front. He was like a rooster in a henhouse, flirting and laughing with the ladies from the class of 1935: Beatrice, Marion, Yvonne, Therrell, Penny, and Cornelia. Cornelia, who had been valedictorian, was feeling great. "I took one of my, I call them my 'Michael Jackson pills,' so I could make it today." She laughed, but then in all seriousness added, "I only take them sometimes. I don't want to get addicted."

Therrell, the daughter of a prominent doctor who had driven a giant black Cadillac to make house calls, recalled that her father "was a general practitioner. We didn't have as many specialists in those days. He would go to the house. He would go to you. If you came to the office, it was one dollar. I had the books. One dollar—the name and the one dollar. If he went to your house it was two dollars. He would spend many a Sunday afternoon riding around trying to collect two dollars. Do I remember it? I remember them giving him chickens or something if they couldn't pay the dollar. It was just, you know, amazing."

The announcer was moving things along. "We get to the part where you use these clappers again. I know that you've been using them all along. We're going to do the roll call of the classes by decade, starting with the present and going back to the past. So, we'll start with the decade of the 2000. Those who are Dunbar graduates from the decade of 2000, let's hear your clappers." An uncomfortable silence with one or two claps in the distance.

"Oh, you have a few." He hurried along. "Decade of the '90s. Decade of the '80s, '70s, '60s, '50s. Wow! It's nice to have the '50s here and nice to see you, and I know you appreciate being seen." The roll call was like an audio representation of Dunbar's history, the further back the announcer went, the more robust the reaction. "The decade of the '40s. The '50s and '40s are still vigorous, huh? The '30s. The '20s. Is this table '51? Is this table '51? Fifty-one, the graduates—we got some people there from the classes of 1928, 1929. I think we just stand for them. One of the ladies from the class of '28 has a yearbook with her, so after the program you may stop by and look at some history. By the way, there is a person

Dr. Graves, Alison Stewart, and the ladies of the class of 1935,
at the Dunbar Gala, October 2009.

from the '20s who wasn't able to make it. Her name is Alberta Addison. She is one hundred years old."

Vince Gray, then the chairman of the city council, was also honored that day for his long career in public service, but was distressed by the disconnect between Old Dunbar and New Dunbar. "You know what really bothered me about that dinner that I went to, lunch or whatever, we went to out there and that was, after you got past about 1975 or '80, there was almost no alumni. Where are those alumni? There needs to be some outreach to find the folks who are younger at this stage. And I'm not sure that this isn't a reflection of the comfort zone that people are operating in at this point. You know, from the '40s and '50s and '60s and '70s, who they were at Dunbar and are comfortable with those folks. We're not comfortable with the ones who came out in the '80s and '90s, so we don't do much to bring them in. Yet, frankly, it's obvious there will be a day when there is no more alumni federation if you don't bring the younger folks. So, I'd like to—I'm reaching back, you know, to accomplish that."

A video was shown, a deeply dramatic historical perspective of the high school and its great achievers. When a picture of the 1977 building came into view, a few boos were heard, a general grumble arose, and one lady vigorously put her thumbs down. The Old Dunbar grads still have emotional attachments to the 1916 building. When it was destroyed, some took bricks and pieces of the building, which they display in their homes. One woman has an original cornerstone in her backyard, surrounded by lovely plants and ivy.

After the film, the director, from the class of 1951, made his way to the podium with something to say. "We all have a responsibility, and we should feel good about this legacy and the pathfinders that have brought us to this day, but if we leave our school the way it is, that legacy will be lost forever. Our young people that are attending the school now will be lost in this fast-paced, moving world. So each of us—I don't care how old we are, how disabled we are—we have a responsibility to take this video and what we got from this today and continue to work and help our young people be a part of this society, not followers but leaders."

Bridging that divide has been a long-term goal of the Dunbar Alumni Federation. It's one of the reasons it holds this big event every three years. Its officers—James Pittman (Dunbar 1951), Brigadier General Elmer Brooks (Dunbar 1949), and Carrie Thornhill (Dunbar 1961)—tried to walk the fine line of celebrating the past while recognizing the present-day challenges facing Dunbar and its students. Classes are encouraged to sponsor students, not just at reunion time but also throughout the year. Lynettra Artis, class of 2001, is perhaps one of the biggest success stories of alumni involvement. "I've wanted to be a lawyer since I was nine years old," Lynettra recalled as she crossed her long legs and leaned back on a tufted couch in the lobby of the Henley Park Hotel. She was dressed in a laid-back yet professional outfit because she was due at work shortly. She is an attorney specializing in contract law. She grew up in a single-parent household with a mother who was a legal secretary. "My mother struggled," is how Lynettra describes the way her mother moved the family from place to place to make sure Lynettra could go to a good school. By ninth grade she was enrolled and on scholarship at a private Catholic school, but she knew it was taking a toll. "Georgetown visitation—too expensive. Bus money, tuition, uniform. I told my mother at the end of my ninth-grade year, I am going to the local school, which was Dunbar. It was a block away." Her mother was not happy about the decision. She worried about the neighborhood and she worried about her bright child's future. "I told her I am going to get As anywhere I go, so don't worry about that. It was better for Mom;

she had two other kids to think about. I didn't need much. I didn't want much." Lynettra knew that one of her brothers was on the edge. While she was in law school, he was in jail as a result of his association with a gang. Lynettra never had a problem. She made friends and she made straight As. "Mrs. Hilton couldn't stand it," Lynettra said as she smiled, showing off her immense dimples. Her English teacher marched her into the principal office and made her enroll in pre-engineering. "She said it [school] was too easy for me and I needed a challenge." By senior year Lynettra had the grades and scores to get into college and she zeroed in on Amherst. "Dr. Graves found out where I was applying; he told me to write a letter about why you want to go there and what you want to do with your education. As soon as I wrote that letter alumni came out of the woodwork! I don't know what I did, I cannot tell you, but that letter was important." Lynettra had tapped into the connection between Amherst and the Dunbar of yesteryear. One hundred years earlier Robert Mattingly was the first of a long line of Dunbar graduates to go to Amherst. Lynettra's interests sparked something in the alumni, maybe a call to action to help a young woman who would make something of her opportunity. "It was definitely the Amherst thing. At the time I didn't know there had been this direct connection for years, but for decades Amherst hadn't thought about Dunbar." She could not believe her luck. Money poured in. "Amherst graduates just came out! I asked myself, 'Is this happening right now?' Throwing money my way, my mother's way, so she wouldn't have to worry about me. It was beyond my dreams. I knew I would have to struggle. I promised her you are not going to pay a dime for college. That is not your worry; worry about the other two. I got a merit scholarship. I did not have to pay. I had food in my belly. I had transportation home for holidays, Christmas, summer. I came out with best college education and had to pay a little, little amount of money." She enrolled in Howard Law School and was living the dream. "I don't know if it is true but Dr. Graves used to say that I helped get the alumni excited again."

In 2008, the federation awarded close to thirty scholarships to seniors. One such scholarship recipient was Sydnee McLeoud, who began to cry when she explained how much the help meant to her. "I'm so grateful and appreciative because a lot of people don't even get to go to college, or have this help and support. And I am so grateful." A 2008 graduate, she was in tears thinking about what the scholarship would mean to her and the teachers who helped her apply. "I was blessed to have a teacher, Miss Townsend, Miss Gloria Townsend. She teaches banking and credit, and she saw something in me and referred me to the class of '36. The scholarship, it was a four-year-plan scholarship to just go—books, schooling, everything just taken care of."

The scholarship means a lot to this young woman with serious responsibilities. "I would have had to get financial aid. I know nothing about financial aid, so that's a big struggle. I actually have a one-year-old son, so this is going to change a lot for him too, because I would like to be a teacher and for him to even go to the school or see Mommy's doing something. If he would like to be a teacher or help out in any type of way, it's all just so great and nice. I can't tell you, but I'm so grateful."

Sydnee, like a lot of students at Dunbar, didn't really have a sense of the school's history or any old school alumni. "I did not know that classes did scholarships or anything like this. This is all very new to me. My grandmother actually graduated '62, and my mother was '89, I think. I've never heard anything about this at all."

The generational divide is wide and deep. Time and time again, Dunbar graduates told stories of despair about encounters with young black youth.

Lonise Robinson, class of 1946, was a devoted teacher in the system for years. "I found that in some of the poorest neighborhoods, those parents were just as concerned about what their children are going to do, and they wanted to cooperate to the fullest. But now it's a whole new kind of idea out here, now, that they are owed something, and they can come with the clothes and their long fingernails and the weaves and whatnot, and the children are just going to the devil."

"And I don't see how the fellows walk with those pants, with the crotch way down there," her husband, Floyd, also class of 1946, chimed in. An eighty-something James Grigsby couldn't help himself one day getting out of the Metro stop in Southeast Washington. He tapped a young man on the shoulder and told him to pull up his pants and have some self-respect. "I know he could have knocked me down, but I had to do it."

Then, a big moment at the reunion arrived. The alumni were about meet the team chosen to turn around Dunbar. Many already had their opinions about Rhee, but the new Dunbar administration was still new, just two months into its tenure. A tall, barrel-chested, white-bearded man took to the microphone. The room grew quiet.

"Good afternoon," he said in big, booming voice.

"Good afternoon," the entire room responded.

"You know, before I came here today, my right knee was hurting, and I thought it was because I was aging, but the pain is gone now because I am inspired by what I see in this ballroom. You know, my name is George Leonard. I'm part of a company called Friends of Bedford, and we come out of New York. And, you know, we didn't know that much about Dunbar, but when we entered the building last year we were very upset with what we saw. Students were in the hallways. Violence was just about on every floor. Learning was not happening in that building, from what I could see, at any level that you would be pleased with."

There was a stir in the room. "Who is this again?" one lady whispered to another. It was an uncomfortable moment for some.

"They are from New York. They are going to run the school," Dr. Graves replied.

"Hmm," was the response.

Leonard continued, "There were no classrooms. There were spaces, open space, and the rest that resembled a prison, and the mentality of the students and the staff in no way represents the legacy of the school as important as Paul Laurence Dunbar."

There was something about his presentation that was irking some people. It seemed to be a case of "How dare you call my ugly sister ugly?" Still George Leonard continued, seemingly unaware of the rumbles in the room.

"I have learned so much today, more than I've learned in the first year. I observed the school in operation. But I will tell you this: the Friends of Bedford will not let you down. We are charged with the mission of turning this school around. We had long talks with so many people in DC to try to understand how did this school end up in this condition after reading about all the success and all the scholars that have come out of that school. Please explain to me how this school can exist this way with the name Paul Laurence Dunbar as the name of the school. I did not like the answers to the questions! So, at that point I realized that I have to take it upon myself to make the changes that I know need to happen at a school like Paul Laurence Dunbar with a legacy that rich."

Leonard was on a roll with no signs of stopping. "I circled Charles Drew's picture. It was on the walls. I circled it. So, students said to me, 'Who is that?' Yeah, right. And that was my reaction. Wow. There's a lot of other pictures I have to circle for you so that you could understand what building you're in and what it represents. I sat her down, and I explained to her who Charles Drew was. And when I was in New York, I had a club that was called the Charles Drew Institute, and little did I know that I would be involved in a project that was going to turn the school around where Charles Drew graduated from."

His presentation reached a crescendo. "We will not let you down! I promise you!" He was almost yelling.

"We did not come to DC to play games. We left our families in New York to come for this mission. And our wives, you know, they're saying, you know, come back home, and when my wife walked that building she said to me, 'Now I understand why you cannot come back home, because there is no way that a school should be in that kind of condition.' We will not let you down."

The reaction of the alumni was mixed.

"I was impressed, but I also felt, why do they have to get somebody from outside? Why can't they do this? Why do they have to spend money to have someone come to the school? And, we know it's filthy. We know there are rats running around. We know an open classroom with a bunch of adolescents—are they insane? So, I don't see, why did they have to waste money getting a bunch of foreigners—when I say, 'foreigners,' they're not part of the system here—to come in and tell them and show them what to do?"

Some praised what seemed to be Leonard's tough-love stance.

"It's about a stable, that in order to clean that stable out, they had to run, like, a river of something through it to clean it. They got a lot of lousy teachers who haven't been properly trained, who are busy trying to wear designer clothes. They are not interested in the truth. They are interested in the salary they get. Now, I admit, teachers are not paid worth—they are not paid what they should get. They educate these stupid basketball players who make millions, and they get nothing," said one Dunbar alumnus.

"He is so enthusiastic, and he really meant what he was saying. Now, I don't know how he's going to go about it," said another.

Leonard ended his speech with a bold prediction: "You have folks who have sacrificed so much for Paul Laurence Dunbar to be the kind of school that it was. There is no way that we are going to stop at what we're doing in DC until Paul Laurence Dunbar is the number-one high school in DC. We have to be the role model for that community, and after being here today . . . I was already fired up before I came here. Now, it's a whole different type of energy that comes out of me, and I will go back on Tuesday and I will tell those students, 'Keep a-plugging away.'"

14 FROM BED-STUY TO SHAW

GEORGE LEONARD WAS SURPRISED that some of the alumni had grumbled at his blunt assessment of modern-day Dunbar. For all his sophistication, the French cuffs, the suspenders, and deliberate speech pattern, George Leonard could come at people in an unvarnished fashion. "I thought they would appreciate the fact that we were honest." He hadn't really expected to make a full-on podium-pounding speech, but something had moved him that day.

Niaka Gaston, chief operating officer of Friends of Bedford, is Leonard's former student. He can finish his mentor's sentences, and Leonard can do the same for him. "Yeah, we could see the discomfort in some of their faces, because they love their school, but we're not talking about what your school *was*," Gaston acknowledged. "We're not talking about . . . we don't want you to love it less."

"It is the unfortunate reality of what this," Gaston gestured around at the off-, off-, off-white cinderblock walls and eye-frying fluorescent lights, "what this is." The Bedford team was sitting in a big conference room within a classic high school main office. It was a springlike day in March 2010, but you couldn't tell inside of Dunbar because windows are few and often high up on the walls, near the ceiling. Their BlackBerrys were buzzing. Their laptops were lined up on three six-foot-long folding tables arranged in a *U* shape so the members of the team could see each other. Often they made eye contact, a nod here and there, acknowledging some e-mail that popped up on a screen. A whiteboard had some notes that would only make sense to them.

Almost two years earlier, Friends of Bedford had been among the candidates being interviewed to partner with DCPS at four of the under-performing area high schools: Anacostia, Ballou, Coolidge, and Dunbar. A member of Leonard's extended family was a graduate of Coolidge and knew of the results Leonard and his team were achieving in New York. Introductions were made. After earning a reputation for a series of successful programs that provided inner-city kids with the tools they needed to compete on state and college exams, Friends of Bedford moved on to a big project: Bedford Academy in Brooklyn, New York.

It was simple. They started a successful public high school in Bedford-Stuyvesant, where one-third of the population lives below the poverty level and unemployment hovers around 17 percent.[1] The student profiles were similar to that of an average Dunbar student. Many were from single-parent homes or weren't being raised by their parents at all. About 63 percent of Bedford Academy students needed free lunch. But here's the big finish: 95 percent of Bedford Academy students graduated and most went to college, including several to the Ivy League.[2]

Originally Friends of Bedford was slated to take over two of the other DC high schools set for restructuring, but then they were asked to come take a look around Dunbar. "We got to Dunbar, and wanted to run back out. It was a dungeon," Niaka Gaston recalls with a laugh, the kind of laugh that lets you know the subject is anything but funny.

"It was very gloomy," Leonard added.

"Dark and dirty carpet . . ." Gaston continued.

"The ramps—"

"The ramps!"

"The ramps," Leonard echoed what everyone thought. "It was a mixture of a prison and parking garage. There were kids everywhere."

"Kids everywhere."

The team left and was settling into preparing to tackle Coolidge and Anacostia High Schools. Rhee wanted them to take on Dunbar. "We cannot underestimate our children and what they are capable of if we provide the right environment for them," she said. She believed Bedford could create that sense of expectation.

We brought in the Friends of Bedford. We put a significant amount of resources in building walls in the school, with trying to sort of paint and clean and pull up the old moldy carpeting and that sort of thing. And is the school perfect now? Heck no, far from it. But can you notice that a shift is occurring, absolutely. And so for kids, many of whom have been in an environment for years where they've been suggested to low expectations and poor quality, in terms of what they were being provided, in terms of an educational academic program, et cetera, you know, a lot of people think, well, when you get to these older kids, sixteen-, seventeen-year-olds that are so hardened that it's too late, right? And what the children at Dunbar show you is, it is not too late. You can talk to seventeen-year-olds who are overage, under-credited, and you talk to them about what they want to do, and they still have a sense of hope and aspiration around what they eventually want to do. And that's what I think is amazing about our kids, and in the long term is what's going to allow this school to change course very quickly is because of the students. And again, as long as we are doing what we're supposed to be doing as adults, the kids are going to arrive to those expectations very quickly.

Friends of Bedford were signed to a three-year, seven-figure deal. "We went through an emotional roller coaster," Gaston jumped right back in. "When you see the conditions that these students are in, and that quite honestly—and this is not to blame anybody, OK? Everybody's to blame, right? That their place is such a situation of failure, of guaranteed failure, and that's OK, you know?" His laugh of incredulity bubbled back up.

"You get this mixture of emotions. First you're just shocked, because this can't be America." He laughs again.

And that's how you feel. This can't be 2009, 2008—this can't be now. Then you become upset. Because now the reality sank in that this is actually happening, and this continued to happen for some decades. Then now you're excited about the prospect of jumping in this, but then you get this rage about you, because now you're getting angry, and you don't know who you're angry at, but you're angry. And then we came back to being hopeful and determined to take this on.

This hope was not only because of the future, but because of the past as well. "And for us, I mean, once we went back, and the research on Dunbar, geez, it was our honor."

Gaston finished up with his hand on his chest. This group was not one that could be described as humble, but in this case they were all sincere.

"Our honor," Leonard softly echoed his former student.

Leonard had been a biology teacher. He had originally wanted to go to medical school but didn't get in because, as he admitted honestly, he didn't have the grades. With a college degree heavy on the biology, he did a short stint as a drug rehab counselor in Brooklyn, New York. At the suggestion of a friend, he considered teaching, something he had no real desire to do. Yet he got his license and was on his way.

His protégé had a similar story, but with very different origins. "I wanted to be a healer," the thirty-something Gaston claims. With his long dreads tied in the back, trailing down his suit, and his round spectacles, if you said he was Spike Lee's boho baby brother, someone would believe you.

"My wife tells me now—well, she told me a couple years ago, you know—you said you wanted to heal? Well, that's exactly what you're doing. So, even though I didn't do what I sought out to do, I have absolutely no regrets. I think that this has allowed me to do so much more than what I was searching for." Gaston had more in common with some of the Dunbar students than anyone realized. He had nearly fallen through the cracks more than once, but had teachers in his high school and college who picked him back up.

"See, I sat where they sat. I mean, I'm from Bedford-Stuyvesant. I was homeless. My family were—they were drug members, they were committing crime. I get this. I mean, I get all of their stories . . . when you hear the things that they've gone through. But I was them. Or, I was a step away from being them. I remember being in college and not totally prepared for college. And I went to Columbia University from Boys and Girls High School in Brooklyn. I wasn't totally as prepared as I should've been."

One day Gaston went to the dean and said, "I don't know if this is going to work out."

"So, what are you going to do if you leave?" the dean asked.

"I'm going to go home—either I'm going to end up selling drugs, or I'm going to die. That's that."

Gaston has empathy for the issues Dunbar students face. "That's their—that's many of their options, I mean, growing on all the other things that happened to them. I didn't, thank God," he said laughing. "He helped me work through that. They deserve as many opportunities as I've had, and when I look back at my life, I'm not successful because of myself. It's because of what others have done for me. I've had phenomenal educators. Mr. Leonard was my biology teacher in high school. I've been blessed with mentors and others who have helped to keep me focused. I want to give that to everybody, and we've committed to doing that."

The Bedford model is based on five tenets listed in this order on the organization's website: parental involvement, academic rigor, culture and climate, community engagement, and discipline. They are heavy on the tutoring, the teacher training, small academies, Saturday classes, with the work being done during school, not after. Parental involvement turned out to be a big issue. Dunbar's 2008 quality school review by DCPS noted that there was a "significant lack of parent involvement" and that parents reported "limited and inconsistent communication from the school." The Bedford team found the parents who did come in were defensive and ready for a fight. "I don't blame them." Leonard said. "They have not been treated well." Leonard and his team get charged up when they discuss the Bedford philosophy to envision, engage, and encourage, producing what they call the "cycle of success."[3] It is a great sales pitch.

At this point in the meeting Leonard displayed a little of the arrogance that some in the District, including some members of the local teaching staff, found irritating. "We're educators, and we feel that we can take on any challenge, and we were so successful in New York, we were ready for the next challenge or the next step, or whatever it looked like. And we realized that this is clearly the next step, because of what we saw."

They saw a building that was obviously broken and sick. The DCPS masters facilities plan included a 2008 assessment of the building. Dunbar's condition assessment read as follows:

ADA Compliance–Unsatisfactory
Convey Systems–Unsatisfactory
Electrical–Fair
Exterior Finish–Fair
Interior Finish–Poor
Plumbing–Poor
Roof–Poor
Structure–Fair
Technology–Poor

Carpet tiles were moldy. Paint was peeling. Some gym equipment was broken and worn beyond use. The roof was unstable. However, even before repairs, the first order of business was a housecleaning; the place was filthy. One teacher claims he and an accomplice sent moldy tiles to the *Washington Post* and that helped "motivate" DCPS to move the process along.

The effort was part of what was called the Summer Blitz. Seventy schools needed to be stabilized, including Dunbar.[4] Doors fixed. Gym equipment patched. Garbage thrown out. The only problem was that the job was done so quickly that many valuable artifacts from Dunbar's golden years ended up in the Dumpsters, including an original Elizabeth Catlett print similar to the one that hangs in New York's Museum of Modern Art. A portrait of one of the school's original founders, William Syphax, donated to the school by Mary Gibson Hundley, was found outside in a shopping cart with some discarded Christmas decorations.[5] The history of the school was lost on many who were there; they didn't even know what they were trashing.

Physically, the building needed to be reconfigured. Teachers had done their best to create a better atmosphere, stacking file cabinets to create makeshift walls. It was a huge change to have walls put up so the students could be in individual classrooms. Dunbar II was built to accommodate twenty-four hundred students. Then Dunbar had anywhere between eight hundred and nine hundred students on the books, of which about five hundred showed up every day. That was a lot of unused, and more importantly unattended, space. Violence in the school was not uncommon.

The fifty-nine-year-old Leonard recalled finding a kid lingering in the halls. The young man was hauled into the office for cutting gym.

"This student who was so disgruntled in here. . . . And he didn't want to talk. 'I'm angry; my life is in the toilet. I don't even want to talk to you with that tie on. And I just want to be left alone until that bell rings so I can go to my next class that I may cut also. But I got to get away from you. Because you represent everything that's bad in my life,' " Leonard recalled, giving words to the boy's frustration.

Leonard sat and talked to the kid for half an hour. "The reason I was able to break through, [was] because we had a conversation for about thirty-five minutes, which probably is the longest he's ever spoken to anybody that represents what I represent. But he gave me enough information so that I understand what he's angry about. And when that bell rang, he couldn't wait to get out of here. But I made it uncomfortable for him to be quiet, to hold his head down, and to accept the reality that, at the rate he's going, he's not going to graduate. And he didn't like that. That I was telling him that he's not going to graduate. Because I got his attention, I guess.

When the teenager got up to leave he asked, "So, now you think that I'm not going to make it?"

"You think you're going to make it? You're cutting classes, and your grades are ridiculous," Leonard replied, displaying his edgy forthrightness. " 'So, you think 'I'm not going to make it' because of that? Wow. Yes. You think you are?"

"I'm going to make it," the kid said. "I don't care what you say."

"Wow, that's the best thing you've said all day"

"Don't tell me I'm not going to make it." The student became sullen and withdrawn again. And then he looked up. "So, you think something's wrong with me?"

"No, it's probably with everybody else but you." Leonard wasn't there to make him feel better about breaking the rules.

"I wanted to make sure before he left here, that he knew it's not OK for you to be the way you are, because he doesn't want to be judged. 'Don't judge me. Let the bell ring, you know, you're out of my life,' " he said, voicing the student's inner monologue. " 'But I want to feel comfortable with being messed up.' And I wouldn't allow that, because I'm going to challenge him until I couldn't. And when he got up, I said, 'All right, so I'll see you later,' and he just kept walking. You know, 'I'm not saying good-bye to you.' But, what's my follow-up? It doesn't end there. He thinks it ends there. Because when you turn around, he's not going to see me. I don't disappear. But in his mind, I disappear for life. We called his parents. We're having a conference with his mother and him, and I'm going to stay in his face until he realizes that you're going to do it the way we say, or you may not be a Dunbar student then. Their final exchange brought the light."

Leonard continued, "He said, 'I already get kicked out of a school already because I curse people out.'"

"So, you've learned from your mistakes."

"'I haven't learned from my mistakes.'"

"Well, you haven't cursed yet in here. That's called growth."

Leonard concluded, "So, he's quiet again. Because he doesn't want to hear what makes sense. But it's up to us as educators, and as the right people, as the right adult, to turn that boy's life around. Whether we win or lose, we have to make the attempt. That's what was missing in DC with most of the adults who were teaching in these schools."

The other thing that was missing, in Leonard's opinion, was an open conversation about mental health issues.

So you have to—because you know that it doesn't always start with a shining star. You know? The diamond in the rough. And you have a lot of those students here that can really rise to the occasion. And that's why we feel it's important to have a mental health component attached to our school, because of what they suffer when they're children—because a lot of them need therapy that they never receive, and that can be a factor as to why they're not learning well. So, and we want to bring that in here. We want it really intense though—we want it to be like a mental health unit here, where practitioners can really meet their needs. But that's going to take, you know, major dollars. But we feel that's the future. With mental health attached on one side, and dorm on the other for kids who can't go home.

In the first year with Friends of Bedford, 48 percent of the teachers were replaced. The number would grow to 60 percent. "They lacked necessary tools that you need to offer instruction to this population." Leonard clarified what he meant: "[With] students of this competency, which is mainly elementary school, you need a teacher that is able to be patient enough to know that you have to teach them where they are and then bring them up, not try to have a standard that they can't meet, so that you end up failing 80 percent of the class. So if you're failing 80 percent of the class consistently, and you're waiting for something to happen so that can turn around, you'll just continue to fail them. So [with] teachers that weren't clear on how to properly educate children who have a scholastic profile that's similar to fourth or fifth grade, then a better school—or a different school—would probably be best for them." Some people and programs had to go for budgetary reasons, including the Dunbar High School Band, the same one that performed in the inauguration. It no longer existed, although the school had to clamp down on some grifters who were going door to door in the neighborhood claiming to be students raising money for new band uniforms for the nonexistent Crimson Tide group.

Leonard noted there were teachers who were effective and invested but they simply did not have the support they needed to succeed. As Leonard continued to expound on his philosophy, in walked a very focused man. He was high energy and tightly wound, with the build of a bantamweight boxer. When Leonard motioned to him to come join the conversation, the man waved it off. With some force Leonard gestured again for the man to come over, and he finally did.

"I don't have time for this now. I need to be in the halls."

"Come on, it's for a good cause. She's writing a book about Dunbar."

"Maybe later, maybe later." The man bounded out of the room and began to walk the halls of the schools. He could be heard saying, "I do not want to see you in my halls!" Stephen Jackson was the new principal of Dunbar High School, chosen by the Friends of Bedford.

Principal Jackson slowed down for a few minutes at the end of the day to answer some questions. Even when he was sitting still, he gave the impression that he was on the move.

"In order to be a principal, especially at an urban high school, you should not be in your office, because you cannot run a building from your office. You run a building from being in the hallways, being in classrooms, being in the cafeteria. Making sure that the building is being run properly. You cannot see anything by being in the office. Rarely do I have meetings in my office during the day. And that is only because that in order to turn schools around, the principal must be visible. The principal must greet the students in the morning. They must see them off in the afternoon. They must talk to them during the day. We have about nine hundred students here, and I practically know the name of every last one of them."

Jackson is all business when he talks about Dunbar. "My biggest challenge is that the school did not have systems, structures, policies, and procedures. In addition to that, you really didn't have a lot of experienced people. So, therefore, you know, we are now putting in systems, structures, policies, and procedures to help organize the school. And generally when the school is out of control, it's out of control because you don't have those systems in place or you may not have strong leadership."

A former chemistry teacher, Stephen Jackson had been principal at two other large high schools, one in Brooklyn and most recently one in Mount Vernon, New York. The current mayor of Mount Vernon described the city's diversity like this: "We have priests, and we have hoodlums."[6] Mount Vernon High School is bigger than Dunbar—nearly twenty-two hundred students. It went through spasms of violence that were regularly featured on the evening news. Jackson's task was huge, but he broke it down to the basics: establish systems and introduce uniforms and smaller learning communities. Each met with varying levels of success.

But most importantly, Jackson got to know the students. "So, every school I generally went to turn around I noticed that there are similar challenges. And those challenges are that they don't have usually strong leadership. But more importantly, they don't even have the structures, the systems, the procedures, the policies that are in place, and basically that's what we were able to do." In his personal statement distributed to the alumni, he refers to himself as a "change agent in the urban educational settings."

"When I visited the school," Jackson said of his first time at Dunbar, "they were, number one, dressed inappropriately. You know, some of the young ladies dressed in very revealing clothes. In addition, the young men were all over the place. I mean I didn't see much adult supervision. I walked by classes with students just hanging out with no teachers, and anytime you have a situation where there's no real adult supervision, then you're going to have chaos. So, it was very chaotic. But the one thing I know about children is that they love and respect structure. And because we came with structure—like I said, in the beginning they were resistant, but because we came with structure, they begin to respect what we did, but more important, we were very consistent. And the first thing for me, in terms of the consistency, is making sure they were in class and making sure that they wore uniforms. And for me, for most of our children, that is one of the first things about being in education that gives them some structure. Being in class and more important, wearing the uniforms, because that to me is important for structure. Because some of them don't have the structure in their homes."

And he is true to his word. In a firm but gentle manner, he let one young woman know she had to go home and come back in the standard polo shirt in the school's colors, and pants or a long skirt. And when she said, very sweetly, looking up at him, "But Mr. Jackson . . ." he made it clear that just looking cute was not going to work. The kids respond to Jackson, and he clearly enjoys being with them. He jokes with them. Sometimes he speaks like them, which might make a very traditional teacher cringe. He is firm and clear and respectful. He has provided structure, and the kids seem to respond. Tough love isn't just a cliché in his world.

An informal poll of some students in the library revealed they didn't mind the uniforms, especially two freshmen. One girl, though, did not like the crackdown on cell phones at all. Her reasoning: "I *need* my phone."

Jackson had very specific goals and a strong sense of ownership about Dunbar's future. And he seemed to be his own man. So why would someone who had run such big programs come to work for someone else in a district far from home? Jackson said it was personal. He had gone to Howard and frequently stressed his ties to DC.

The principal had also spoken at the alumni luncheon back in October and was clear he wanted to be considered part of and work with the community, saying:

I'm honored to be at Paul Laurence Dunbar Senior High School for several reasons. Number one, not only is it a historical black institution, but many of my family members graduated from Dunbar. My grandfather's oldest brother graduated in the late 1920s. My aunt graduated—my great aunt, which is my grandfather's youngest sister—graduated in 1934, in the class of 1934, and then I had a host of uncles and cousins who also graduated. In fact, some of you may even know my great uncle who was a boxer here, in DC, Billy Banks. That's my uncle, my great uncle. . . . I spoke to Aunt Ada yesterday. We had a long conversation, and we talked about the importance of restoring Paul Laurence Dunbar. Most of my family is from DC. My mother was born here, and when Mr. Leonard contacted me in New York to come down here—I already turned around two schools in New York, and to be honest with you, when they asked me about turning around a third, if it were not Paul Laurence Dunbar, I would have turned them down. But because of what the school represents to me personally, I am here. We are working together. It's a tremendous amount of work, but I'm sure all of you were hearing some of the good things that we are doing at this particular school. I love this school. I love the work that many of you have done over the years, and I guarantee you, you give us a few years, not only will it be one of the best schools in DC, it will be one of the best schools in the United States of America.

Leonard and Jackson had a history. Jackson has said that, when he was a young educator, Leonard had mentored him along the course of his twenty-year career in New York.[7] He describes them now as colleagues, even though technically the Friends of Bedford hired Jackson. "They're managing the school," he said, clarifying their roles. "George Leonard and the Friends at Bedford, they manage two schools: Coolidge and Dunbar. Basically they sit down with me, and we collaborate, all right? I'm known for turning schools around, OK? They brought me down to help them turn the school around. So, we collaborate about what should be done, you know, how it should be done. Sometimes we agree, sometimes there may be disagreements, but that's fine, you know. The bottom line is that we work as a team to ensure that students get what they need in order to have a full high school experience. But more important, we focus on education more so than anything else."

At the end of Dunbar's first year under the stewardship of the Friends of Bedford and the hands-on management of Principal Jackson, it was time to breathe. There had been so many changes: the restructuring, a slew of teachers shown the door, new faces in the classrooms, and a new code of conduct. By June 6, there was a need for a pure celebration of the students and their achievements: the school's commencement. The event was held at Cramton Auditorium on the campus of Howard University. Being on Howard's campus gave the event a certain gravitas and an aspirational undertone. It seemed fitting considering the expectation that Dunbar's academic spirit could be revived.

Cramton Auditorium had been designed by M Street graduate Hilyard Robinson, and it was known for its unobstructed views of the stage. A news crew was set up in the back of the auditorium to cover the event, not really there to document the graduation but rather to get some video for the evening news. On stage at this commencement would be Mayor Adrian Fenty and his challenger in the 2010 race, City Council Chairman Vince Gray.

The tension on the stage was thick and dark, in stark contrast to the humidity-free, gloriously sunny June day. The nice weather was a huge relief from the winter of 2010. DC had pulled through a series of huge snowstorms. In the first week of February alone, DC had seen thirty-three inches of snow.

The future of Dunbar High School may have been forever altered by all that precipitation, which residents called Snowmaggedon. Mass transit stopped. School was canceled for a week. Mayor Fenty's seeming incompetence became a national sport as jokes abounded and the $100-million-a-day government shutdown became part of the American conversation. DC insider and shoot-from-the-lip MSNBC host Chris Matthews fired off his complaints on national TV: "We've got a very sophisticated mayor this time; everybody liked him for a while. And I'm telling you, it's time for a competition in the next primary 'round here. I think somebody's gotta run. This city needs a little better effort right now. I'd like to see some action."

Matthews was prescient. Mayor Adrian Fenty's reaction to Snowmaggedon 2010 was a fail. The drumbeat that "Fenty must go" began, but the anger about the cleanup was just an offshoot of a deeper discontent with what some considered his aloof governing style, and very specifically, his choice for the schools chancellor, Michelle Rhee.

After two and a half years as chancellor, if you said "Michelle Rhee" in a conversation in DC, it would be like saying, "I don't vaccinate my kids" or "I just got a new Hummer—it matches my other one." People would decide who you were and what you believed in right then and there. By that time, Rhee had fired hundreds of teachers, closed twenty-four schools, and pissed off the teachers unions—stepping on toes and earning accolades. Many admired her kids-first mantra and weed-whacker approach to bureaucracy. Jay Matthews of the *Washington Post* was an early adopter on Rhee and the Friends of Bedford. He summed up Rhee's appeal this way:

> She is putting in charge of these schools the best principals and energetic principals she can find, ones who stay in teaching, and giving them the power to hire their own team of teachers and giving them the power to fire those teachers pretty quickly who don't work out. And then empowering them to run their schools in ways that make sense to them and their team. And as part of that, to make that work, she got the foundations to promise her a lot of money so she could pay these people more and have a better chance of keeping these very bright and energetic people long term [than] if they were being paid enough . . . you know, to satisfy their moms.[8]

Referring to the slew of young Teach for America recruits, he said:

> That's what she's tried to do. And it's hit all kinds of bumps. Although she's been in the job longer than I thought she was going to be. I thought this is going to flame out much sooner. I didn't appreciate how much the politics and feelings in the city were in her favor. I didn't realize how deep was the outrage and depression at the state of the schools.

While her message of improving the schools and putting kids first couldn't be argued with, the way she went about it was another thing.

One of Rhee's critics along the way was Councilman Gray. Gray was nonplussed when it came to light that the chancellor had rearranged some difficult school budget cuts previously approved by the city council. Rather than cut money from a summer school program, Rhee chose to find $9 million in part by firing 266 teachers in the fall of 2009.

When Rhee appeared before the city council a month later, it looked like one of those congressional hearings where some bank CEO or military officer has been summoned to the table to answer questions and be publicly scolded. Neither Rhee nor Gray backed down. The exchange was recorded and still lives on YouTube.

GRAY: Why didn't you tell this council that you chose to do something else? Do you think that's inconsequential to say, "I'm not going to do summer school, I'm just going to fire a bunch of people that will add up to 9.1 million dollars." You think that's OK?

RHEE: I think that in times when you are making difficult decisions, that things don't always happen in an ideal manner. Just as, let me just give you an example here, when you cut our budget by $21 million, you did not call me to ask me if it was OK to cut summer school—

GRAY: We don't have to—

RHEE: Now hang on a second, wait a second. And the thing is, I don't actually blame you for that because you were under a tremendous amount of pressure. You were under a time constraint. I understand that you had to make those budget concessions.

GRAY: First of all, this was a public process at which a vote was taken, and it became the law of the District of Columbia. Why did you choose not to follow with the law?

RHEE: Because I did not—

GRAY: The law was . . . Did you know that the mayor signed that budget also?

RHEE: Yes, I do.

GRAY: So, did you tell him that you were just simply going to flout the law?

RHEE: What I told him was that I was going to make the decisions that I felt was in the best interest of children.

GRAY: Irrespective of what the law said?

RHEE: No, because we would have ultimately sent down the reprogramming that we would need to.

GRAY: Ultimately. What difference does that make? You already ripped the people, what difference does that make then? It's moot. You rip . . . you took $9.1 million that we had said we were going to reduce summer school, you then said I'm not going to do that because I don't like it . . .

RHEE: Correct.

GRAY: . . . so I'm going to rip the people. So what difference does a reprogramming make at that stage? These people sitting out here lost their job because that is the decision you made . . .

RHEE: Correct.

GRAY: . . . so what was the council supposed to do at that point?

RHEE: Well, I think that the bottom line is that I am the agency director—

GRAY: Well . . .

RHEE—you commented earlier in my infinite wisdom, I was hired to run the school district. I got a 13–0 confirmation vote from this council, so I assumed—

GRAY: I was a part of that.

RHEE: Exactly, so I assumed—

GRAY: I didn't confirm you to be a single authority, however. I confirmed you because I hoped that you would follow the law.

RHEE: Correct, but you also confirmed me believing that I had the skills, knowledge, and abilities necessary to be able to manage this agency effectively.

While Gray did not like Rhee, he loved, loved, loved, loved Dunbar High School. Seated in his large city council office on one of the many wood-and-leather chairs, he leans forward as he speaks.

"Dunbar was still a school that . . . had enormous academic rigor," he said. "The teachers were people who were highly intellectual, highly accomplished folks who probably became teachers because, in their field, they couldn't get jobs otherwise: physicists, chemists, mathematicians—very highly accomplished people—very rigorous in the educational requirements, and worked closely with the homes. You know, and highly respected. And that's why I'm not . . ."

Clearly Gray was getting ready to let loose on the chancellor. "Teachers were revered, especially African American teachers. I mean, there was doctor, lawyer, teacher. And to see what's happened to these African American teachers, the way they've been treated, it has just hit outright in this African American community in the city. And, this chancellor doesn't get it. She doesn't see it."

Rhee's firing of so many teachers struck a particular nerve in the black community. "Michelle Rhee doesn't understand middle-class black people," Gray said, without any anger, but as more of an analytical conclusion. He was referring to the role of teachers in the black community. Historically, the caliber of people who became teachers were men and women who would have been Rhee's classmates at Cornell, if they had been born forty years later.

"Of course, she doesn't have that kind of background, so it doesn't mean anything to her. She's catching the brunt of it because she's tone deaf. But, you know, you had teachers who worked closely with the home, that were great role models. You had—it was a much more closely knit environment than what you have now."

However, Gray does not have nostalgia for the days of Dunbar's glory, the pre-1954 segregated days, that some older folks will quietly say under their breath was a better day for Dunbar. "You knew what you were being excluded from. . . . We already were into a period of desegregation of schools, but Dunbar was never really desegregated. I don't think Dunbar's ever been desegregated. It's still as African American today as it was back when there was segregation. Those who think that, you know, education for African Americans might have been better, the problem I have with that is that what you don't get is the social education that is vital, because that's the world you're going to live in."

Gray's world was the one of working-class, segregated Washington. He grew up in a one-room apartment near Dunbar. "My parents—neither one of my parents finished high school." His mother didn't work, but his dad did everything he could for the family. "My father worked two jobs. My father worked in the hospital in the daytime and drove a taxicab at night. He worked long hours. I think he worked himself to death, actually. You know, and that's the myth about Dunbar, also, that the perception, you know, it was kind of rich black folks who were sending their children. It was pretty much working-class folk. I know when I went there, Dunbar was already in transition. It wasn't the Dunbar it was in the '30s and the '40s and even early '50s. Because now folk are going there because they lived near Dunbar. That's how I got there."

Gray's adult career has been one of public service laced with politics. He headed an organization to advocate for the developmentally disabled and mentally ill. He was the executive director of Covenant House in the District. He'd been a successful councilman where he was now chairman. He was thought to be calm, thoughtful, and accommodating. And at this point in his life, after becoming a widower in his late fifties, he was being nudged toward running for mayor of his hometown.

With all this conflict simmering from the preceding year, Councilman Vincent Gray, Mayor Adrian Fenty, the Friends of Bedford, Stephen Jackson, Dunbar alumni, guests, and honors students took their seats on the stage at Cramton. There was last-minute jockeying for aisle seats as the graduates walked in, the young men in black caps and gowns, the young women in crimson. A young man who had graduated from Dunbar a few years before and was now a security guard at the Brookings Institution was there to cheer on his younger sister. He was proud that she was headed to college, and he politely asked for an aisle seat so he could get a good picture of his little sis.

Chairman Gray (Dunbar 1959) seemed like a natural choice to be commencement speaker. That's what some students and faculty, including Principal Jackson, had thought when they invited him. The Friends of Bedford had officially invited Mayor Fenty. The commencement speaker's position appeared to have been double-booked, so thought some alumni and students, and the principal.

Gray opened the event to great cheers. "You are part of the Crimson Tide," he told the students to applause. "You are wearing the red and black with great pride. You are carrying the name of one of the greatest people in the history of this country, that is Paul Laurence Dunbar."

He later told a reporter, who videotaped the interview, that he was not pleased to have been what he saw as "bumped" from the speaker's slot. "I was asked verbally if I would do this, and I agreed to do so for those who asked informally. Those were people associated with the school, faculty members who said that the faculty had come together and the students wanted me to do this as well."

He made a point that was not lost on anyone watching the clip. "This is the high school I graduated from. Some things ought to be above politics and be sacrosanct, and that is when you have an opportunity to come back and be a part of your own high school, that is an absolutely wonderful moment."[9] The politics Gray was referring to was the fact that he was now officially challenging Adrian Fenty; Vincent Gray was running for mayor.

Fenty's turn at the microphone didn't go quite as well. It was enough to make the TV reporter jump up to make sure the camera was rolling. They'd set up to get some b-roll of the two candidates; what they got was some incredible audio. As Mayor Fenty greeted the students, the booing started. It did not last long, and there were cheers too, but the boos were loud enough to make the evening news. The mayor was unfazed.

"Dunbar class of 2010," he addressed the graduates, "the world is ready for you to make your mark. Dunbar's mantra is where the tradition of excellence continues. And that couldn't have been a more worthy goal. Keep pushing yourselves. Don't ever take no for an answer. Never accept any excuses from why a challenge cannot be met and why a problem cannot be solved."

When a reporter asked about the mix-up, a genuinely bewildered Fenty said, "I didn't even know this was an issue until you guys asked me. I didn't know anything about it." He composed himself and continued. "I really do feel that everyone was here in a positive spirit on behalf of the kids. And I think that's what matters."[10]

A year later, Fenty, Gray, Rhee, Leonard, and Jackson would all have new jobs.

15 | THE FALL

IF YOU HAD LOGGED on to the DCPS website in early August 2010 to find out who was the principal of Dunbar, your answer would have been someone named TBD. When Leonard and Jackson had stood a few feet apart handing out diplomas just two months earlier, the Gray/Fenty drama wasn't the only dissension festering on that stage. The working relationship between the Friends of Bedford and Stephen Jackson was not working.

It was an arranged marriage of sorts. Their styles didn't mesh. Bedford was nuanced, Jackson direct. Bedford was planning for the long term; Jackson was in the here and now. The Bedford team reveled in its New York-ness; Jackson adopted DC as his hometown. Bedford had the full support of Chancellor Rhee; the alumni loved Jackson. Publicly they all put up a good front, especially on August 28, 2010, when Dunbar was the rally point for Al Sharpton's "Reclaim the Dream" march on the anniversary of Dr. King's "I Have a Dream" speech.

For years, because of its history, Dunbar had attracted visitors and been used as a backdrop or photo op. First Lady Barbara Bush was a commencement speaker, Robert Kennedy met with students, musician Alicia Keys visited in celebration of Women's History Month, and even Richard Nixon had greeted students back in the day. For Sharpton's "Reclaim the Dream" event, Dunbar felt like the appropriate venue at which to start the march; so many of its graduates had been early civil rights leaders and fighters for equality. Graduates had worked to change the law and education.

Dunbar was the right place and would be in the national spotlight that day. A stage with a full sound system was set up on Dunbar's field behind the school. The bleachers around the track began filling up as early as 8:00 AM. Tripods were plunked down on the media platform, and TV correspondents prepared their intros. Within the first five minutes of the scheduled list of speakers, both Jackson and Leonard were on the stage, welcoming the crowd. Later, Leonard would reveal he was surprised at Jackson's appearance and introduction as the principal of Dunbar, because he no longer officially held the post. Still, both men shook hands and smiled. It was not a day for conflict, especially given that the real Dunbar superstar of the day was a student named Bianca Farmer, whose heartfelt speech gave hope for the next generation and reminded everyone what was really at stake:

> We can reclaim our families, we can reclaim our schools, we can reclaim our streets, and we can reclaim our pride. We have to do this so that we can reclaim a promise for a better tomorrow. I challenge my peers, brothers, and sisters to remember how far we have come and to not allow our legacy to be put in vain. Reclaim the dream. Thank you.

By the fall of 2010, Michelle Rhee was a household name, the result of an intense press campaign for the documentary *Waiting for Superman*, made by the Academy Award–winning director of *An Inconvenient Truth*. It revealed to the rest of the country what people in the District had known for a long time: the public school system in DC was rotting.

The film had made a big splash and provided an enormous platform for Rhee's work and her movement. For months the documentary had been showing in small screenings to select groups of tastemakers and media people. There was incredible buzz, to the point of noise, around the movie, Rhee, and her reform movement. Oprah Winfrey booked Rhee on her show and declared her a great leader, a "warrior woman." By this time, if any paper or blog ran a story about Rhee, the comments section would be jammed with opinions supporting her plan and salient objections to what she proposed. And sometimes the posts would contain hateful, disgusting, and racist remarks. She was a liar or a savior.

During this moment when education reform was front and center in the zeitgeist, Mayor Fenty doubled down on Rhee. Instead of distancing himself from the controversial woman he had hired, they visited schools together. She made speeches at his events. A popular media meme began to evolve: the Washington DC mayoral election was a referendum on Michelle Rhee and all the changes she had put in place.

On September 14, Vincent Gray defeated Adrian Fenty in the Democratic primary. On that day he became the presumptive mayor of Washington, and ultimately Michelle Rhee's boss. The director of *Waiting for Superman*, Davis Guggenheim, a DC native, had followed Rhee for a year. He hoped Gray would consider keeping her. "She's a very polarizing figure. I think she's a hero, and I think she was doing the essential work. And I think if you stopped what she was doing, it would be a tragedy. So my hope is that the new mayor will find a way to continue what she's doing because it really—you could tell it was working."

Michelle Rhee resigned one month after Fenty lost. Some of the people she put in place would not only survive but thrive. Her number two, Kaya Henderson, rose up the ladder to become interim chancellor. Others would not make it to the end of the year.

On the Monday before Thanksgiving, a fifteen-year-old girl went home and told her mom she had been raped by six Dunbar students in the school, near a lower-level stairwell, during school hours. The following day six young men were arrested and charged with aggravated sexual assault. The story began to circulate and made the local news just as the school was closing for the holiday. Classes resumed the following Monday, and over the next nine days the school went through a seismic shift.

After the alleged assault, rumors about the level of safety in Dunbar's halls were no longer being considered hearsay. By numerous accounts from faculty and students, and the interim chancellor herself, there seemed to be behavioral relapse at Dunbar. George Leonard was acting as interim principal, but he was also managing Dunbar and Coolidge.

"I felt that Leonard did an outstanding job the first year until he became principal," retired librarian Charles Phillips recalled. He liked the team of Jackson and Friends of Bedford and had high hopes for what they might accomplish together. "Leonard had the special ability to communicate to everybody. He made you feel wanted. He made you want to feel that you could do better than you're doing, even if you were the worst teacher there. You could do better if you were the best teacher. You still had to do better."

However, that fall Phillips noticed an uptick in crude behavior. Gambling. Sexual displays. He said something was just "off" that fall. "Things changed. Students didn't even know who Leonard was when he became principal." Discipline in the halls was spotty. "Leonard spent too much time in the office and not enough time in the halls, standing in the halls. When he was in the hall, these kids ran. They didn't hang around. When he wasn't in the hall . . . chaos."

A young Teach for America teacher walked out of the school and took her story to the *Washington Post*. She claimed Dunbar was a hostile and dangerous environment. Even though, after reviewing the evidence, the district attorney dropped the sexual assault charges against the Dunbar male students on November 30—without explanation—the Friends of Bedford had become the ones under investigation.

On December 8, George Leonard and his team were summoned to meet with Interim Chancellor Kaya Henderson and members of her senior team. The next day a letter went out to Dunbar parents.

> Dear Parents and Guardians of Dunbar Students,
>
> In order to provide your children with a solid education in an environment that promotes their growth and learning, I have made significant changes at Dunbar Senior High School beginning this week. I shared this information with you last evening through a telephone message.
>
> We are committed to ensuring that all students and staff are safe and that Dunbar Senior High School returns to an environment where all teachers can teach and students can learn. In partnership with the Dunbar community, a plan is in place that will touch on many aspects of Dunbar's operations. This plan will require immediate action over the next two weeks, and will be followed by longer-term work designed to further support teaching and learning.
>
> Leadership. As of today—Thursday, December 9th—Dunbar will be led by a new, but familiar, interim principal. Stephen Jackson

was principal of Dunbar during the 2009–2010 school year. He was reappointed interim principal of Dunbar yesterday. Friends of Bedford will no longer manage or have oversight over Dunbar.

Principal Jackson will lead a Dunbar that is orderly, well-run, and conducive to your child's learning. In the coming days, he will announce other steps that will be taken in order to improve the Dunbar climate.

Safety. Both MPD and the Roving Leaders have assigned additional officers to Dunbar in order to ensure security of students and teachers. Portions of the building not in use have been secured and closed off. Non-functioning cameras and other security equipment have been repaired or replaced.

Parent and Family Engagement. A parent meeting has been scheduled so that you will be able to discuss with Principal Jackson these changes and other matters important to you. The meeting will take place on Monday, December 13th at 6:00 PM in the Dunbar library.

Interim Principal Jackson is supported by a team made up of administrators, counselors, and others who will be present at Dunbar over the next several weeks. Along with Dunbar leadership, faculty, and staff, they will address issues of neighborhood safety, school facilities and operations, student support, and family engagement.

I am confident that these changes will result in a stronger Dunbar that will better serve your student. We look forward to your engagement in this process, and we will continue to update you as these plans go forward.

Sincerely,

Kaya Henderson, Interim Chancellor

"Why do I think it didn't work out? I think there are a couple of reasons." Kaya Henderson paused for a moment to think. It had been a few months; things had calmed down and now she had a little perspective. "On the one hand, I think, what Friends of Bedford was able to do in Brooklyn was very different than the situation here for a couple reasons. One, in Brooklyn they started a school from scratch. So, you know, they took a group of ninth graders and grew their school over time, as opposed to taking an existing four-year institution that is, you know, already has kids across all four grades. And they were able to build a culture, as opposed to trying to change a culture. They were also here responsible for two schools at the same time, Dunbar and Coolidge. Whereas, I think, in Brooklyn they were able to devote 100 percent of their time and attention to one school."

This would become the prevailing narrative in the District, repeated again and again, whether or not it was true. Henderson didn't pile on in a way that many others in the media and in the school did. Her analysis was evenhanded.

"I also think that there are some challenges—to be really fair to them—in being able to operate in a charter context where you can do sort of whatever you want and having to operate in a school district context."

Henderson showed her considerable skills as a diplomat, as well as her steeliness, when pushed on the subject. "I think, you know, I think when we, DCPS, engaged in this new kind of a relationship, I don't think that we had—this was the first time we ever did this, right? So, I don't know if we had all of the supports necessary." The comment was an example of twenty-twenty hindsight and Henderson knew it. At the time it seemed to make sense. She continued, "We *had* worked out the appropriate amount of supports and the appropriate amount of accountability. We were kind of figuring this out together. And I think that also affected Friends of Bedford's ability to be successful at Dunbar. I think it was a host of things. I think, you know, there's a little bit of blame to go around to everybody."

As for the tensions between Leonard and reinstalled Principal Jackson? "Let me be clear," her tone hardened, dramatically. "That was *their* hire. . . . While technically all principals are DCPS principals, they brought Principal Jackson down from New York. We didn't know him before this. That was their choice to run Dunbar." In a job where she doesn't get to laugh a lot, she cracked a small joke, soaked in truth, about wanting a drama-free year. "My primary hope is that kids have an uneventful school year."

George Leonard believes one thing to be true: "They made a big mistake pulling us out of that school." He and his team—Niaka, Bevon, and Derrick—were working in their familiar setup of tables in a U shape, with laptops open and stacks of reports and data piled up. Only this time they were at Coolidge High School where, for the time being, they were still the managers and where they'd had more success. For nearly two hours, the Bedford group swatted down accusations, knocked off all of the criticism that led to their expulsion, and presented the names and dates to back up their claims. They pointed to their accomplishments, from cleaning up the school to a rise in students testing proficient or advanced in reading, an uptick from 18.2 percent to 31.9 percent at Dunbar.[1] From what they had witnessed, they believed an action plan they had presented before they were canned was still being used. At times their arguments and claims seemed feasible, but at other times they sounded downright paranoid. They realized they had made two critical errors: underestimating the political climate of Washington and failing to put their hubris aside.

"We came here to educate," said George Leonard, shaking his head. "Getting caught up in the political end and the negativity? No, no, no, I am not getting caught up in that. We came here to do that job that was in the school building. We didn't know we were going to have to educate all of DC." Even though no voices were raised, their anger was palpable. With their natural way of picking up where the other left off, Niaka Gaston added, "We are not politicians, and we are not sorry for it."

They definitely weren't politicians. They didn't compromise. They didn't adjust to the situation. Their modus operandi led to professional Darwinism. The group that adapts to its environment survives. Just because one survives doesn't mean that person or entity is in the right; it just means it found a way to exist in its current environment. Friends of Bedford's "we know better than you, plus we are from New York" attitude did little to endear them to DCPS and some of the Dunbar alumni. When a mailing went out from the alumni association touting the goals Bedford wanted to achieve at Dunbar, someone from the class of '43 sent it back with a note that read, in part, "Why in the world are you mailing out these objectives and the names and pictures of Leonard, Thompson, Cerisier, and Gaston, all of Brooklyn, NY? We Dunbarites are very dissatisfied with your article featuring out of towners and Dunbar High School."

If Bedford saw something that was interfering with the plan, one of them would speak out. At one point they publicly criticized the cutting of staff midyear as well as the way teachers were evaluated through a program called IMPACT.

"We went around saying things like 'IMPACT is stupid!' Now the person responsible for IMPACT is now the chancellor. I said it was a dumb idea to have an RIF [reduction in forces] in October. Who does that?" They called out a scheduling administrator for putting all the kids, eight hundred of them, at lunch together. They decided against AP classes because they believed they were window dressing at this point because the kids did not do well. Friends of Bedford seemed to be running Dunbar as a charter school, which it wasn't—they still answered to DCPS. It was an off-kilter relationship. They were given a lot of leeway at first. One of the Bedford officers confessed, "It still worked while Michelle Rhee was at the helm because she understood that's who we are. She would defend us. We really didn't understand the extent to which she protected us."

Leonard knew the end was coming. "When [Rhee] stepped down, we knew our project would be in jeopardy. Fenty and Rhee [were] the governing body. When Gray won, it started to rain on us. She left in October, and we knew then that our safety net was gone." The Friends of Bedford were confronted with the reality that their detractors had been keeping score.

When presented with their reported failings, they rebutted each and every one. On the charge that they bumped Vince Gray from graduation? Not true. That the school wasn't secure? Friends of Bedford had asked for security but were denied. In fact, in its first report submitted to DCPS there is a detailed budget for the security the Friends of Bedford requested. The Bedford report requests,

An increased number of security agents to manage the movement of students, not only throughout the building, but also into and out of the building.

Better trained agents who are qualified in handling disruptive students and student conflict.

The use of proactive agents willing to engage students who are cutting and/or violating the rules and regulations of the school and DCPS.

The partner [Friends of Bedford] is currently awaiting a decision from DCPS regarding its ability to hire an outside security company to replace or supplement Hawk One services.

It is the intention of Friends of Bedford Inc, to manage the security service if DCPS allows.

After Hawk One went bankrupt in 2009, the Bedford team broke the rules and hired its own security company to supplement the replacements. DCPS removed the Bedford hires. Chaos in the halls? A load of bad kids were transferred into their school, and problems followed. They didn't respond quickly enough to the alleged sexual attack? They wanted to wait until the police investigation was conclusive. The teacher who walked out and talked to the *Washington Post?* She wouldn't accept that there were certain legal channels they had to go through in order to discipline kids. They had an answer for everything.

What seems to have been lurking around the edges of the difficulties was the disintegrating relationship between Friends of Bedford and Principal Jackson. By this point, it was a case of he said/he said about what had happened between them. Things got so toxic that lawsuits were filed and subpoenas sent, including one to a *Washington Post* reporter. All that eventually went away, but the bad feelings did not. Jackson felt undervalued and dismissed. Friends of Bedford felt deceived, describing the events as a coup staged by a former friend. Jackson saw Bedford as being in over its head and not tuned in to the immediate needs of the students.

By this time, the Friends of Bedford knew all of its members would be returning to New York soon. They questioned whether or not DC was really ready for reform.

"Denial," Niaka concluded. "They are in denial. They are not about change."

"They refuse to move the citizens to the point where they can be competitive in this country," Leonard said. Not clarifying exactly who "they" were, he continued, "DC is a farm, and what they are growing is human athletes. And if they don't become professional, they go back on the street. Most of the graduates are still on the eighth-grade level. That is the sad truth."

Gaston's next remarks summed up why he believed the Bedford-DC experiment couldn't work. "They saw us as reformers who were actually here to reform, and instead of allowing us the time to do the job, they found reasons to make excuses. Michelle Rhee's mistake." He did concede one point, however. "We are arrogant. We are. I am going to say it, because we are great. We know what is right, and we know that we are going to fight for what's right."

They would have kept on talking if not for a warning announcement over the PA. Another massive snowstorm was going to hit DC. Teachers should prepare for an early dismissal. All the men rose, put on their hats and coats, and headed for Coolidge's exits as the students started to leave.

"We need to be in the halls and outside," George Leonard said.

It snowed ten inches overnight. Mayor Gray had been in office for twenty-three days. Jake Tapper, a reporter from ABC News, tweeted to his followers: "Dear Mayor Gray, it's been snowing for hours and I haven't seen one snowplow. You there?" As former Mayor Fenty had already found out, in DC the power shift changes like the weather.

Spring 2012

In Dunbar's library, Principal Jackson gives some advice to a member of the debate team, something about presentation.

"Awww, Mr. Jackson . . . ," says the young man.

"It is true. Believe it," Jackson insists as he walks over to sit at the head of a long table. It is close to 6:00 PM. Principal Jackson is in the library to attend just one more meeting before the end of a long day that started with him greeting students in the morning. In walks one of the ladies from the front office with a piece of birthday cake for him, from an office party he had to miss. "Thank you, Miss Hayes."[2] He nods to her. She gives him a big smile back and then takes the plate as others trickle in for the meeting.

"Relationships, relationships, relationships" are one key to Jackson's leadership at Dunbar High School. He'd been back at Dunbar just over a year. "Most of the children in the building knew me and when I came back they were so happy to see me. The kids said, 'Oh, Jackson is back. We know what we have to do.' So everybody was in class, and everybody basically wore their uniforms. I didn't have any problems. So that I came back the first day, children knew, 'Well, this is Mr. Jackson.' They even told the little freshmen, 'That's Mr. Jackson.'"

Before he was reappointed principal, Mr. Jackson had been working as a consultant in the school, a position agreed upon after the collaboration with Bedford disintegrated. "Unfortunately we did not agree with how the school should be turned around. When they told me that they wanted to do certain things, I said, 'Well, respectfully, Mr. Leonard, that does not work.' And they did not listen. So, therefore, at the end of the year, I said, 'I will not work with you again. I am resigning my position as principal, and you can do what you need to do.' And unfortunately, because they did not know what they were doing, in terms of turning schools around, the school spiraled out of control. The day I left is the day the school spiraled out of control."

Teachers tell anecdotes of as many as fifty students in the halls if no authority figure was around, and about colleagues who, by Christmas, had taken all of their personal days for the year because work was so stressful.

When Jackson returned, he got the security DCPS promised and some latitude to do things his way—in the short term. "Fortunately we were able to put certain things in place where, you know, . . . it stabilized the school." One teacher described it as *Law & Order* with a caring side. Stephen Jackson will speak about himself in the third person, often. Of his return he said, "The students know Mr. Jackson loves them. And oh, I love my students and they love us. And we take care of our students. And we build relationships with our students." Jackson relates to the students on several levels. When the young black man Trayvon Martin was shot in Florida and was described as being suspicious for wearing a hoodie, Principal Jackson joined the young men in his school in protest one day by wearing a hooded sweatshirt.

Jackson describes his method as "nag and nurture." The students are regularly reminded of disciplinary action, including supervised study and the enigmatic "Jackson's list." "Generally, we call up their parents. If a student gets into another argument with another student, we bring in staff members where they are able to mediate between the students, and generally we don't have anything after. But if we do, you know, the last thing we do is suspend 'em. We may suspend 'em for a couple of days. We may suspend them for a longer period depending on their infraction, but . . . I want to knock on wood that we haven't had many fights in this building at all. We diverted the fights because kids know if they fight, the hammer comes down on them very hard. The language . . . that they have used in the past, you know, they don't use the same type of language, although you may hear it here or there. But all you have to do is 'Ahem!' Or 'Oh, I'm sorry. I'm sorry.' So it's a different attitude because kids feel they're in a nurturing environment."

Students with an interest in science can enroll in smaller academies focusing on technology and engineering. "In addition to that, we've created a tenth grade academy. Just for tenth graders. Then we have the eleventh and twelfth graders that are in the towers. But the tenth graders, they have their own area. Ninth graders have their own area. The eleventh and twelfth graders have their area. We've also created another lunchroom so the ninth graders eat by themselves. And then the following period, the tenth graders eat by themselves. The eleventh and twelfth graders eat together upstairs. So we built, over last summer, a brand-new lunchroom downstairs, separately, just for the ninth graders and just for the tenth graders." The ninth graders are also required to take an 8:00 AM class that focuses on their futures. They wander in, some of them still putting on the belts they had to take off to make it through the metal detector at their entrance. One day the first half of the period was dedicated to creating a five-year timeline. The students were asked to make a collage, a storyboard, about their hopes and dreams for five years down the road. A group of giggly girls are busy pasting pictures of wedding dresses on their large pieces of cardboard. In the second half of the period the students were asked to prepare questions for a group of volunteers, professionals who were brought in to talk to the students about career options.

"Because we've created a learning environment for students in the ninth and the tenth grades, exponentially they are learning. So we separated them, and fortunately for us, the ninth graders are not picking up certain habits of the older folk." Jackson laughs a knowing laugh.

The meeting is about to begin. A few local politicians stroll in, a couple of coaches, alumni, and a few members of city government. An agenda is distributed, and an attendance sheet is passed around. Everyone is here for the monthly meeting to discuss the new $122 million Dunbar Senior High School.

16 | NEW NEW SCHOOL

WEARING WHITE CONSTRUCTION HATS and holding shiny new shovels, politicians, educators, and alumni dug into a big pile of earth churned up for the occasion. It was a cliché photo op, but the sentiments felt that day were something rare in such a political city: they were genuine. Once the dirt started the fly, the crowd hooted with joy.

The ground breaking for the new new Dunbar High School was an emotional occasion for those who gathered on the school's backfield. "A marvelous day!" cheered a class member from 1969.[1] A former educator who loved teaching in the first building, Dunbar I, recalled a better time: "The original school was an absolutely beautiful edifice. I enjoyed my tenure there. I loved the children and the administration. I loved the community that was Dunbar. I loved the community that we formed."[2] For many, November 17, 2011, was a step toward rebuilding Dunbar on all levels.

Laid out in the offices of the firm of Perkins Eastman the drawings showing the elevation, landscaping, and interior cutaways of Dunbar III could have covered an average conference table three times over, maybe four. Matt Bell, one of the firm's principals, stroked his salt-and-pepper beard as he explained why his team had pursued the Dunbar project.

"We like to do schools because we think they're really the sort of anchors of communities, so this one looked like a great opportunity to fix something that seemed to have gone haywire with the '70s building. And we think we can. We thought at the time, when we went after it, that it's a good project for us because it has—it's an urban school, and a tight, urban site, so we know how to do those sorts of things. We like building in DC. We have a lot of experience in the process of DC."

Perkins Eastman, formerly EE&K, has designed libraries and public parks around the world and in the District. Not long before the Dunbar project, the firm executed a streamlined, elegant, and seamless addition to a Victorian school in Foggy Bottom that was designed in the late 1800s. Even though Bell has the demeanor of a seasoned vet who has "been there, done that, flew back business class," he was obviously intrigued by this opportunity. "It's a very high-profile project, not the least of which because it's in the nation's capital, but also because of the history of this particular school. So, we've teamed with Moody-Nolan; they're the largest minority architecture firm in the United States. So, there's a lot of constellation of things that sort of come together."

"The whole history resonated with us," said Patrick Williams of Moody-Nolan. "One of the things we pride ourselves on in the firm is what we call 'responsive architecture' to come up with solutions early on in the process." Williams, who has been working on K–12 architecture in the District for fifteen years, sees this moment as one that will restore some faith. "I think it is actually really accomplishing something that, quite frankly, a lot of people—a lot of students, teachers, and even a lot of alumni—probably thought this would never happen in their lifetime."

The team of Perkins Eastman/Moody-Nolan was chosen after a yearlong contest. When the Office of Public Education Facilities Modernization (OPEFM) announced that any interested firm could submit a proposal, there was only one requirement: Capture the soul of the 1916 building. In the two-pronged process firms first had to submit a narrative, a vision of the work that was proposed. The next phase was to submit a design.

The OPEFM was created in 2007, specifically to address the enormous structural problems in the city's schools. At the time there were four thousand open and unresolved work orders involving thirty-three schools. Before there could be any discussions about designing new campuses, the schools needed to be stabilized so they would be safe. Once that was accomplished, the next phase was the progressive modernization of the middle and elementary schools. On the high school level, the projects would be singular, wholesale, onetime events.

The entire district-wide overhaul, funded by bonds and taxes, could take as long as ten years. As for the budget, the numbers fluctuate, much to the chagrin of the city council, but the bill in the end will be close to $2.5 billion.³ Roughly $122 million of those funds have been allocated for Dunbar III.

Building the new Dunbar is an enticing venture, but certainly one with strings attached. So many different groups feel ownership of the school. The reality of the situation—attempting to please alumni, the current administration, teachers, parents, students, and government agencies, all while respecting the history of the school—would be tricky. For all involved, there seemed to be a tacit agreement not to screw it up this time. Most people felt that Dunbar II had evolved into the equivalent of an educational Death Star.

About the only people in the process who had somewhat kind things to say about the sprawling structure were the architects working on Dunbar III. Partially out of professional courtesy and intellectual objectivity, Sean O'Donnell, another Perkins Eastman principal, can articulate what was supposed to have been advantageous about the 1977 building. A soft-spoken, bespectacled man with a sense of architectural history, O'Donnell knows how to get beyond the visceral reaction most people have to Dunbar II.

"It was part of the modern movement of doing things differently in some ways, and created a new architecture for a new age. And I think we've learned a lot about scale and context and things since then. We're trying to celebrate the urban environment more than those buildings were trying to refute the urban fabric." Indeed, the external problems of DC had informed how the schools were built.

"I think there was also an introversion of those open school environments, that it was, you know, let's focus on what we're doing here internally and not recognizing the sort of powerful connection that the environment has." O'Donnell is very excited about the opportunity to introduce light into the school life of Dunbar students. He points to entire walls of glass that will illuminate the halls during the day, and be a visual invitation into the school for the community. "The idea of glass and transparency, openness and sort of an opposition to the '77 building, which was doing that [concrete] for maybe the right reasons. It was trying to be energy efficient, but we've learned a lot about how to do energy-efficient buildings without removing all the windows since then."

As part of the strategy to help maintain the building, the team decided to go for LEED platinum status. Leadership in Energy and Environmental Design (LEED) certification is based on the number and effectiveness of environmentally advanced applications in a design. The more applications, the more points, and number of points determines the building's silver, gold, or platinum status. For example, Dunbar III will feature geothermal heating as well as water-collecting units to support reusing rainwater in the building systems. The new school will also use high-end, more expensive materials that last longer, such as terrazzo flooring for the high-traffic areas.

But before any earth was moved, or pen was even put to paper, the architects from both Perkins Eastman and Moody-Nolan went straight to the source to find out what made Dunbar meaningful to the students who had gone there. They interviewed alumni who told them stories about dances in the armory, lunches eaten on the steps, and the watchful eyes of the teachers down the corridors. "We looked at the history of the building. We looked at the yearbooks, and we started with the people, first and foremost," says David Shirey, the project designer.

He recently oversaw another DC modernization project that added a new two-story, 43,000-square-foot addition to a 1932-era, 17,900-square-foot elementary school. He has been working closely with all of the different communities concerned with construction. He goes to the school regularly to participate in the monthly update meetings in Dunbar's library. The meetings provide an opportunity to air concerns and ask questions. Shirey takes notes when the coaches say they want to make sure the sports fields will be a certain way. He responds to a community leader who reports that dust is making its way into the homes surrounding the site.

Shirey says many of the design elements arose from stakeholders' feedback. "So, in looking at the project, we started with the people, and we started with the academic history, and then the cultural history, and that very quickly brought us back to the architectural history of the armory, of the way the school was sited on First Street." The armory, at the top of the gorgeous staircase, was the entryway to Dunbar in all ways. It was where social functions were held. It was where you met your friends. It was where class pictures were taken. It was the heart of the school, with all the arteries running to it and through it.

"There was that formality of entrance and formality of the building wrapping the athletic and the private, semipublic spaces on the back side. So we tried to take that, those elements and those ideas, and look at how best we could site the building. A lot of it really built off that plan. In fact, we had them here. One of the things, I grabbed a set of drawings, and I know this doesn't work very well for audio . . ." Shirey finds what he was looking for and explains that the new school will return to the 1916 school's footprint. Dunbar III will go back to the site of Dunbar I.

In the 1970s, to accommodate the new sports field, Dunbar II was pushed two streets over and dropped right in the middle of the neighborhood. Patrick Williams describes it this way: "It was like a stake was just planted down." The new building will not only return to the old location, it will also be reminiscent of the 1916 building. "The academic wing on this side, and the administration wing on this side. In some ways, you can almost think of them as this miniature campus of three buildings."

Because urban schools can't sprawl like suburban schools, designers have to build up. As they learned from Dunbar II, however, an immense multiramp tower is not the solution. "You have the four-story classrooms. We have the pool, the gym, and the theater. The arts wing. We have the administration and then, just like the section of the 1916 building that [rose] above the entry, . . . the library. We've done the same thing on the second floor and put the media center in the library, right on the corner of First and N Street. We are defining these different zones of the more civic-minded, the pure academic classroom laboratories, and then the administration and the media center. We create this distinction because [we] assume [students don't spend] an entire day in the classroom. They're going to have electives. They're going to be engaged in arts in some fashion. They're going to be engaged in physical education. So there's going to be that transition. So in some ways by using the program we're able, we hope, we believe, to create that sort of, the conditions at least for that kind of interaction again that used to happen in the armory."

While at least one critic sniffed that the design was too safe and perhaps too reverential, the architects did not make a twin of Dunbar I.[4] Dunbar III will have a knock-out sports complex, unlike the 1916 building. The new building also has to be compliant with the Americans with Disabilities Act, so there can't be a grand external staircase. And of course, there is the issue of security. Anyone who enters Dunbar now

Concept renderings of the new Dunbar III.

Perkins Eastman and Moody-Nolan

has to go through a metal detector. "A balance we find ourselves having to negotiate these days are the security aspects of the school," Shirey says with a sense of determination.

It's a problem they want to solve. The plan for the new school is a mix of preventative and passive measures. "And so how can we do that? How can we create the idea of passive security that . . . when you walk through there's not a sense of, 'I'm being watched all the time.' And quite frankly, if we can kind of remove that idea, then you can remove one-half of what some folks call 'the prison mentality.' When people feel they're being watched, they respond one way. When people feel that they have to watch someone else all the time from a position of authority, they respond in a different way."

Shirey points to a walkway bridge that goes across the main open atrium. "How can we maintain safety? And how can we maintain those sight lines? Well, when you're seeing the folks, and you're engaging the administration on a regular basis, we think there's a benefit to it. Provided it's not in a punitive side, right? So that's part of why we have the assistant principals on each floor. And they have a glass wall that looks down the corridor. So when the students are coming through, it's not a surprising thing to interact with the assistant principal on a regular basis." Shirey points to a walkway, a bridge that spans the new armory and points to one of the sight lines they've created. "You walk by, you can wave. You see, it's not the only time that you engage with the administration, when there's a problem. So hopefully that also can help foster that sense of community between the students and the authority to where the idea of going to an authority is not only when there's a problem. Or only if there's a problem for the students."

"There will be metal detectors built into the architecture," Patrick Williams notes. But, he explains, with the right budget and design, the detectors can be fairly undetectable if placed in the surrounding support walls. "There are new, streamlined ways we can do this; we integrated them in the curtain wall system actually and aligned it with the main wall. Visually with the rhythm of the curtain wall."

The entrance of Dunbar III—a large, welcoming plaza—will face O Street, which will be reopened. On the outside of the building, the school's name will be displayed on a singular tower, harkening back to the original two towers that flanked the entrance of Dunbar I. A funny thing happened over time as well. The name of the school changed a bit. It has always officially been Dunbar High School. When the 1977 building went up, the exterior read DUNBAR SENIOR HIGH SCHOOL. Lately, its banners and letterhead referred to it as Paul Laurence Dunbar High School. On the recent plans, displayed on a tall brick tower are big, bold letters that read vertically: D U N B A R.

Paul Laurence Dunbar will get his due. His likeness and his poem "Keep A-Pluggin' Away" will be embedded on a wall directly facing the entrance. The history of the school will be built into the building so it won't be forgotten and can't be discarded. The great heroes of Dunbar will never have their pictures placed in crooked plastic frames again. Their accomplishments will be displayed on stainless steel plaques integrated into the architecture.

"Throughout the building, we have about 220 of these," Shirey says of the plaques that will be in the floors. "There have been so many incredibly successful people that have come through this institution, not necessarily this building, this institution of Dunbar, frankly. . . . The fact that there are six Dunbar graduates that are on stamps. There is a level of record that was demanded that is hard to meet."

Shirey points out that the wall of superstars, eighteen plaques in the Armory below Dunbar's image, is meant to be an aspirational tool. A plaque is reserved for someone who had made a grand contribution. "Not just 'Congratulations, someone's the valedictorian,' and now you get permanently remembered. There's a level of success, the bar being that high. It helps define what the expectations can be, and then here are the resources to help achieve it, to help achieve these expectations."

Not all the plaques will be filled when the school opens. "You'll notice there are two kinds of plaques. There's the one identifying folks who have achieved, but frankly, the bulk of the plaques, maybe two-thirds, 60 percent, we want to make blank. 'Cause I want the students to come through these spaces every day. They're walking down the arts corridor, and there's blanks in the arts corridor. You know, they're walking down the civic, or in front of the theater, or in front of the gym, and there's blanks in front of the athletic corridor there in front of the gym. You know, you want them to walk by and say, 'See that one there? That's me. In a few years that's gonna be me.'"

There's a real romance attached to the building of this new school. The architects are into it. The students are into it. The administration is into it. There's so much hope pinned on this one building. Sean O'Donnell and his team are aware of the expectations. "We want to create a center of community here that's open and inviting, and you know, it becomes maybe a place [where] Dunbar grows back to the prominence that it had. There's this administrative transition that's occurring now, and so with the architecture, maybe there's the opportunity to reconceive of the place in its entirety. And I'm not party to what's happening with the administrative side, but hopefully this is the opportunity again for Dunbar to reassert itself, in DC certainly, and put it back up to even the regional stage that it used to be on."

There was a moment of candor from one of the architects. The new building has a bridge, a walkway over the armory. When asked about kids who might throw projectiles—or each other—over the side, Matthew Bell looks over his glasses and answers, "To a certain extent, the architecture can only solve so many of those problems."

17 | BACK TO THE FUTURE

It would be a great fallacy to give segregation credit for the lucky combination of events which produced Dunbar. The school didn't want to be segregated, and one can easily imagine conditions that would have maintained its traditions to the present day. The Dunbar experience does show that all the talk about racially balanced classrooms, or innovative curricula, or that matter of racial limits on intelligence is simply beside the point. Education is an art influenced less by the criteria of social science than by the self confidence of the teacher and the eagerness of their pupils.
—Wall Street Journal, *June 30, 1975*

A building can only do so much. The architect was correct.

The English Teacher

Matthew Stuart is writing on the chalkboard in his room, #702. It's near the top of one of the towers. The little bit of natural light comes in from a series of small rectangular windows about ten inches wide that are close to the ceiling. He is getting ready to continue a classroom discussion of Ayn Rand's *Anthem*. He wants his students to explore the thesis that the individual can be programmed to lose all desire for self-realization if a higher power has all the control.

Slowly students amble in, all wearing the correct uniforms but with disregard for the school's no–cell phone policy. It is a twelfth grade class full of seniors who will be graduating with the class of 2012, hopefully. Well, the class isn't actually full. Only fourteen of the thirty-eight students have shown up.

"Good morning," says Mr. Stuart. Most of the students respond. One boy is in a conversation that is loud enough for all of his fellow students to hear. And that may be the point. "I feel so bad it was Mother's Day, and I didn't have anything for my moms—anything. She got me an iPhone." He smiles a smile that revealed he wasn't actually that concerned, but now everyone knows he has an iPhone. Mr. Stuart sees a chance to engage the kid.

"Well, you could have given her a gift that didn't cost any money, like cleaning your room," Stuart offers.

"Whaaat?" another student butts in, not really understanding the idea of an act being a gift.

Stuart tries another route. "Or you could pick her some flowers."

"Ain't no flowers growing in the ghetto," responds a thin, sweet-looking kid with shoulder-length braids who simultaneously slammed his body into a chair while dropping his backpack on the floor with a thud.

"Just dandelions," chimes in his friend. Mr. Stuart smiles. At least the kids heard him.

Stuart stands before them, an even-tempered, nice-looking twenty-something white guy wearing a tie and slacks. In a few weeks he will be getting married. But before then he has to get his students ready for their final exams. From 11:40 AM to 1:00 PM he really digs into the concepts at hand while slowly pulling the students along.

"What is collectivism?" he asks. When no one responds, he calls on kids individually and through a series of questions helps them get closer to the answer. He refers to his students as "ladies and gentlemen" when he wants their attention. He asks two young men to take turns reading a passage out loud. A girl in the corner wants to know what the word "transgression" means.

"Transgression. Who can tell her what it means?" There are a few mumbles. Stuart offers, "If you are on your cell phone in school, that's a transgression."

A little bit later, when one student who has been looking bored and sullen all class blurts out the perfect answer to a question, Stuart congratulates him. Scoffing is heard in the corner. The young man throws his hands up and says, "Don't hate!" A girl who is seriously overweight and slightly unkempt grows agitated when she refuses to believe a certain fact is true. "NO!" she yells. Her reaction is a little bit startling, but Mr. Stuart seems accustomed to her lack of control.

About thirty minutes into the class another student asks if he can have the handout of the reading assignment they are currently discussing. Through it all, Matthew Stuart smiles, keeps his cool, ignores what deserves ignoring, and plows on. He constantly asks the kids, "What do you think? What do you think?" When one kid has a very basic question, Stuart points to a student he knows is well prepared and motions. "Help her. Tell her what the answer is."

Occasionally a student gets up and walks over to show another student something on a phone. In one case, a new tattoo is being displayed. Stuart watches, makes eye contact with the girl but keeps going. She heads back to her seat. It's a double period, which requires a marathon mentality. He knows he has to maintain the momentum to keep the students involved, or at least not be disruptive to those that do want to listen.

"What I have . . . is that students are great with ideas. You give them a new idea, and they just get all wide-eyed about it. Like, they love that. They think that's the coolest." That's what he loves about his classes. The challenging part for him comes from a failure in the system. "What I was told, and accepted on an intellectual level, but just still couldn't, like, grasp, when I got here is just how terribly—how far behind on basic reading skills some kids are. I taught twelfth grade here. How is it that some students get to the twelfth grade without blending their sounds yet— not being able to blend t and h into a 'th' sound for 'thunder' or 'this'? And, that's an actual student this year. That's hard because, what does a twelfth-grade education mean for you as an individual?"

It leads to acting out from time to time. In class, a hulking student with shiny, raisin-sized rocks in his ears gets up and moves around the room, time and time again. He can answer some of the questions but gives a look like it is an imposition to do so. "He has a grown man's body and a grown man's thought process, without the academic skills behind it," Stuart says. "And there is a difference between being a smart person and being able to succeed, like, with As in school. 'Cause he's very bright . . ."

But what will become of him?

Stuart doesn't dumb down his class lectures, but he does have to break them down into small, digestible parts. Sometimes that doesn't work. He tried *The Red Badge of Courage*, but his students did not take to it and he got blank stares in class. *Macbeth?* A big hit. "They liked the murder, and they really liked Lady Macbeth's personality. They loved her. They *loved* her."

Teaching wasn't on Stuart's radar as a kid growing up in Ohio. "In elementary school it was the range of firefighter and plane pilot. But I started thinking about it more seriously in my sophomore year of college, like, around 2006, and started working as a Sunday school teacher to test the waters. Never did anything with education but applied to Teach for America in my senior year. I was accepted and was excited to come to DC for that. Since then, I've gone on just to make sure I got the full licensure, so I'm keeping up with that."

Stuart was part of the Teach for America wave of 2007. He has now been at Dunbar for three years. It was his first and only professional teaching job. He graduated from Michigan State in May 2009, came to DC in June, and was teaching by August. He was a few months shy of his twenty-third birthday. After an intense and fast-paced crash course at the Teach for America boot camp, he was assigned to Dunbar one week before school started.

After weeks of preparing for his first class, he got an unwelcome surprise right off the bat. "So, I started planning my units. Actually found out the first day that I wasn't teaching the class they told me I was. I was told [I would be teaching] Read 180, sort of the remedial freshman/sophomore. But then it was twelfth-grade English." It is a world of difference teaching fourteen-year-olds with learning disabilities when compared to teaching seventeen- and eighteen-year-olds who may or may not have been just pushed through the system. "It's a big jump. And, that was with the Friends of Bedford—that's when they were in charge of the scheduling it."

He still has tough feelings about it. "I've never been lied to about my class since then." Caught off guard, he had his first introduction into the rough waters of being a public school teacher in DC. He was aware that he was walking into a school that was in the beginning steps of restructuring mandated by No Child Left Behind. "Aware, but only aware. That doesn't mean understanding. It doesn't mean understanding causes or being able to evaluate it. I knew that a lot of the staff had disappeared from the year before. I knew that there was a management group and they were telling us the ways that they would support us. If a student curses in your class, they will be like, 'Here's the protocol.' It's mostly discipline. Mostly discipline, and they promised us working Promethean boards, which eventually came. And it makes a big difference. Technology and discipline—those were the promises."

Stuart tells a familiar story. Kids with troubled home lives. School budgets cut drastically. The number of electives for students has been slashed to the point that one of his seniors that day said she was done with school after second period—she had nothing else to do. A student pops his head in, midclass, to ask for a pencil. As for supplies, Stuart does what he can. He judiciously hands out pencils and pens to students who come to class without a writing instrument.

For the most part, the students show Stuart a good deal of respect. "You stay, is the biggest thing. The first year, as much as anything, is just getting tested out, and the students want to know what your reputation is. I mean, since tenth grade, they've known that I was the twelfth-grade teacher," he says, putting it in plain terms. He was not one of the Teach for America candidates who split when the two years were up. "So, I mean, I come to work every day. There's always a lesson. And, I've been here for a while. If you care, that's all they need."

In passing, Stuart mentions how impressed he's been by two other educators on staff: the veteran girls' track coach Marvin Parker and the newly promoted head football coach, Jerron Joe. Coach Parker was recruited from a private Christian school and Coach Joe had been the assistant football coach and knew Dunbar well.

The Football Star

"Way to stay on top of it!"

"Depth! Depth! Depth!"

"Huddle up!"

The Dunbar High School football team is working hard on a sweaty August evening. It is 91 degrees at 5:00 PM, and squads of young men push to perform on the Cardozo High School football field. It's ironic that the Dunbar team is practicing on Cardozo's turf. Cardozo was once

Central High School, the all-white high school built the same year as the original Dunbar. Central got a full athletic field; Dunbar did not. The team is practicing at Cardozo because the Dunbar field is all torn up; the city is going to build Dunbar a new state-of-the-art field once Dunbar II is demolished. Cardozo is also undergoing a modernization like Dunbar—finally, equality of facilities almost one hundred years later.

"I can't believe it is almost time for school," says Jerron Joe before he jogs back onto the field and returns to his team. It is the first practice of the season, so Coach Joe is paying attention to his players' tempo and watching their alignment. Some of the players are just naturally gifted. One kid catches the ball so effortlessly you might suspect there is a magnet in the ball and one on his hand. A wiry receiver can jump so high it seems like a special effect. During one drill a young-looking receiver misses the ball over and over again. The last time the kid gets closer but still doesn't catch it. Coach Joe shouts out, "Good. That's good. You listened. You did the right thing."

Not long ago, Jerron Joe was in the same position. He graduated from Dunbar in 2004 and returned to his alma mater. At twenty-five, he became the youngest coach in the history of the legendary Crimson Tide football program.

Joe looks quite a bit different than when he was a student. Gone are the braids, his hair now short. A trim goatee is still in place. He is compact and strong with a youthful look. Even though he looks young, his first question to his players is one from an old soul: "I ask, 'What are you going to do when the ball goes flat?' I use the terminology that 'the ball always will go flat. Whether you are Dan Marino, Peyton Manning, or Michael Jordan, your career will be over. But what I want to get across to my players is that with education you always have something to fall back on."

Jerron knows that with so many Dunbar players in the NFL, like his high school friend Vernon Davis, his players have stars in their eyes just as he did. He believes his returning to the school after a tremendous high school football career proves his point. "Because they know that, with me being a coach, that I'd love to be playing professional football right now. Unfortunately, the ball went flat in my college days."

Jerron was both a scholar and an athlete in school. He was a starting cornerback who broke a record. "My junior and senior year, I made all the honors. After my junior year, the *Washington Post* voted me the best undersized player in the league because I was five nine, 160. My junior year I led my entire league in interceptions. Going into my senior year, I was recruited heavily by the Ivy League schools, Georgetown, because I had excellent grades as well. I actually finished the top male at the top of my senior class. I had a 3.8. It was ten girls that beat me out. I finished eleventh." He received a full scholarship to the HBCU North Carolina Central University (NCCU) where he graduated with a degree in physical education in 2008. At NCCU he simply didn't have the sports career he hoped for and doesn't make excuses. "I would like to think, because of injury, my career in college wasn't as good as I wanted it to be."

But just the fact that Joe made it to college is another lesson for his students. When he was their age, he was essentially on his own. "When I was younger, I lived with my mom, my two brothers, and my stepfather. So, basically, middle class. I led the good life. My mom did what she could to take care of me and my brothers. She did an excellent job."

His mother, who also graduated from Dunbar, had been a police officer but became seriously ill and couldn't provide for her family any longer. "She got sick. I moved from a four-bedroom—separate living room, dining room, kitchen, two-sided basement, big front yard, back-yard, three bathrooms—to moving into a housing project before I got to high school because she got sick. So, my story is always good because I had family members from here who didn't do so well. I had family members that did. But, it's all about decision making."

Joe could have gone one way, but he chose another, with the guidance of his mother and another police officer, a man who coached high school sports and became a mentor to him. Joe had someone there who had his back, and he had the seeds his mother planted. "The things that she instilled into me as a child up to the age of twelve, thirteen, whatever it was when I moved out, I didn't let that—I didn't let society take over me. I tell these kids all the time, 'Don't be a product of your environment.'" He is grateful to his mom for what she could do, and she was there at the school the day his big promotion was announced.

Joe is tough on his own players in the same way but realizes they are coming from some challenging circumstances. He knows what the deal is when you are a young African American man in DC and was reminded of it one day after practice. "Two young white cops pulled me over. I had a Ford Mustang. It's nice. And I was dropping one of my kids off. And I'm young. And we're crossing paths. I'm at a stop sign. They're at a stop sign. And then we drove past each other. I'm looking through my rearview mirror—they're about to pull me over. This was very recently—the first thing that he said was, 'What are you doing around here?' "

Joe gets a little irritated recalling the story. "I don't have the right to? Did you see my tags that say DC? So he says, 'License and registration.'

"I say, 'Can I ask, why are y'all pulling me over?'

" 'Your headlights.'

" 'Y'all pulled me over from the front—and my headlights was working.'

"I got out the car and checked them after they left. Basically, I was in a high drug trafficking area with a nice car. They said, 'Well, do you have any drugs or weapons we need to worry about?' I said, 'No. I'm actually an educator.'

" 'OK.'

"So, at this point, I'm getting frustrated. They go, run my tags, come back.

" 'Are you sure you don't have . . . ?'

" 'Didn't I tell you guys I'm an educator? Matter of fact, I'm also the head coach over at Dunbar.' The officers response: 'Oh, well, you need to get these boys right so the Redskins can win.' "

Shades of Jo-Jo Stewart and Leon Ransom in 1944.

Coach Joe knows what his students are up against but urges them to somehow push past it. Joe, who is not that old and doesn't even look his age, is as serious as can be when he says, "You know how they say that babies are raising babies? Nobody wants to take on the responsibility of being the parent and holding their child accountable. I tell my kids all the time that football teaches you life lessons: teamwork, time management, working through adversity. There are so many life lessons you'll learn through football. That's the same thing with class."

Joe's decision to come back to Dunbar recalls the day when M Street/ Dunbar graduates returned to their alma mater to try to make things better. Returning to a place you know so well creates a level of familiarity or a bond that can take a new teacher a few years to develop. Joe believes the ball going flat in college was meant to be.

"I didn't always know I wanted to teach, but I did know that I wanted to be a mentor."

The Girls' Track Coach

A tall girl with impossibly long and strong legs leads the way through a maze of cement halls that are sorely in need of a paint job. As she heads down the stairs and through a set of red metal doors, it is hard to keep up because her stride is brisk and each step covers a significant amount of ground. She's not that talkative or expressive, but when she reaches Coach Parker's office and sees him, a big smile breaks out.

In the basement of Dunbar High School, something special has been happening. Coach Marvin Parker has pictures plastered everywhere of his championship team. Since Parker arrived in 2005, the Dunbar girls' track team has been on an upward trajectory. They are city champions. From day one, he told the girls he expected nothing less. "We are going to leave a legacy. We are going to build a tradition for women at this school."

A former military man who had been stationed around the world from Germany to Jersey, Parker settled into life as a husband and father while working as an accountant. In his spare time he coached track at a Christian private school near his home in Maryland. One day at a meet he was approached about taking over for Dunbar's retiring coach.

"Before I decided, I spent a season watching and observing. I was coming from a private school. I have structure and discipline. It was easy." He lets out big chuckle when describing what he noticed about the Crimson Tide's lady runners. "It was like, *Wow!* Some of these little girls need a swift kick!"

But then he leans back in his chair and nods his head, in the way he probably did seven years ago when he signed on.

"I think I can take this challenge. That's my competitive spirit in me." And he was eager to work with some athletes who he could tell were gifted. "I was impressed that there were a lot of talented kids here who were undisciplined."

Parker's drill includes early morning practices before school, starting before sunrise. At night his runners were instructed to do a series of exercises including push-ups and sit-ups. They were told to do research and then write papers on athletes who had excelled in their particular race. And taking a page from the 1928 Dunbar handbook he even sent home a worksheet explaining the need for a balanced diet, telling the parents to "stop giving these girls biscuits and gravy." Parker's delivery is a hilarious meld of Martin Lawrence meets a handsome preacher. And that describes his look too.

"I was told, there is no way you are going to get inner-city girls to practice at five o'clock in the morning. It is not gonna happen. Yeah it is! Because I am going to eliminate all their excuses." The excuses included: "I have no way to get to school," "We aren't going to win anyway," and "My mom won't let me." One by one, Coach Parker knocked them down. He would pick up girls himself at their homes—as early as 3:30 AM some days—to get them to practice. After the first summer of training, the girls won their first, second, and third meets.

"The parents couldn't wait to get them out of the house. 'Come get 'em!'" he shouts imitating someone's Madea-esque mom. "I had great parent participation for the few who had parents. Some are in group homes." Parker has runners who are in foster care. One girl was virtually homeless. Another suffered from abuse. Within his team, he created an alternate family for his runners. He would take them to IHOP and show them inspirational movies such as *Remember the Titans*.

In describing the team spirit, Parker makes a fist, though not in an aggressive way. His fist symbolized unity: the strength of five fingers together is greater than each finger on its own. "You can't get between the fingers. What happens in the family stays in the family. What happens in the track office stays in the track office. I will encourage you. Use words like family. Love, togetherness, camaraderie. Using words like that. That's what that is."

He is very clear that the track team is not a social club, and anybody who signs up has to pass a series of first-time challenges. There are no excuses. It is a rule that if it is below forty degrees, high school athletes can't practice outside. No problem—Coach Parker has the girls train the school parking garage. The team's success started to attract students who might have fallen through the cracks. One day a girl named Samantha approached him in the hall. She wanted to be on the team.

"I heard this girl's a fighter. Off the chain. 'Do I want this kid on my team?' I have some crazy kids, but do I need to add another one? OK. I'll be cuckoo for Cocoa Puffs, I'll bring her in. And this kid had a work ethic that was unbelievable, also with a God-given talent. God blessed her with genetics."

Marvin Parker, Dunbar girls' track coach and dean of students.

Getty Images

Watching these athletes run or jump or sprint leaves you wondering how the human body is capable of such feats. They are all muscle and grace. Yes, they are young and in shape, but the intensity and focus on the girls' faces is as mesmerizing as their speed and agility. Teenage girls with focus like that should be good students too. And they have to be if they want to be on Parker's team, despite Dunbar's academic reputation.

"After being around these girls, they are intelligent young ladies. But the reputation of DC schools is that these kids were plumb dumb and had no clue. I just walked in this building and found out it was just not the case. Some of the girls—straight brilliant." When he did start asking why some of the students weren't trying, the answer was both trite and true. "I asked them, and they said it was peer pressure. They were trying to keep a false image. 'I'm Saratoga. . . . I'm from Seventh and O,'" he says, putting on the voice of a teenager trying to act hard. "I broke it down to them how stupid it was. Nobody owns nothin' in DC! The federal government owns everything in DC. You are representing neighborhoods and projects that care nothing about you."

He hadn't realized the depth of the girls' inspirational deprivation until he started taking them on the tours of colleges where they had track meets.

"When we went to Virginia Tech I met with the director of pre-engineering. He took the girls all around, went in the dorm rooms. You should have seen their faces. I could have just cried." The girls had no idea life could be like that.

Coach Parker brings speakers, frat brothers, and recent college graduates to the school to talk to his students. "I never have to win another championship, but my girls *have* got to go to college." His demeanor changes when he thinks about the bigger picture. He is very, very serious about the way he believes adults should talk to kids. "We need to start telling the truth about these things. You want to break the cycle, break the chains, break the cycle of having babies, staying in DC, going on Section 8, never leaving the 'hood." He stresses that they are ladies. When he realized that some of the girls were uncomfortable in the tight running shorts and were receiving unwanted attention, he helped design a more modest running skort for the girls.

He can point to every girl in a recent team photo and name where she is in college. Morgan State. Coppin. The good reputation of his team has helped him recruit talented runners to come to Dunbar, which until recently wasn't easy. Parents did not want to send their kids into *that* building, and they weren't too keen on the academic statistics coming out of the school.

One student who took the leap was Angela Bonham. Bonham had been attending a progressive high school in the District that had a 100 percent graduation rate and a 100 percent college acceptance but a small track program. Bonham is a natural athlete. She is fast. She's a golfer and a gifted math whiz. She was also extremely shy. Coach Parker promised Angela and her family that she would get a good education and be part of a championship track team if she came to Dunbar. By her senior year Angela had seventeen individual city titles in cross-country, indoor, and outdoor track, and she earned a four-year academic scholarship to George Washington University.

In a few minutes of her spare time, heading home from a campus job and wearing a flowing floral skirt and ballet flats, she looks tiny sitting on a bench in Union Station. "Dunbar isn't as bad as people make it seem, OK? There are some bright kids that come out of Dunbar. And if you keep them interested, then they will do what they have to."

Her first impressions of Dunbar were not bad, but she remembers that it was confusing. "The rules were really relaxed before I got there. 'Cause I got there, and I saw half the kids wearing school uniforms. And, I wasn't sure if I was going to be wearing a uniform or not, because I figured like, everybody's wearing the same thing—what's going on? And nobody told me about anything."

She arrived during the school's first year of restructuring and was placed in the rigorous pre-engineering program. "There were problems with the kids. They did whatever they wanted to do. Walk the halls and anything they wanted to do. So they had us in, like, a section in the school. And when Bedford came they kind of integrated us more. So, we were with the chaos, but it wasn't as much chaos because they had controlled a lot of the mess."

She never regretted coming to Dunbar, though. "It's good to know that I came out of a school with great history, because I could be the next person, you know?" The track team helped her come out of her shell and even become a bit of a team jokester, masterminding one specific trick involving Twizzlers that is now an inside joke. She really admires Coach Parker for all he did for the team. She says, "When I started at Dunbar, I knew no one and was just another athlete that transferred to be on a better team; however, when it was time to leave, it felt like I was leaving my family."

Coach Parker is not just a coach at Dunbar; since 2009, he has also been the dean of students. He was invited in by George Leonard and Friends of Bedford, who told him they liked what he was doing with the track team and asked if he could spread a little of that magic around the school at large.

Parker gave what was probably the most sober and fair assessment of what went right and what wrong with the Friends of Bedford's short tenure. "I liked the Friends of Bedford. I think the FOB had the right idea and didn't execute the plan properly. But this is not New York. I sat in the meetings, and they were taken aback with the kind of kids [at Dunbar]. You can't come in here and think you are just going to talk to those kids—you got to get in their face with the authority of a drill sergeant but the love of a father. Their plan wasn't translating. They didn't understand it was a political town. They would have worked if they had listened. But they were really full of themselves, so they didn't listen. I liked them. I appreciated what they wanted to do. I could see that [Leonard] was pushing the school in the right direction, but you were making promises you couldn't keep. And you can't do that in DC."

Parker has continued to work at the school and is very happy that Stephen Jackson is back as principal. "Mr. Jackson believes in surrounding youself with folks who are about getting the job done."

In getting the job done, Parker has had his own political run-ins. When he first got to Dunbar, he made a lot of noise about the inequity in funds for girls sports. He says Title IX was not in effect. "It was all football, football, football, football. Nothing against the football team, but come on! You know?" And he has been questioned repeatedly about driving the girls to the school for practice.

He and Principal Jackson are working every rule in the book to make sure the school is full of children who want to be there. He knows how many infractions can lead to transfer. He resents what he calls the charter schools dumping problem kids back into the DCPS school system. He recalls one young man who had transferred into the school with straight *F*s, who wouldn't leave the hallway. The young man had no interest in class. He wanted to do what he wanted to do. Parker asked him to move along to class.

"Fuck you," he said—and then tried to run away from the *track* coach.

"Let me hip you to something, young man. Who you think you foolin'? I am going to call your mother. "

"You can call my mom."

The mother was shocked when Parker told her the kid was suspended. "You are going to suspend him for being in an unauthorized area? He can't get in-school suspension?"

"No. No. Your son has straight *F*s. Your son has not been to a class. I am sending him to you. This is not a babysitting service. It's not. This is a house of learning."

The Future

As you exit the school, it is impossible not to see the new construction of Dunbar III. Parker and Jackson are thrilled about the facility. He goes to the architectural update meetings to ensure that the athletics program will be represented. And in a move that may seem like karma, Dunbar II will be demolished to make way for the new sports complex. A shiny new school will certainly sweeten his recruiting pitch.

Parker favors old soul music when he drives, and his satellite radio station of choice has the O'Jays in heavy rotation. "That's real music," he says. Driving away from Dunbar and toward the convention center, the gentrification in the area near Dunbar is obvious. Young blonde women in Lululemon yoga pants are walking their Labradors, and Kohler bathroom fixture boxes sit on the curbs. Coach Parker has a realization about his team as he turns the corner, "Yeah, I guess sometime soon I may have my first Caucasian runner."

Dunbar is in the 20001 zip code, which by one demographer's account had the tenth-largest increase in white residents in the whole country over the last decade. In 2000 the white population in the area was 5 percent, and in 2010 it was 32 percent.[1] There are a lot of new dog parks, which seems to be the symbol for gentrification.

Matthew Stuart is one of the few white teachers at Dunbar, which has led to some interesting exchanges. "I mean, most of the time, it's just funny curiosities [such] as—'Mr. Stuart, how do you get your hair to do that?' It's like, 'Well, that's—it sometimes curls when it gets longer, naturally.' So, it's more like, curiosity and, like, it's not even about you, but it's just—if it's something that's new they want to know."

Matthew Stuart has a few questions of his own when the subject turns to Dunbar and demographics. "Are you going to be able to help the students who are here, whoever they are? And, then, the second question is: What is that group of students going to look like? So, what do you want the school to be?"

The new school can accommodate eleven hundred students, though there aren't that many attending Dunbar now. So who will fill this new, sleek school? The old Dunbar model, focusing on college prep, is being used at Banneker High School, which is 85 percent African American, with academic metrics and a graduation rate that mirrors Old Dunbar's. Dunbar is and will continue to be a general population school.

It is expected that Dunbar III will take on students from another area high school, the academically struggling Spingarn, which is slated to close. Principal Jackson hopes to recruit all kinds of students to the new state-of-the-art Dunbar High school through advertising. The school recently received a major $300,000 grant, and while most of the money will go to extended-stay programs, Jackson has earmarked close to $25,000 for a marketing campaign about Dunbar's promise. Radio ads were produced highlighting Dunbar's historic significance and its athletic dominance. The school has an inviting new website.

So what will the newest incarnation of Dunbar be? Is this $122 million building for the current population or a potential population down the road—the ones who may live in the expensive new condos that have gone up not far away? The year 2012 marked a milestone for the city: DC became no longer majority African American. The famous U Street corridor, the once elegant and busy black epicenter, was burned out in the riots. It is now trendy restaurants and cupcake shops. Just up the street from the school is a proposed development called City Market at O. The developers are promising six hundred residential units and a hotel, plus thousands of square feet of retail space. And the harbinger of all things upwardly mobile, a Trader Joe's, is slated to open soon a short distance from Anna J. Cooper Circle.

A young woman named Olivia moved in behind Dunbar four years ago because she liked the commute to work and the price of real estate. She belongs to a social circle of young multiculti women who have bought their first homes near Dunbar within the past few years. The back of her house looks out on one of the school's parking lots.

"That lot has been known to harbor a lot of criminal activity. When I first moved in it was a place where people would dump stolen cars. They would meet to do drug deals." She would find her driveway blocked by cars when there were basketball games. "It's not the best view from the back of my house."

She was excited when she found a flyer for a community meeting about the new construction. Only a few neighbors showed up. Some people at the meeting were unhappy because they said the school was going to block their afternoon light. Olivia liked what she heard and thinks the new school orientation will help reduce crime. Also, her view is going to improve dramatically, "I'm happy because there will now be a soccer field behind my house." She was impressed when she heard about Dunbar's history. She hadn't known.

There are more than forty schools in the United States today that are called Dunbar. Most are in African American neighborhoods and have varying degrees of academic success. Dunbar in Baltimore is an academic gem, while Dunbar High School in Chicago was the scene of recent shootings. Dunbar High School in Washington, DC, could make history again and extend its legacy. Given the demographics of the area, given that one in seven new marriages involves partners of different races,[2] and given that the founders of Dunbar were originally in favor of integrated schools but did the best they could under awful legal conditions, Dunbar's new place in history could be as the first truly, organically integrated school in Washington, DC. If that happens, the lessons of Dunbar will have been learned and the legacy of quality education, for all, no matter the color of one's skin, will continue.

A lot of things have changed in the five years since Dunbar was forced into restructuring and the new school was conceived. Mayor Vincent Gray was warmly welcomed to his position and then went through a dismal period during which some suggested he should step down. Kaya Henderson continued to follow the policy of evaluating teachers and shedding those who did not make the grade. Rodney Chambers now heads up a music nonprofit. And the Friends of Bedford began the application process for a charter school in DC, only to withdraw the application. They returned to New York, where they are now having success with middle schoolers and have opened a dynamic afterschool program in Brooklyn. Angela Bonham is thriving at GWU. And several of the people interviewed and featured in this book have died: Lawrence Graves, Commander Wesley Brown, Billy Taylor, Elizabeth Catlett, Dr. James Bowman, and Joe and Carol Stewart. And in August of 2013 the new Dunbar High School will open.

A $122 million facility is exciting for all involved, but external and self-inflicted wounds continue to affect the Dunbar community. On March 13, 2013, just blocks from the new building thirteen people were injured in a drive-by shooting. Dunbar's principal told the media he was concerned about retaliation violence. And in what the papers dubbed a result of win-at-all-costs, sports-first mentality, the 2012 Crimson Tide football team had its city championship title revoked for allegedly using an ineligible player. As this book went to print Coach Joe could only say an appeal was in the works. A DCPS spokeswoman confirmed the appeal process. She added, "No disciplinary action has been taken on Coach Joe. He remains head coach."

Dunbar High School will attempt to rebuild itself day by day with a new building, new teachers, new students, and perhaps even a new culture. Maybe it was a sign of good things to come when last spring on a sunny day, something that sounded like music could be heard in the parking area in front of the school. At the end of a single-file line of students was was a big kid with a big drum strapped to his chest, pounding out a percussive backbeat. There was a small group of musicians, a sax player here and a trumpet player there, marching in line, working out what appeared to be the beginning of a song while working on a formation. Maybe this version of the band wasn't as flashy or as fierce as the Crimson Tide that marched down Pennsylvania Avenue in 2009, but the Dunbar High School marching band was back.

ACKNOWLEDGMENTS

THANK YOU TO: WILLIAM and Isaac Wolff, Jane Dystel, Jerome Pohlen, Michelle Schoob, and everyone at Chicago Review Press, James Edwards, Kimberly Springle, Matt Martinez, Eric Nuzum, Kelly Caldwell, Barbara June Carter, Philip Prem Das, James Bruce, Louis Campbell, Tom Sherwood, Lisa Crisp, Mayhugh A. Graham, Pete Stewart, Jon Meacham, Ida Jones, Joellen El Bashir, Richard Jenkins, the Dunbar Alumni Federation, Teddy Gebremichael, and Casey Klein.

NOTES

Chapter 2: Teaching to Teach

1. Constance McLaughlin Green, *Secret City: History of Race Relations in the Nation's Capital*, (Princeton, New Jersey: Princeton Press,1967), 47.
2. Kate Masur, "Washington's Black Code," *New York Times*, December 7, 2011; "Washington Jail Site, African American Trail," Cultural Tourism, www.culturaltourism dc.org/things-do-see/washington-jail-site-african-american-heritage-trail.
3. Green, *Secret City*, 25.
4. Anacostia Museum and Center for African American History and Culture, *The Black Washingtonians: 300 Years of African American History*, Anacostia Museum Illustrated Chronology (Hoboken, NJ: John Wiley and Sons).
5. Ibid.
6. *Manual of the Board of Trustees of the Public Schools of Washington City* (M'Gill and Witherow, 1863), 18.
7. Report of the Commissioners of The District of Columbia, Volume IV, The Government Printing Office, Washingotn, DC, 1905, 88.
8. Kimberly Prothro Williams, *Schools for All: A History of DC Public School Buildings 1804–1960* (Washington, DC: US Department of Interior, 2008), 1.
9. Samuel Yorke Atlee, *History of the Public Schools of Washington City, D.C.* (Washington, DC: M'Gill and Witherow, 1876), 1–2.
10. J. Ormond Wilson, *The Report of the Commissioner of Education for the Year 1894–95* (Washington, DC: Government Printing Office, 1896), 1,681.
11. J. Ormond Wilson, *Eighty Years of the Public Schools of Washington 1805–1885: Report of the Commission of Education* (Washington, DC: Government Printing Office, 1896), 1,674.
12. Ellen M. O'Connor, *Myrtilla Miner* (Boston: Houghton Mifflin, 1885), 12.
13. O'Connor, *Myrtilla Miner*, 12.
14. O'Connor, *Myrtilla Miner*, 13.
15. Myrtilla Miner to Harriet Beecher Stowe, Myrtilla Miner Papers, Library of Congress, Washington, DC.
16. Elijah Green, interviewed by Augustus Ladson, 156 Elizabeth Street, Charleston, South Carolina. *Before Freedom,When I Just Can Remember: Twenty-Seven Oral Histories of Former South Carolina Slaves* (Winston Salem, NC: John F. Blair Publisher, 1980), 65.
17. Myrtilla Miner Papers, Library of Congress, Washington, DC.
18. Myrtilla Miner to "Dear Friends," 31 July 1851, Myrtilla Miner Papers, Library of Congress, Washington, DC.

19. W. H. Beecher, Letter to Solicit Funds, Reading, Mass., December 1865, Myrtilla Miner Papers, Library of Congress, Washington, DC.
20. O'Connor, *Myrtilla Miner,* 56.
21. Myrtilla Miner Letter to Friends, 1852, Myrtilla Miner Papers, Library of Congress.
22. Letter to Myrtilla Miner from student Marietta Hill, Myrtilla Miner Papers, Library of Congress, Washington, DC.
23. Myrtilla Miner to friends, 1852, Myrtilla Miner Papers, Library of Congress, Washington, DC.
24. Reverend Wm. H. Beecher accounting records, May–July 1856, Myrtilla Miner Papers, Library of Congress, Washington, DC.
25. Myrtilla Miner Letter, 3 May 1854, Myrtilla Miner Papers, Library of Congress, Washington, DC.
26. Lester Wells, "Myrtilla Miner: A Paper Before the Madison Historical Society," September 12, 1941, Library of Congress, Washington, DC.
27. O'Connor, 121; "Wide Enough for Our Ambition: D.C.'s Segregated African-American Schools (1807–1954)," Humanities Council of Washington, DC, www.wdchumanities.org/bigreadexhibit/exhibits/show/dcsegregatedschools.
28. *Encyclopedia Britannica Online,* "Myrtilla Miner," www.britannica.com/EBchecked/topic/383669/Myrtilla-Miner.
29. Miner Normal School, School Rules and Terms, Washington, DC, July 1, 1876.

Chapter 3: The Law Giveth and the Law Taketh Away

1. Letitia Brown and Elsie Lewis, "Washington in the New Era 1870–1970," Publication of the Education Department of the Smithsonian, February 1972, 4.
2. "Charles Sumner: A Featured Biography," www.senate.gov/artandhistory/history/common/generic/Featured_Bio_Sumner.htm.
3. "The Old Senate Chamber: The Caning of Senator Sumner," www.senate.gov/vtour/sumner.htm.
4. Green, *Secret City,* 69.
5. Donald Roe, "The Dual School System in the District of Columbia, 1862–1954: Origins, Problems and Protests," *Washington History,* Fall/Winter 2004–2005.
6. *Special Report of the Commissioner of Education on the Condition and Improvements of Public Schools in Washington DC submitted June 13, 1870,* Government Printing Office, Washington DC, 1871.
7. Ibid.
8. Mary Gibson Brewer to Carter G. Woodson, 18 March 1935, Association for the Study of Negro Life and History.
9. Willard B. Gatewood, *Aristocrats of Color: The Black Elite 1880–1920* (Fayetteville: Arkansas University Press, 2000), 39–40.
10. E. Delorus Preston Jr., "William Syphax, a Pioneer in Negro Education in the District of Columbia," *Journal of Negro History* 20, no. 4 (October 1935): 448–76.
11. Robert E. Lee House Arlington Memorial, "Pitcher," www.nps.gov/museum/exhibits/arho/exb/slavery/medium/ARHO6694_Pitcher.html.
12. The Special Report of the Commissioner of Education, "The History of Schools for the Colored Population," Volume 1, Part 1. Washington, DC, Government Printing Office, 1896.

13. *Inhabited Alleys in the District of Columbia and Housing of Unskilled. Hearing before A Sub-committee of the Committee on the District of Columbia*, Washington DC, Government Printing Office, 1914.

14. James Borchert, *Alley Life in Washington Family, Community, Religion, and Folklife in the City, 1850–1972* (Urbana: University of Illinois Press, 1982), 14.

15. Ibid., 149–50.

16. *Annual Report of the Colored Schools in Washington & Georgetown 1871–1872: George F.T. Cook Superintendent*, January 23, 1873.

17. Lawrence Otis Graham, *The Senator and Socialite: The True Story of America's First Black Dynasty* (New York: HarperCollins, 2006).

18. *Special Report of the Commissioner of Education on the Condition and Improvements of Public Schools in Washington, DC*, submitted June 13, 1870, Government Printing Office, Washington, DC, 1871, 28.

19. *Report of the Commissioner of the District of Columbia for the Year End June 20, 1905*, vol. IV, 71.

20. Ibid., 372.

21. *Fourth Report of the Board of Trustees of Public Schools of the District of Columbia*, 1878, Washington Gibson Brothers Printers.

22. Allen Lessof and Cristof Mauch, *Adolf Cluss, Architect: From Germany to America* (New York: Berghahn Books, 2005), 151.

23. *The Rise and Fall of Jim Crow: A Century of Segregation, The Civil Rights Act Declared Unconstitutional*, 2002, www.pbs.org/wnet/jimcrow/segregation2.html.

24. Rayford Logan, *The Betrayal of the Negro: The Negro in American Life, The Nadir 1877–1901* (New York: Da Capo Press, 1954).

25. Editorial, *Washington Bee*, December 18, 1886.

26. Richard Kluger, *Simple Justice: The History of Brown v. Board of Education and Black America's Struggle for Equality* (New York: Vintage Books, 1975), 68.

27. United States Department of the Interior, National Register of Historic Places Inventory Nomination Form, "M Street School," September 26, 1996, 3.

Chapter 4: It's the Principal

1. *Questionnaire: Negro College Graduates Individual Occupational History*, Anna Julia Cooper Papers, Manuscript Division, Moorland-Spingarn Research Center, Howard University.

2. Ibid.

3. Louise Daniel Hutchison, *Anna J. Cooper: A Voice from the South* (Washington, DC: Smithsonian Institution, 1982), 1.

4. Anna Julia Cooper, "Higher Education of Women," *A Voice from the South*, 1890–91.

5. Ibid.

6. *Questionnaire: Negro College Graduates Individual Occupational History*, Anna Julia Cooper Papers, Manuscript Department, Moorland-Spingarn Research Center, Howard University.

7. Anna Julia Cooper letters, Anna Julia Cooper Papers, Manuscript Department, Moorland-Spingarn Research Center, Howard University.

8. George Jenifer, "The Myrtilla Miner Normal School," *Crisis*, April 1917.

9. Report of the Board of Education to the Commissioners of the District of Columbia, 1902–1903, 193.

10. Charles Lemert and Esme Bhan, *The Voice of Anna Julia Cooper* (Oxford, England: Rowman and Littlefield, 1998), 20.

11. *Questionnaire: Negro College Graduates Individual Occupational History*, Anna Julia Cooper Papers, Manuscript Department, Moorland-Spingarn Research Center, Howard University.

12. "Colored High School—Delay in Acting Upon Charges Unsatisfactory," *Washington Post*, September 19, 1905.

13. Editorial Page, *Washington Times*, June 26, 1902.

14. *Washington Times*, September 21, 1902.

15. District of Columbia Board of Education Notes, September 6, 1905.

16. "Negroes on Race Question," *New York Times*, September 27, 1903.

17. "Colored High School—Delay in Acting Upon Charges Unsatisfactory," *Washington Post*, September 19, 1905.

18. Advertisement, *Colored American*, October 3, 1903.

19. Elizabeth McHenry, *Forgotten Readers: Recovering the Lost History of African American Literary Societies* (Durham, NC: Duke University Press, 2002), 157.

20. "Colored High School—Delay in Acting Upon Charges Unsatisfactory," *Washington Post*, September 19, 1905.

21. Ibid.

22. Anna Julia Cooper, "A Negro Dialect," *A Voice from the South*, 1891.

23. Mary Helen Washington, *A Voice from the South*, "Letter from Annette Easton to Leone Gabel, October 1, 1977," Smith College archives.

24. *Cumming v. Board of Ed. of Richmond County*, 175 U.S. 528, December 18, 1899.

25. Minutes of the Board of Education of the District of Columbia, March 1904.

26. *Report of hearings before the subcommittee on the several school bills relating to the reorganization of the schools of the District of Columbia*, Washington, DC, Government Printing Office, February 26–March 13, 1906.

27. "Colored High School—Delay in Acting Upon Charges Unsatisfactory," *Washington Post*, September 19, 1905.

28. Louis Harlan and Raymond Smock, eds., *The Booker T. Washington Papers* (Champaign, IL: University of Illinois Press, 1977).

29. "Director Hughes Heard," *Washington Post*, September 23, 1905

30. "President Resigns; Endowment Gone," *New York Times*, April 29, 1910.

31. Organic Act of June 20, 1906, Current School Board—34 Stat. 316, ch. 3446, The Basic Authority of the C Alain Locke Papers Box 1-1 Folder 45; Manuscript Division, Moorland-Spingarn Research Center, Howard University.

32. Anna Julia Cooper Papers, Manuscript Division, Moorland-Spingarn Research Center, Howard University.

33. Ibid.

Chapter 5: Bricks and Mortarboards

1. Hearing before the Subcommittee of House Committee on Appropriations for the District of Columbia, Appropriations Bill 1912 (Washington, DC: Government Printing Office, 1913).

2. Jacqueline Moore, *Leading the Race: The Transformation of the Black Elite in the Nation's Capital 1880-1920* (Charlottesville: University Press of Virginia, 1999), 89.

3. *Fourth Report of the Board of Trustees of Public Schools of the District of Columbia, 1878,* Washington Gibson Brothers Printers.

4. House Appropriations Bill 1906, 147.

5. National Rifle Association of America, Annual Report 1908, 17.

6. "Bride to Share in Oyster Wealth," *New York Times,* April 26, 1921.

7. Bulletin of the Maryland Agricultural Experiment, College Park Maryland, 1907, 234.

8. "The Mansion at Strathmore, History & Architecture, www.strathmore.org/media/pdf/MansionHistory_final.pdf.

9. "Ashford Criticizes Oyster," *Washington Herald,* October 27, 1907.

10. *Minutes of the Board of Education of the District of Columbia,* May 7, 1913.

11. Kimberly Prothro Williams, *Schools for All: A History of DC Public School Buildings, 1804–1960* (Washington, DC: US Department of Interior, 2008).

12. Hearing before the Subcommittee of House Committee on Appropriations for the District of Columbia, Appropriations Bill 1914 (Washington, DC: Government Printing Office, 1913), 147.

13. *Minutes of the Board of Education of the District of Columbia,* October 20, 1908.

14. Minutes of the Board of Education of the District of Columbia, Entered in to the minutes a letter from Jay J. Morrow, October 30, 1908.

15. "Hacker Mentioned for Ashford's Job," *Washington Times,* May 28, 1909.

16. "Ashford in Alarm," *Washington Herald,* January 18, 1910

17. "Officials Endorsed by Trade Committee," *Washington Times,* 1911.

18. Hearing before the Select Committee of the United States Senate, Select Committee to Investigate the Public School System, March 9, 1920, 1253.

19. Marie Anderson Ittner, "William B. Ittner: His Service to American School Architecture," *American School Board Journal* (January 1941): 1.

20. Elizabeth Armstrong Hall, "Schools of Thought," *St. Louis,* May 2005, 1.

21. District of Columbia Board of Education Meeting Notes, vol. 6, 1912.

22. Ibid.

23. Hearing before the Select Committee of the United States Senate, Select Committee to Investigate the Public School System, March 9, 1920, 1252.

24. "Accepted Design for the New M Street High School," *Washington Star,* March 28, 1914.

25. Ibid.

26. "Colored High School Goes to First Street," *Washington Star,* April 29, 1911.

27. Dayton Aviation Heritage National Park, Exhibit, "The Young Writer," Dayton, Ohio.

28. Paul Finkleman, ed., *Encyclopedia of African American History, 1896 to the Present,* vol. 1 (New York: Oxford University Press, 2009).

29. "Wilbur and Orville Wright Timeline, The Wilbur and Orville Wright Papers," http://memory.loc.gov/ammem/wrighthtml/wrighttime.html.

30. Marvin McFarland, ed., *The Papers of Wilbur and Orville Wright, vol. 2: 1906–1948* (New York: McGraw-Hill Book Company, 1953), 696; Mary Kay Carson and Laura D'Argo, *The Wright Brothers for Kids: How They Invented the Plane* (Chicago: Chicago Review Press, 2003), 11.

31. "Paul Laurence Dunbar: From the Academy of American Poets," www.poets.org /poet.php/prmPID/302.
32. Some news reports say 1,150; others say 999, and some say 1,175.
33. Commissioners of the District of Columbia, Annual Report 1917, vol. 6, 267.
34. His ex-wife Alice Dunbar Nelson attended as well.

Chapter 6: Old School

1. Class Notes, *Liber Anni* (Dunbar High School yearbook), 1923.
2. Dunbar High School Student handbook, 1922, 1 Sumner School and Museum Archives.
3. Garnet C. Wilkinson, M Street 1898, was principal from 1916–1922. He was promoted to assistant superintendent of schools.
4. Dunbar High School Student Handbook, 1922, 3. Sumner School and Museum Archives.
5. Mary Brewer, "The Budgeting of the Assignment" (address before Dunbar faculty), November 29, 1928.
6. Otelia Cromwell, "A High School Generation, September 1921–June 1925, Dunbar High School, Washington, D.C.," December 10, 1925, Table II.
7. Dunbar High School Student Handbook, 1925, Sumner School and Museum Archives.
8. "Cleanliness and Neatness," Dunbar High School Student Handbook, September 1925, 81.
9. Booker T. Washington, "Up from Slavery": Booker T. was originally coined by General Armstrong.
10. Allison Davis, Burleigh Gardner, and Mary Gardner, *Deep South: A Social and Anthropological Study of Caste and Class*, (Chicago: University of Chicago Press, 1941), 16.
11. "School Mourns Death of Assistant Principal," *Dunbar Newsreel*, December 1948, 1.
12. Courtland Milloy, "Dunbar Grads Still 'Pluggin' Away'; Class of 1925 Promises at Reunion to Keep Applying Lessons Learned," *Washington Post,* June 24, 1985, C3.
13. Mary Gibson Hundley Papers, 1897–1986, Schlesinger Library, Radcliffe Institute, Harvard University.
14. "The Black Renaissance in Washington, DC; Jessie Redmon Fauset," http://dc librarylabs.org/blkren/bios/fausetjr.html.
15. Lorraine Elena Roses and Ruth Elizabeth Randolph, *Harlem's Glory: Black Women Writing, 1900–1950* (Cambridge: Harvard University Press, 1996). 520.
16. ACHE TV interview program of Dr. Eva B. Dykes, Oakwood College, Papers of Eva B. Dykes, Manuscript Department, Moorland-Spingarn Research Center, Howard University.
17. DeWitt S. Williams, *She Fulfilled the Impossible Dream: The Story of Eva B. Dykes* (Hagerstown, MD: Review and Herald Publishing Association, 1985), 15.
18. Ibid, 37.
19. "Dunbar Graduates Find Varied Work," *Washington Star,* April 22, 1928.
20. Sandra Fitzpatrick and Maria Goodwin, *The Guide to Black Washington: Places and Events of Historical and Cultural Significance in the Nation's Capital* (New York: Hippocrene Books, 1991), 109.
21. "William Allison Davis:Psychologist, Social Anthropoligist, Author and Educator," www.esperstamps.org/heritage/h17.htm.

22. Dan MacGilvray, "A Brief History of the GPO—The Auto Age," www.access.gpo .gov/su_docs/fdlp/history/macgilvray.html.
23. John Davis Letter to Gordon Davis, Courtesy of the Davis Family private papers.
24. Dewey & LeBoeuf went bankrupt in May 2012, and Gordon Davis became a partner at Venable.
25. University of Chicago Centennial Catalogues, "Allison Davis-Education," www.lib .uchicago.edu/e/spcl/centcat/fac/facch25_01.html.

Chapter 7: Chromatics

1. Jacqueline Trescott, "Too Good to Tear Down?" *Washington Post*, March 1975.
2. Brad Snyder, *Beyond the Shadow of the Senators: The Untold Story of the Homestead Grays and the Integration of Baseball* (New York: Contemporary Books/McGraw-Hill, 2003), 9.
3. George Johnson, "The Present Legal Status of the Negro Separate School," *Journal of Negro Education* 16, no. 3 (Summer 1947), 288–89.
4. Edward Christopher Williams, *When Washington Was in Vogue: A Lost Novel of the Harlem Renaissance* (New York: Amistad-HarperCollins, 2004), 92.
5. Ibid., 22.
6. Walter White, *A Man Called White: The Autobiography of Walter White* (Athens: University of Georgia Press, 1948, 3.
7. Ibid. 137.
8. Minutes from the Board of Education of the District of Columbia, September 12, 1904.
9. Daniel J. Sharfstein, *The Invisible Line: Three American Families and the Secret Journey from Black to White* (New York: Penguin Press, 2011), 137.
10. "Court Must Draw the Color Line," *New York Times*, June 3, 1910.
11. Robert B. Jones, "Jean Toomer's Life and Career," *American National Biography* (New York: Oxford University Press, 1999).

Chapter 8: Coming of Age

1. Richard Seven, "Hazel Markel, 92; Distinguished Herself In Radio and Print Journalism," *Seattle Times*, December 13, 1991.
2. Kelly Quinn, *Making Modern Homes: A History of Langston Terrace Dwellings, a New Deal Housing Program in Washington, D.C.* (College Park, MD: University of Maryland Press, 2007), 169.
3. Mary Gibson Hundley Papers, 1897–1986, Biographical sketch, Schlesinger Library, Institute, Harvard University.
4. Letter from Dean of Admissions at Sarah Lawrence College to Mary Hundley, Mary Gibson Hundley Papers, 1897–1986, Biographical sketch, Schlesinger Library, Radcliffe Institute for Advanced Study, Harvard University.
5. "Court Asked to Evict Teachers," *Afro American*, April 19, 1941, 24.
6. Houston, Houston & Hastie to Mr. and Mrs. Frederick F. Hundley, 26 June 1942, Scheslinger Library, Papers of Mary Hundley.

Chapter 9: Right to Serve

1. "Army & Navy, 22 Officers," *Time*, February 28, 1944.

2. Bernard Nalty, "The Right to Fight: African American Marines in World War II," World War II Commemorative Series, www.nps.gov/history/history/online_books/npswapa/extContent/usmc/pcn-190-003132-00/sec14.htm.

3. Jonathan Sutherland, *African Americans at War: An Encyclopedia* (Santa Barbara, CA: ABC-CLIO Publishing, 2004), 562.

4. Henry Herge, *Navy V-12* (Paducah, KY: Turner Publishing, 1996), 39.

5. "Midshipman Signs Up Here," *Afro American*, June 26, 1937.

6. Mission Statement, United States Naval Academy, www.usna.edu/about.htm.

7. "Army and Navy: In Again, Out Again," *Time*, July 19, 1937.

8. "No Unpleasantness in Middy Resignation," *Indiana Recorder*, July 19, 1937.

9. Bradley Olson, "He Pressed on Despite Rough Seas," *Baltimore Sun*, February 2, 2006.

10. Robert Schneller Jr., *Breaking the Color Barrier: The U.S. Naval Academy's First Black Midshipmen and the Struggle for Racial Equality* (New York: NYU Press, 2005), 177.

11. Ibid., 178.

12. Colonel James A. Moss, *Manual of Military Training*, (Menasha, WI: George Banta Publishing, 1917), 1.

13. United States War Department, *Infantry Drill Regulations:Changes Nos. 1-19*, United States Army, April 15, 1917.

14. "The Competitive Drill M Street High School Wins," *Washington Bee*, May 27, 1911.

15. CSPAN-Brian Lamb Q&A with Colbert King, May 31, 2009, www.c-spanvideo.org/program/307940-1.

16. Dr. Lawrence Graves to Paul C. Johnson, March 14, 2010.

17. Benjamin F. Butler, *The Negro in Politics. Review of Recent Legislation for His Protection—Defense of the Colored Man Against All Accusers. Address of Gen. Butler in North Russell Street Church, Boston, Monday Evening, May 8th, 1871*.

18. Virginia Department of Historic Resources, Marker Number V 26, 1993.

19. Benjamin O. Davis Jr., *American: An Autobiography* (Washington, DC: Smithsonian Institution Press, 1991), 2.

20. Ibid., 69.

21. "The Charles Drew Papers 1941-1950," *Profiles in Science*, the National Medical Library, National Institute of Health (Bethesda, MD: US National Library of Medicine).

22. William Elwood, *The Road to Brown* (film transcript), produced by University of Virginia, 1990.

23. "We Don't Try to Be Different," *Time*, May 6, 1946.

24. Ibid.

Chapter 10: *Bolling, Not Brown*

1. Kluger, 514; Genna Rae McNeil, *Groundwork: Charles Hamilton Houston and the Struggle for Civil Rights* (Philadelphia, PA: University of Pennsylvania Press, 1982), 188.

2. Michael Gillette, *The Texas Book: Profiles, History, and Reminiscences of the University— Blacks Challenge the White University* (Austin: University of Texas Press, 2006), 142.

3. George Strayer, *The Report of a Survey of the Public Schools of the District of Columbia* (Washington, DC: Government Printing Office, 1948), 216.

4. Report of the Meeting of the Dunbar Alumni Association with Superintendent of Schools Dr. Hobart M. Corning, November 18, 1946, Franklin Building, Washington DC.

5. "Legends in the Law: A Conversation with James Nabrit III," *Washington Lawyer*, July/August 2001.
6. Kluger, 520.
7. Milton Korman, *Bolling v. Sharpe*, 347 U.S. 497, closing arguments, December 11, 1953.
8. Jeanne Rogers "No Quick Integration Seen in D.C. Schools," *Washington Post*, May 18, 1954, 4.
9. Ibid.
10. Thomas Sowell, "The Education of Minority Children," *Education in the Twenty First Century* (Stanford, CA: Hoover Institution Press, 2002), 79–92.
11. Baltimore Afro-American, January 5, 1954.
12. "Danger on the School Board," *Washington Post*, February 10, 1954, 8.
13. George Strayer, *The Report of a Survey of the Public Schools of the District of Columbia* (Government Printing Office: Washington, DC, 1948).
14. Jeanne Rogers, "Integration a Unique Problem Here," Washington Post, May 23, 1954.
15. Ibid.
16. Ibid.
17. *Minutes of the Board of Education of the District of Columbia*, September 22, 1954.
18. *Minutes of the Board of Education of the District of Columbia*, September 22, 1954.
19. *Minutes of the Board of Education of the District of Columbia*, , November 17, 1954.
20. Ibid.
21. Letter to the Board of Education, *Minutes of the Board of Education of the District of Columbia*, October 7, 1954.
22. *Minutes of the Board of Education of the District of Columbia*, , March 17, 1954.
23. Charles Lofton, Principal's Letter, *Liber Anni* (Dunbar High School yearbook), 1955.
24. Thomas Sowell, "The Education of Minority Children," www.tsowell.com /speducat.html.
25. Testimony of Dr. Garnet C. Wilkinson, *Minutes of the Board of Education of the District of Columbia*, vol. 67, January 4, 1950.

Chapter 11: Elite versus Elitism

1. Conversation retold by Dr. James Bowman, James Bowman Oral History Interview, Oral History of Human Genetics Project, Session #1, June 26, 2006.
2. Dawn Rhodes, "Dr. James E. Bowman, 1923–2011: U. of C. Professor an Expert in Inherited Blood Diseases and Population Genetics," *Chicago Tribune*, September 30, 2011.
3. John Easton, "James Bowman, Expert on Pathology and Blood Diseases, 1923-2011," *University of Chicago News*, September 29, 2011.
4. Kambiz Foroohar and David Glovin, "How Nemazee Used Harvard Degree Swindling Banks of $292 Million," *Bloomberg*, March 21, 2010, www.bloomberg.com /apps/news?pid=newsarchive&sid=a8w3j0T3Xbrc.
5. Interview with Dr. James Bowman at UCLA, Oral History of Human Genetics Project, June 26, 2006
6. Harvard Law School's Charles Hamilton Houston Institute for Racial Justice, Annual Martha's Vineyard Forum, "The Dunbar Story: Achieving Success in an Era of Segregation," August 18, 2010.

7. *Liber Anni* (Dunbar High School yearbook), 1939, "James Bowman."

8. Other similar communities include Sag Harbor, New York; Highland Beach, Maryland; and Idlewild, Michigan.

9. Stanley Nelson, *A Place of Our Own* (film), Interview with Professor Manning Marable, PBS–Independent Lens, 2004.

10. "The Dunbar Story: Achieving Success in an Era of Segregation," Charles Hamilton Houston Institute for Race and Justice, Martha's Vineyard, MA, August 18, 2010.

11. Wolfgang Saxon, "H. Naylor Fitzhugh, 82, Educator and Pioneer in Target Marketing," *New York Times*, July 29, 1992.

12. *Mr. Soul The Movie, Ellis Haizlip and the Rise of Black Power TV*, February 2012, Daniel Pollard and Melissa Haizlip Producers, www.mrsoulmovie.com/aboutthefilm.htm.

13. Elizabeth Catlett in Conversation with Henry Louis Gates Jr., W. E. B. DuBois Institute for African and African American Research, Harvard University, Cambridge, MA, April 18, 2011.

14. Ibid.

15. Karen Rosenberg, "Elizabeth Catlett, Sculptor with Eye on Social Issues, Is Dead at 96," *New York Times*, April 3, 2012.

16. Elizabeth Catlett, Lecture, Harvard University, April 18, 2011.

17. Austen Bailey, "New Acquisition: Elizabeth Catlett the Sharecropper," *Unframed*, August 3, 2011, http://lacma.wordpress.com/2011/08/03/new-acquisition-elizabeth -catlett-sharecropper.

18. Parts of this interview were edited at Dr. Taylor's request. He had suffered a stroke and would forget items and then recall them later in the interview.

19. Remarks of President Barack Obama, Congressional Gold Medal Awards Ceremony for Senator Edward Brooke, Washington, DC, October 29, 2010, www.whitehouse.gov.

20. Edward Brooke, *Bridging the Divide: My Life,* (New Brunswick, NJ: Rutgers University Press, 2007), 214.

21. Tamar Lewin, "Wellesley Class Sees 'One of Us' Bearing Standard," *New York Times*, April 14, 2007.

22. James Nabrit III, e-mail interview, July 24, 2012.

23. William MacDougall, "Negro Tired of Excuses, Says Nabrit," *Washington Post*, June 30, 1963.

24. Don Robinson and Leon Dash, "Thousand Quit Classes in Howard U Boycott," *Washington Post*, May 11, 1967.

25. Gregory Tignor, "Living Black in Washington: A Pictorial History," 3, 2002, Courtesy of the Tignor Family.

26. "Integration Doing Well, Says Eastern Principal," *Evening Star*, September 20, 1956.

27. Marine Hoffman, "Reestablishing the Good Name of EHS," *Washington Post*, October 29, 1963.

28. Eastern High School, *Rambler* (yearbook), 1969, 98–99.

29. Ibid.

30. Mary Stratford, "DC School Board Polled on the Track System," *Washington Afro American*, December 15, 1964.

31. "Mrs. Butcher Assails Critics of Negro Pupils," *Washington Post*, February 3, 1956, 29.

32. Ibid.

33. Willard Clopton Jr., "Eastern Principal Accused," *Washington Post*, March 10, 1968.

Chapter 12: New School

1. Mary Hundley Gibson to *Washington Star*, 3 November 1973, Mary Hundley Gibson Papers, Schlesinger Library, Cambridge, Massachusetts.
2. Neely Tucker, "The Wreckage of a Dream," *Washington Post*, August 24, 2004, B1.
3. Keith L. Alexander, "More Recollections of D.C. Riots Following Dr. King's Death," *Washington Post*, April 6, 2008.
4. Appropriations Committee, Capital Outlay Project Schedule, Fiscal Year 1966, 1,264.
5. Urban Renewal Plan for the Shaw School Urban Renewal Area, January 9, 1969.
6. Jeanne Rogers, "Dunbar High Plays a New Role; It's Now a Neighborhood School," *Washington Post*, January 23, 1957.
7. Ibid.
8. Lawrence Feinberg interview, August 2, 2012.
9. Ronald Kessler, "Spread of Drug Use in Schools Perplexes Washington Officials," *Washington Post*, March 20, 1970.
10. Lawrence Feinberg, "Years Bring Change to Dunbar High School–'Black Elite' Institution Now Typical Slum Facility," *Washington Post*, December 28, 1969, D1.
11. Patricia Sullivan, "Charles Sumner Lofton; Principal at Dunbar During Civil Rights Era," *Washington Post*, August 10, 2006.
12. Ibid.
13. Ibid.
14. Entire conversation in *Minutes of the Board of Education of the District of Columbia*, June 27, 1972.
15. William Raspberry, "Dunbar: Victim of Mediocrity," *Washington Post*, April 25, 1975.
16. Charles Bryant, Robert Bryant, Hector Carrillo, Robert de Jongh, Amarian (no first name given in the presentation), Preliminary Submission Dunbar Senior High School Replacement, Washington D.C., 1970–71.
17. Wolf Von Eckhardt, "Design for an Urban Setting," *Washington Post*, December 11, 1971, E1.
18. Ibid.
19. Jacqueline Trescott, "Old Dunbar High School: Too Good to Tear Down?" *Washington Star*, March 1975.
20. Ibid.
21. Michael Kiernan, "Council Blocks Dunbar Razing," *Washington Star News*, April 1, 1974, B4.
22. Ibid.
23. *Minutes of the Board of Education of the District of Columbia*, vol. 131, June 24, 1974.
24. Letters to the editor, *Washington Star*, March 25, 1975.
25. Paul W. Valentine, "60 Dunbar Students Talk to Mayor," *Washington Post*, March 31, 1976.
26. R. C. Newell, "New Dunbar High School Opens, Still Facing Some Old Problems," *Afro American*, April 16, 1977.
27. Cynthia Savage, "Pranksters Kill Purpose of New Escalators," *Dunbar Newsreel*, Fall 1977.
28. Lawrence Feinberg, "We Must Have Pride in It; New Dunbar a Challenge to Students," *Washington Post*, April 13, 1977, C1.

29. "Minority Review Report of Alternatives to the Demolition of Paul Laurence Dunbar High School," May 23, 1977, 2.
30. "Walls Come Tumbling" (photo caption), *Washington Post*, June 5, 1977.

Chapter 13: Children Left Behind

1. District of Columbia Public Schools, Quality School Review Report, Restructuring Achievement: A Model for Improving Schools which Continuously Fail to Make Adequate Yearly Progress, January 2008, Dunbar HS, 2.
2. Ibid., 7.
3. Ibid., 3.
4. Fast Company Staff, "Gimme an F!," *Fast Company*, August 7, 2008.
5. Interview with Jeff Chu, August 13, 2012.
6. Jeff Chu, "Fixing D.C.'s School System," *Fast Company*, August 8, 2008.
7. Interview with Jeff Chu, August 13, 2012
8. V. Dion Haynes, "Parents Seek Action over Homeless Presence," *Washington Post*, October 23, 2007.
9. Interview with Jeff Chu, August 13, 2012.
10. Bill Turque, "Rhee Has Ousted 24 Principals," *Washington Post*, May 16, 2008.
11. "D.C. Schools Chief Rhee Faces High Hopes for Reform," *PBS NewsHour*, November 19, 2007.
12. Fixing D.C. Schools: A *Washington Post* Investigation, Dunbar High School Open Repair Requests, projects.washingtonpost.com/dcschools/repairs/open/6-2004.
13. District of Columbia Public Schools, LEA School Restructuring Plan, 2008–09, Dunbar Senior High School.
14. Alan Goldenbach, "Getting Up for the Competition," *Washington Post*, December 24, 2008.
15. Linda Wheeler and Serge Kovaleski, "School Shootings Break Out in DC," *Washington Post*, January 27, 1994.
16. Richard Lacayo, Ann Blackman, Cathy Booth, and Janice C. Simpson, "Crime: Lock 'Em Up! And Throw Away the Key," *Time*, February 7, 1994.
17. The White House, Memo, Subject: School Violence Event, January 28, 1994, www.clintonlibrary.gov/assets/DigitalLibrary/BruceReed/Crime/79/647420-tour.pdf.
18. DCPS Office of Data and Accountability, Federally Mandated School Improvement in DCPC, 2009.
19. District of Columbia Public Schools, ELA School Restructuring Plan, 2008–09, Dunbar Senior High School, 7–8.
20. Washington Post Editorial Board, "DC's Odd Resistance to Charter Schools," *Washington Post*, February 14, 2013.

Chapter 14: From Bed-Stuy to Shaw

1. Girmay Zahilay, Community Food Investment Partnership with City Harvest, http://hungercenter.wpengine.netdna-cdn.com/wp-content/uploads/2011/06/Community-Food-Assessment_Bed-Stuy-Zahilay.pdf.
2. Susan Dominus, "A School Succeeds with Extra Study and Little Homework," *New York Times*, May 16, 2008.
3. Innercity Students Can Outperform the Norm," www.friendsofbedford.org/success.html.

4. Testimony of Allen Lew, Executive Director of the Office of Public Education and Education, Senate Homeland Security and Government Affairs Subcommittee on Oversight of Government Management, the Federal Workforce, and the District of Columbia, Friday, March 28, 2008, Dirksen Senate Building.
5. Interview with Kimberly Springle-Archivist, Sumner Museum and Archives, archivist, August 9, 2012.
6. Peter Applebome, "Before Hosting 'Bandstand,' Growing Up in a City with a Complicated Story," *New York Times*, April 20, 2012.
7. Stephen Jackson, Personal Statement, Dunbar Alumni Federation, 2009.
8. Interview with Jay Matthews, January 25, 2010.
9. Christopher Dean Hopkins, "Gray: Fenty Took My Commencement Speaker Slot," *D.C. Wire* (blog), June 7, 2010, http://voices.washingtonpost.com/dc/2010/06/gray_fenty_took_my_commencemen.html.
10. Ibid.

Chapter 15: The Fall

1. Jay Matthews, "Rhee Initiative That Will, Thankfully, Outlast Rhee," *Washington Post*, September 19, 2010.
2. Name changed.

Chapter 16: New New School

1. "New Dunbar Groundbreaking Press Conference", November 17, 2011, www.youtube.com/watch?v=WmB7e8ioGSg.
2. Ibid.
3. "District of Columbia Modernization and Stabilization Project," www.mckissackdc.com/project.aspx?pid=2400178.
4. Phillip Kennicott, "Winning Design for Dunbar High School Scores an Average Grade," *Washington Post*, March 15, 2010.

Chapter 17: Back to the Future

1. Michael J. Petrilli, "The Fastest-Gentrifying Neighborhoods in the United States," Thomas B. Fordham Institute, June 11, 2012., http://educationnext.org/the-10-fastest-gentrifying-public-schools-in-the-u-s.
2. Wendy Wang, "The Rise of Intermarriage: Rates, Characteristics Vary by Race and Gender," Pew Research Center, February 16, 2012.

SELECTED BIBLIOGRAPHY

Alexander, Eleanor. *Lyrics of Sunshine and Shadow: The Tragic Courtship and Marriage of Paul Laurence Dunbar and Alice Ruth Moore.* New York: New York University Press, 2001.

Anderson, James D. *The Education of Blacks in the South, 1860–1935.* Chapel Hill: University of North Carolina Press, 1988.

Avalon, John. *Independent Nation: How the Vital Center Is Changing American Politics.* New York: Harmony Books, 2004.

Buck, Stuart. *Acting White: The Ironic Legacy of Desegregation.* New Haven: Yale University Press, 2010.

Braxton, Joanne M., ed. *The Collected Poetry of Paul Laurence Dunbar.* Charlottesville: University Press of Virginia, 1993.

Close, Ellis. *The Rage of a Privileged Class.* New York: HarperCollins, 1993.

Cromwell, Adelaide M. *Unveiled Voices, Unvarnished Memories: The Cromwell Family in Slavery and Segregation, 1692–1972.* Columbia: University of Missouri Press, 2007.

Lester, Joan Steinau. *Fire in My Soul.* New York: Atria Books, 2003.

Davis, James F. *Who Is Black? One Drop Rule Defined.* University Park, PA: Pennsylvania State University Press, 2001.

Davis, Allison, and John Dollard. *Children of Bondage: The Personality Development of Negro Youth in the Urban South.* Washington, DC: American Council on Education, 1940.

Du Bois, W. E. B. *Black Reconstruction in American 1860–1880.* New York: Free Press, 1935.

Gates, Henry Louis, and Cornel West. *The African-American Century.* New York: Simon and Schuster, 2000.

Fletcher, Marvin E. *American's First Black General: Benjamin O. Davis Sr., 1880–1970.* Lawrence: University Press of Kansas, 1989.

Gentry, Tony. *Paul Laurence Dunbar.* Los Angeles: Melrose Square Publishing, 1989.

Gillette Jr., Howard. *Between Justice & Beauty: Race Planning and the Failure of Urban Policy in Washington D.C.* Philadelphia: University of Pennsylvania Press, 1995.

Graham, Lawrence Otis. *Our Kind of People: Inside America's Black Upper Middle Class.* New York: Harper Perrenial, 1999.

Gutheim, Frederick and Antoinette J. Lee. *Worthy of the Nation: Washington, DC, from L'Efant to the National Capital Planning Commission.* Baltimore: Johns Hopkins University Press, 2006.

Hansen, Carl F. *Miracle of Social Adjustment: Desegregation in the Washington, D.C. Schools.* New York: Anti Defamation League, 1957.

Hare, Nathan. *The Black Anglo-Saxons.* New York: Collier Books, 1965.

Hoy, Suellen. *Chasing Dirt: The American Pursuit of Cleanliness.* New York: Oxford University Press, 1995.

Hundley, Mary Gibson. *The Dunbar Story 1870–1955.* New York: Vantage Press, 1965.

Irons, Peter. *Jim Crow's Children: The Broken Promise of the Brown Decision.* New York: Penguin Books, 2002.

Jaffe, Henry, and Tom Sherwood. *Dream City: Race, Power, and the Decline of Washington, D.C.* New York: Simon and Schuster, 1994.

Jones, Edward P. *Lost in the City.* New York: HarperCollins, 1992.

Kessler, James, J. S. Kidd, Renee Kidd, and Katherine A. More. *Distinguished African American Scientists of the 20th Century.* Phoenix: Oryx Press, 1996.

Kozol, Jonathan. Sa*vage Inequalities: Children in America's Schools.* Harper Perrenial, 1991.

Lacy, Karen. *Blue Chip Black: Race, Class, and Status in the New Black Middle Class.* Berkeley, CA: University of California Press, 2007.

Latique, Casey, and David Salisbury. *Educational Freedom in Urban America: Brown v. Board After Half a Century.* Washington, DC: Cato Institute, 2004.

Liebow,Eliot. *Tally's Corner: A Study of Negro Street Corner Men.* New York: Little, Brown and Company, 1968.

Eliot Manning, Kenneth R. *Black Apollo of Science: The Life of Ernest Everett Just.* New York & Oxford: Oxford University Press, 1983.

Patler, Nicholas. *Jim Crow and the Wilson Administration.* Boulder: University Press of Colorado, 2004.

Pritchett, Wendell. *Robert Clifton Weaver and the American City.* Chicago: University of Chicago Press, 1989.

Provenzo, Eugene F. *Du Bois on Education*. Lanham, MD: Rowman and Littlefield, 2004.

Robinson, Eugene. *Disintegration: The Splintering of Black America*. New York: Doubleday, 2010.

Ross Jr., Lawrence C. *The Divine Nine: The History of African American Fraternities and Sororities*. New York: Kensington Publishing Corp, 2000.

Reef, Catherine. *African Americans in the Military*. New York: Facts on File Inc., 2004.

Savage, Beth L., Ed. *African American Historic Places*. New York: John Wiley & Sons, 1994.

Schneller Jr., Robert J. *Blue and Gold and Black Racial Integration and the U.S. Naval Academy*. College Station: Texas A&M University Press, 2008.

Shenton, James P. *History of the United States to 1865*. New York: Doubleday, 1963.

Solomon, Burt. *The Washington Century: Three Families and the Shaping of the Nation's Capital*. New York: Harper Perennial, 2004.

Tough, Paul. *Whatever It Takes: Geoffrey Canada's Quest to Change Harlem and America*. New York: Houghton Mifflin, 2008.

Touré. *Who Is Afraid of Post-Blackness? What It Means to Be Black Now*. New York: Free Press, 2011.

Travis, Toni-Michelle, and Ronald Walters, eds. *Democrat Destiny and the District of Columbia*. New York: Rowan & Littlefield, 2010.

Tyack, David B. *The One Best System: A History of American Urban Education*. Cambridge: Harvard University Press, 1974.

Williams, Edward Christopher. *When Washington Was in Vogue (A Lost Novel of the Harlem Renaissance)*. New York: HarperCollins, 2005.

Woodson, Carter G. *The Education of the Negro Prior to 1861*. Washington, DC: Associated Publishers, 1919.

Wade Jr., Harold. *Black Men of Amherst*. Amherst: Amherst College Press, 1976.

Whitmire, Richard. *The Bee Eater: Michelle Rhee Takes on the Nation's Worst School District*. San Francisco: Jossey Bass, 2011.

Wiley, Amber. "Concrete Solutions: Architecture of Public High Schools During the 'Urban Crisis.'" Dissertation, George Washington University, 2011.

Young, Whitney M. *To Be Equal*. New York: McGraw Hill, 1964.

INDEX